BE READY WHEN THE SH*T GOES DOWN

BE READY WHEN THE SH*T GOES DOWN

A Survival Guide to the Apocalypse

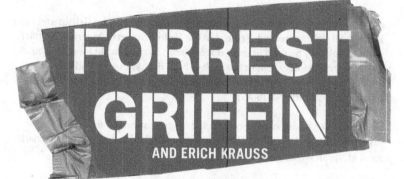

FORREST GRIFFIN

AND ERICH KRAUSS

with Illustrations by Jason Lee

itbooks

AN IMPRINT OF HARPERCOLLINSPUBLISHERS

*it*books

A hardcover edition of this book was published in 2010 by William Morrow, an imprint of HarperCollins Publishers.

FIRST IT BOOKS PAPERBACK PUBLISHED 2011.

Designed by Richard Oriolo

Library of Congress Cataloging-in-Publication Data has been applied for.

ISBN 978-0-06-199826-3

HB 03.17.2021

Dedicated to my friend, Big John Grantham—love ya, brother

CONTENTS

PARENTAL WARNING: ORTBIYAAMBTA–1435

Now that I am a famous author, it has come to my attention that there is no rating system for books. There is a rating system for movies, CDs, and even video games, but absolutely nothing for books. I am sure the reason for this is that kids today are far too lazy to read, even when the subject matter is filthy. In any case, this has to change. When I did the promotional tour for my *New York Times* bestseller, *Got Fight?*, I cannot count how many eight- and ten-year-old kids came up to me and had me sign their copies. Of course I signed their books because it put money in my pocket, but it was very inappropriate for kids that age to be buying my book. Having lost some sleep over the whole matter, I felt the need to come up with a rating system and apply it to this book.

As you can see above, I have given this book a rating of ORTBI-

YAAMBTA—1435, which is an acronym for Only Read This Book If You Are A Male Between The Ages of fourteen and thirty-five. Simple and to the point, am I right? The reason for such a harsh rating is due to all the dirty language, which includes but is not limited to "ass clown," "ball juggler," "cum catcher," "dick sucker," "eel stroker," "felcher," "goo-gargler," "hippie," "ignoramus," "jack-off," "kitty-kicker," "loser," "motherfucker," "narcissist," "ogler," "penis," "queef," "rubber," "stupid," "teetotaler," "urethra," "vagina," "wannabe," "X-ray-glasses-wearing-peeper," "yodeler," "zelcher" (like felcher, only with a Z . . . Don't ask). Notice how I used one swearword that starts with each letter of the alphabet. Genius, am I right? (Note: I do not want to get e-mails saying that I did not use every one of these words in the book. They are all printed above, so yeah, they have all been used.) Anyway, I figure that if you are fourteen, you have probably heard most of these swearwords before, so reading the book won't corrupt your mind too terribly. Your parents might still see you as their little angel, but we both know the truth. Fourteen is the new thirty. If you are under fourteen or over thirty-five, you have most likely heard these words, but the context in which they are used might either give you nightmares about the "bad man" or cause uncontrollable vomiting, depending on which end of the spectrum you fall. In any cause, you've been warned—now go buy your copy! Just don't read it if you're not the right age.

ACKNOWLEDGMENTS

I would like to thank Lucas Rakofsky for not suing me for passing his ideas off as my own ... which, by the way, I have been doing for years ... At least that is what he says.

I would like to thank Chuck Norris for saving America. I have a Total Gym that I've never actually used, but I'm sure it's phenomenal. It's also an excellent clothes rack.

I would like to thank Ben & Jerry for making it so damn hard to make weight. Fuck you, Ben, and fuck you, Jerry.

I would like to thank myself for teaching all of you how to survive the apocalypse. You should thank me as well.

I would like to acknowledge my freshman English teacher, not because she changed my life for the better, but rather because she gave me a B for my apparent incorrect usage of commas. That was bullshit. Nobody with a life has thought as much about commas as I have. If you, want to connect two, thoughts without having to start a new sentence, and rename the subject, use a comma. I mean is, that so fucking hard (comma) bitch! . . . Telling me I don't know how to use commas. I used eight commas in this paragraph, and I did an excellent job.

I would like to thank the chief medical adviser for this book, Anthony Rakofsky, who happens to be allergic to peanuts. As a matter of fact, he is allergic to nuts of any kind. Despite his help on this book, when I start my new utopia in the aftermath of the apocalypse, I will ban people like him from breeding. Seriously, how are people who are allergic to nuts still alive? Talk about pampering the weak! Personally, I have Gladsens syndrome, which is an immune deficiency. Although this too is a pretty big weakness and makes me terrified to shake people's hands, I am bigger and manlier than Anthony, so I will be exempt from any of the postapocalyptic rules or restrictions that I create in my kingdom.

I would like to thank Tucker Max, author of *I Hope They Serve Beer in Hell*, for making me look like a good guy in comparison.

I would like to thank my mother, again. I thank her for everything good I do from now until the day I die. Everything bad I do, like this book for example, I blame entirely on bad sitcoms, violent video games, and heavy-metal music.

I would like to thank Bill O'Reilly and Bill Maher for making me the angriest person on the planet.

I would like to thank yoga instructors for being totally and completely insane. Seriously, yoga will not cure cancer or make your erection stiffer (we all know the only way to get a stiffer erection is to allow your penis to get repeatedly stung by bees).

I would like to thank my management, Zinkin Entertainment, for making it seem reasonable for companies to pay enormous amounts of money for me to do nothing.

Thanks to Zakk Wylde and Eric Hendrikx for supplying the Vehicle of Death section.

Thanks to Frank Scatoni and Raffi Nahabedian.

And finally, I would like to thank coffee for helping me find my inner rage.

A very special thanks goes out to contributing editor Bret Aita for outstanding work. I've never met Bret and don't know what a contributing editor does, but Erich told me he's doing a phenomenal job.

CAUTION

Do not under any circumstances burn this book for heat. It is preferable that you die of hypothermia before you destroy this book.

WARNING

This book was written for idiots by idiots.

NOTE

This book was not tested on animals. It was tested on migrant day laborers. Hey, fuck you, they signed the waivers. No, they couldn't read English, but whose fault is that?

WARNING

To protect the innocent, the names, dates, and places in this book have all remained real. Only the facts have been changed.

WARNING

It is important that you understand that absolutely no research went into this book. Well, that isn't entirely correct. Erich spent about twenty minutes on the Internet, but that was mainly to get the correct spelling of names, which I am pretty sure he still got wrong.

WARNING

There are only four warnings, one caution, and one "note" in this book. There should obviously be a lot more. Please do not sue me.

MONEY-BACK GUARANTEE

In the event of the apocalypse, if the information in this book does not save your life, Forrest Griffin will personally refund every penny you spent on its purchase, including the tax. (Disclaimer: Money must be collected in person, *after* the apocalypse. In the event that you are dead, your family members are not allowed to collect the refund, even if they bring your corpse to Forrest's house in a wheelbarrow.)

FORREST, WHAT THE FUCK ARE YOU THINKING?

So a lot of you are picking up this book and thinking, "Forrest, you're a fighter, and not a particularly good one, what the fuck do you know about surviving the apocalypse?" Or perhaps you're muttering quietly to yourself, "Why should I take advice on surviving the end of the world from a guy who gets hit in the head on a regular basis?" Or maybe you're saying, "Sure, Forrest is the guy I want helping me battle it out in a nuclear wasteland, but he's not necessarily the guy that I want teaching me about water purification." Fine. I can sort of understand your skepticism, so let me explain.

I've learned many lessons during my time on this planet, but at the age of, oh, let's say elevenish, I learned a very important one. If you read my last book, you're probably thinking this has something to do with the time I shit myself while bungee-jumping at Dollywood, but you're wrong. Although that little experience clued me in to the fact that you probably shouldn't eat Mexican food an hour before you dive off a fifty-foot tower, the lesson I am talking about is one of the biggies.

The event that changed my perception of the world and, even more importantly, the people in it, occurred on a beautiful spring afternoon in Augusta, Georgia. School had just let out for the day, and I was heading home with my five best friends in the world. All of them were traveling on their bikes, and I was on foot because my bike had a broken chain. Being fatherless at the time, I had every intention of going to one of my friends' fathers to get the needed repairs, but fathers have a tendency to help out their own kids first. In any case, I was huffing it on foot.

Everything was as right as rain as we made the journey from the schoolhouse to our neighborhood. I kept a decent pace, and my friends did tricks on their bikes to ensure I never fell too far behind. We were telling jokes, laughing, and making plans for the upcoming weekend. But just as we turned onto the street that led to all of our homes, I noticed the face of one of my friends change. It went from the happy-go-lucky face of a typical eleven-year-old to the panic-stricken face you see in horror movies just before a person gets mutilated by a chain saw. At first I thought he was grimacing for my benefit because he was looking in my direction, but then I noticed that he was actually looking over my shoulder.

That's when I heard the snarling, growling beast. Still running, I looked behind me and saw the biggest fucking dog in the world, foaming at the mouth and sprinting in our direction. This rabid rottweiler turned our casual trip home into the Tour de France. All of my friends lifted their asses off their seats and stood up on their pedals, pushing with all of their strength. At first our scattering confused the irate and rapidly approaching dog, which I later named Cujo. He went after the bikes first, but as my friends pulled ahead, he decided to conserve his strength and turn on me.

It was just like one of those documentaries you see on the Discovery Channel where a lion storms into a pack of wildebeests. At first the lion just sort of runs around, but then he quickly hones his laser sights on the weakest, most pathetic creature in the group. In this particular case, I was the pathetic creature because I wasn't currently in possession of a bike.

I sprinted for home, and with the insane mutt having been momentarily distracted by my friends, I had approximately a ten-yard lead, but I could hear the rapid clicking of his long-nailed paws drawing nearer. By the time I could see my house in front of me, my fear had risen to an unimaginable level. If I hadn't pissed just prior to leaving school, my pants would have been soaked. I made this high-pitched piglet squeal that I had never made before and have never made since. Each time one of my feet touched pavement, I was certain it would be the last. Eleven years old and this was it, the end of my life.

In my terror, I peeled my eyes away from my home and turned them on my group of friends, hoping they would somehow save me or at the very least offer me some type of reassurance that everything would be all right. Never in my life had I needed the support of another human being so badly, and I knew that if there was anyone I could count on being there for me, it was my trusted amigos.

Instead of seeing the support I so badly needed, I saw something that will be forever etched into my frontal lobe. My blood brothers, *mi hermanos*, my partners in crime were pointing at me, laughing their asses off. And I am not talking about smiling or even chuckling—each and every one of them was bent over the front of their handlebars, mouth wide open, laughing from the belly. The kind of laughter you get when someone you absolutely hate trips in the school cafeteria and stomach-surfs on their food tray down a flight of stairs, except it was *Look at Forrest get chased by that rabid dog!*

I sprinted across my front lawn, and surprisingly I made it to the front steps. I leaped up them in a single bound and skidded to a stop on the front porch. With trembling hands, I threw open the screen door and reached for the knob. The killing machine was right behind me now, but I had made it. I'd escaped a brutal mauling that if videotaped would have undoubtedly been played over and over again on the nightly news, perhaps even led to stiffer dog laws in the United States, until . . .

The fucking door was locked.

Cujo lunged, but with the screen door having already swung shut on my backside, he bounced off. The instant he landed, he came right back at me. Although my face was pressed firmly against the wooden door, I could feel his hot breath on the back of my legs. For a brief instant I thought that perhaps I was protected, but that's when Cujo put those fantastically long claws to use and began tearing into the metal screen mesh. I tried reaching into my pocket to get at my keys, but there wasn't enough room. I was literally sandwiched between the door and the screen.

In less than a minute I not only felt Cujo's claws tearing into my skin, but I could also feel his wet nose. His game plan became overwhelming apparent—he was attempting to tear a large enough hole into the screen to get his head through, and once he managed that, my legs and butt cheeks would essentially become Alpo.

The fear became so great that something snapped in my mind. I don't want to say I blacked out because I was still awake, but my body somehow started working on autopilot. When my mind refocused, I was clinging to one of the thick, circular pillars that traversed our porch, seven feet off the ground. To this day, I have no recollection of making the four-foot journey from the door to the pillar or even climbing the pillar. To be quite honest, I don't even see how I could have covered that distance without getting mauled.

In any case, I was clinging with all my strength to this pillar and the rabid rottweiler was angrier than ever. It was just like one of those Tom and Jerry cartoons where Tom is clinging to something several feet off the ground, and a pit bull is jumping toward him and snapping its massive jaws.

After what seemed like an eternity, but in reality was probably closer to ten minutes, my mother pulled into the driveway. She saw me clinging for dear life to the pillar, screaming and crying, and then she saw the dog at my feet, leaping into the air in an attempt to reach my flesh. Like a soldier who rushes blindly into the battlefield to save a comrade, my mother exited her car, grabbed a thick branch off the ground, and then stormed up onto the porch. She arched that stick back like a baseball bat and then swung for the hills.

The branch connected with the top of Cujo's head. Unfortunately, my mother's weapon of choice consisted of 90 percent mildew, causing it to evaporate upon impact and cause no harm to the dog whatsoever. It did, however, make Cujo realize that it had a much more accessible meal. It turned on my mom, and while she swung her half-size bat to keep the dog at bay, I leaped off the pillar, pulled my keys from my pocket, and sprung open the front door.

I don't know how my mom did it, but she managed to fight off the dog and back up through the front door. Once we were both inside, we slammed the door and fell to the floor in exhaustion, both of us dripping blood. My wounds most likely required stitches by today's standards, but due to the fact that we didn't have medical insurance, my mom broke out her kick-ass first-aid kit, cleaned the gashes with some peroxide, and then threw butterfly bandages on those suckers. The dog had clearly been rabid, and at the very least we should have been given some antibiotics, but somehow we both avoided dying horrible deaths.

The attack left me with some decent-size scars on my legs and ass, but instead of reminding me of the horrors of that day, they remind me of the important lesson that I learned. The lesson is this: When the shit goes down, even your best friends in the world will abandon you, and most likely do so while laughing their tits off. Whether it's a dog attack or the apocalypse, no one is going to save your sorry ass but you, so you better be fucking ready.

I've spent the last twenty years making sure I'm ready, and now I'm going to make sure that none of you get swept up in fallout. Now you might be thinking, "Forrest, by teaching everyone your secrets, aren't you making it harder for you yourself to survive when the end of the world comes?"

The answer is no, I'm definitely not. Because we both know that if you're reading a book by me, clearly learning from books isn't your thing. So yeah, I'm not that worried. Besides, worst-case scenario, I've got my mom to protect me and I'm pretty sure not even this book will save you from her.

YOU **MUST** PASS THIS TEST . . . THIS TIME I MEAN IT!

A s I've mentioned in all of my high-profile television and radio interviews, my previous book, *Got Fight?*, spent nine weeks on the *New York Times* bestseller list. So what's the problem? Everything that becomes popular too quickly becomes unpopular just as quickly. The clothing brand No Fear ring a bell? No, probably not—see my point. This is not because the product sucks in any way[1]—it is because of you, the consumer. When an army of nerds is seen toting a certain product between the chess club and front lawn of the high school where they receive their afternoon beatings, normal people get turned off from purchasing the product.

---

[1] Of course I am referring to my book, not the No Fear clothing brand, which sucks huge donkey cock—and I mean that in a bad way.

Personally, I want my books to be read by only the cool crowd,[2] so I am going to have to be a lot more selective this time around as far as whom I allow to purchase a copy. In the test below, you will find three types of questions.

The first type question will rate your manliness. I know what you are thinking—"If I passed the manliness test in your last book, *Got Fight?*,[3] can I go ahead and skip this test?" The answer is no. After all, a lot can happen in a year. A woman could have removed your balls and placed them in her purse[4] or you could have finally gotten around to buying that two-hundred-dollar pair of jeans you always wanted. You must prove to me that you are a man now, not sometime in the distant past.

The second type of question will judge your worth as a human being. Essentially, do I even want you surviving the apocalypse? Remember, I have knowledge you need, and I want to make sure you are worthy of receiving it before I slip you my large baton (of knowledge).

The third type of question will judge your Forrest Griffin Survival IQ. It has nothing to do with trying to stuff various-shaped blocks into various shaped holes. In my world, I am only concerned with stuffing one object into one hole. That's right—the object is *knowledge* and the hole is your *brain*! But before I give you this injection of knowledge, I must ensure that you have the necessary cunning, craft, and ingenuity to properly receive it. If you are not ready and I give it to you anyway, it could blind you or kill you or both. Both would be the worst.

This test is more important than the SATs or that test you took after watching the Kmart employee theft video (by the way, I scored a hundred percent on my employee theft test at Food Line—try to top that, bitches!). It will determine whether or not you are allowed to read the book that will help you outrun the death that scorches the face of the earth in the not-so-distant future. So, I highly recommend reclining in your chair, sipping on your chamomile tea,[5] and really thinking each question through before answering.

Tip: If you get stuck on a certain question, answer based on how you think I might react in such a situation. Pretty much all the questions below

---

[2] You know, the people who devour those awesome *Twilight* books.

[3] Did I mention that it was on the *New York Times* bestseller list for nine weeks?

[4] Or a man could have placed them in his fanny pack, which would be much worse.

[5] Anyone that drinks chamomile tea does not deserve to survive the apocalypse. Decaffeinated tea defeats the purpose of tea—it is the same as drinking Near Beer.

FORTUNE COOKIE WISDOM

I want it known that although I have placed Fortune Cookie Wisdom boxes throughout this book, in no way am I racist against Orientals . . . or Asians . . . or whatever they are called these days. They are good at math and have small penises—what's not to like? The reason I use the term is that after consuming a cheap, lousy, Chinese dinner of overfried, MSG-filled dog, the fortune cookie often gives you a pearl of wisdom that makes the meal not so bad. Hopefully, the fortune cookies in this book will make it not so bad, as it contains too much MSG and has the same consistency as fried dog meat.

P.S. My mom, who is as liberal as they come, still calls Asians "Orientals." It is a throwback from a different era and she can't help herself . . . and she loves their rugs.

were situations I found myself in over the course of my filthy life, and my reaction is always the correct reaction, even if it seems like a terrible reaction upon first glance. If you think how I behaved was strange, stupid, or perhaps slightly homoerotic, not only will you flunk the test and fail to be buttered with my hot knowledge, but I will also come to your house and steal one of your lovely pets. If you do not have a pet, I will shit underneath your couch, close all the doors and windows, and turn the heater all the way up.

(Note: If you do not pass the test in this book, you can still purchase a copy; you just aren't allowed to read it.)

FORTUNE COOKIE WISDOM

While shitting under the couch is horrible, it is nothing compared to the upper-decker, which is where you shit in the upper lid of a toilet. Every time you flush, it smells more like shit. Although I have never personally given an upper-decker, in college, me and a couple of friends went to a party, and the two girls who owned the home where the party was being held turned out to be real bitches, so my two friends both shit in the upper lid of their toilet. I was the lookout guy. And no, I didn't ask if they both shat into the upper lid at the same time. I don't want to know those kinds of things. It raises far too many questions.

1. **You step into the octagon with Anderson Silva and things don't quite go as planned. How do you react?**

    a. Remember that the last time you were in this situation you started crying in front of millions of people (e.g., Keith Jardine). Instead of repeating the experience, you immediately bolt from the cage, all the while singing Flock of Seagulls' "And I raaann . . ."

    b. Fight Anderson Silva in the parking lot, except this time you use some type of weapon such as a billy club, baton, or bazooka.

    c. Quickly invent some injury that prevented you from fighting to your full capability, such as glaucoma.

    d. After you wake up, get in the referee's face for stopping the fight.

    e. Throw your hands up into the air and pretend you won. When they announce that Anderson won, begin shouting, "I was robbed!"

    f. Remain in the ring and take your defeat like a man.

ANSWERS

    a. +8 points. Excellent answer. It will cause every reporter and fan to ask you, "What the hell were you thinking?" for the next several months, but at least no one will see you cry . . . again.

    b. -8 points. Bad choice. Anderson Silva is a master with nunchucks as well. Most likely he will claim your weapon and beat you to death with it.

    c. +4 points. I am not a big fan of fighters who make excuses, but if you cite glaucoma as being the reason for your loss, you get the +4 points for originality. However, if you made up a more generic excuse such as a slipped disc, broken foot, or busted hand, subtract ten points . . . Remember, all fighters are injured to some degree during the training process. Why? Because a part of their training consists of actual fighting.

    d. -5 points. After suffering such a terrible loss, the last thing you want to do is get beat up by Mario Yamasaki. It would be a career killer.

    e. -5 points. An excellent way to look like an even bigger jackass.

    f. -2 points. Now I know that I said this was the proper way to handle a loss in my previous book, but I am now retracting that statement in an attempt to make myself feel manlier. If you chose this answer, fuck you! You think you are better than me? You try getting beat by Anderson Silva and then sucking it up for a postfight humiliation interview.

2. Which way is north?

   a. Toward the mountains.

   b. Over by that lake.

   c. Down by the stream.

   d. Toward that mangrove forest.

ANSWERS

   a. -5 points. No, stupid, the mountains are in the south.

   b. -5 points. The lake is in the southeast. Either your compass is broke or you have eaten too many paint chips.

   c. +8 points. Correct. You score big!

   d. -8 points. While you were trying to answer this question, I made a voodoo doll in your likeness and I'm currently sticking pins into its genital region.

3. You get completely wasted in a bar and at the end of the night you somehow end up in a cougar's apartment, getting it on. While the two of you are engaged in hot, sweaty, sloppy sex, she cocks her head back from the doggie-style position and says in a sweet and maternal voice, "Honey, you ain't been in me for the last five minutes." How do you react?

   a. Despite her intense disappointment, you down a Powerade and attempt to get back into the game.

   b. Curl into the fetal position and began to weep.

   c. Robe quickly, make small talk for approximately five minutes, and then spend the next four days hoping that you never see her again.

   d. Ask her why the fuck it took her five minutes to speak up.

   e. Apologize and then spoon with her for the rest of the night.

ANSWERS

a.   -5 points. I am not a big fan of quitters, but you got to know when you are defeated. If you couldn't keep it up when you thought you were the biggest stud this sweet lady had bedded in her short fifty-five years, you most certainly won't be able to keep it up while she is doing her nails, texting her friends, and playing tennis on the Wii. If you chose this answer, you are either a sadomasochist or are overly determined to achieve something you probably shouldn't have attempted in the first place.

b.   -5 points. Absolutely pathetic . . . While you're at it, might as well have her change your diaper and take your temperature with a rectal thermometer. (Come to think of it, that might actually get me excited again . . . I am sure Freud would have something to say about that; after all, that woman was old enough to be my mother.)

c.   +8 points. This is the correct answer because it's how I reacted. I really truly hoped that I would never see her again, but just like my hopes to strut into the octagon and give Anderson Silva a critical beat-down, it didn't work out for me. Not long after this emasculating experience, I saw her at a restaurant while I was eating with a group of friends. I sank so low in my chair only my forehead could be seen over the top of the table—not an easy thing when you're six three. (Note to self: Never tell anyone about this traumatic experience.)

d.   +5 points. Who allows you to beat on their backside for five minutes without saying anything? Who does that? Unfortunately, a combination of the alcohol and the humiliation of her statement shut down my two remaining brain cells and prevented me from asking this question. If you should find yourself in this exact situation and have the gall to inquire about the meaning behind the delay, please e-mail me the answer. I still want to know . . . It is more like a *need*, really . . . The more I think back on that experience, the more horrible it becomes. I remember I had that drunk sweat going, and I was literally drenching her back. It was super gross.

e.   -5 points. Do you really want to smell mothballs, talcum power, and Chanel No. 5 all night? Yeah, didn't think so.

f.   God, this is really confusing. I can't remember what answer goes with what question.

4. Early in your MMA career you agree to fight Dan "The Beast" Severn. Instead of trading strikes, he repeatedly takes you down and lies on top of you. He has on his trademark black underroos, his mustache is tickling your neck, and his barrel chest is squashing your innards. In an attempt to get under his skin and turn this into an entertaining fight, what do you whisper into his ear?

  a. You looked thinner on TV.

  b. Magnum PI called, and he wants his mustache back.

  c. You look like a fat Freddy Mercury, anyone ever tell you that?

  d. You better hurry this up—you've got that seventies porno to make later.

  e. Hey, do you and Don Frye share the same mustache because I have never seen the two of you together.

  f. If you let me up, I will give you a shirt for Christmas that reads MUSTACHE RIDES 5 CENTS.

(P.S. No need to check Sherdog.com. Yes, I lost that fight.)

ANSWERS

  a. +3 points. I said this to him and meant it. The dude was huge, and when you fit all that mass into those tiny shorts, it is kinda disturbing.

  b. +5 points. If you watched the fight, you know just how boring it was. I had my head pinned up against the cage for the majority of it, giving me plenty of time to think up remarks. I felt this was one of the better ones. As a matter of fact, I think it even made me crack a smile.

  c. +5 points. Although I have been told that Tank Abbott used this insult while commentating on one of Severn's fights, I came up with it all on my own and whispered it to him while he was lying on top of me. Scary to think that Tank Abbott and I have the same sense of humor.

  d. +8 points. Not sure when I said this to him in the fight, but I thought it was more original than my other rips.

  e. +5 points. Another good one. Seemed to upset him too.

  f. +6 points. I didn't say this, but it would have been funny. The first time I saw that shirt it was on the back of a sixty-year-old woman in Juárez, Mexico. Thinking she had a great sense of humor, I went up to her to ask her about her shirt, but she didn't speak a lick of English. Obviously, she didn't have a clue what her shirt said.

5. **You are heading into the desert to escape the aftermath of the apocalypse, and you get to bring one person with you on your journey. Which one of the following would it be?**

  a. Stripper

  b. Doctor

  c. Wilderness Man

  d. Plumber

  e. Prostitute

  f. A Navy SEAL

  g. Little Person

ANSWERS

  a. -5 points. Stripper: Despite what you might be inclined to believe, a stripper has very little value in the desert. Come to think of it, a stripper has very little value period. This is due to the fact that while she was growing up, her father told her she had very little value. I know what you are thinking, "But, Forrest, what if I want to go out with a bang!" If that's your goal, you should have picked a prostitute. A stripper is like a car that starts but won't actually take you anywhere (except to the ATM). In addition, she is going to find a way to talk you out of your water, shelter, food, and any dignity you have left.

  b. +5 points. Doctor: Although there are no medical instruments or supplies in the desert, doctors are smart people who are fairly good at improvising. If you picked a doctor, I give you +5 points. However, if the doctor is a psychiatrist, subtract 15 points. Unless, of course, you are a stripper. If you are a stripper and selected a psychiatrist to wander with you in the desert, give yourself +15 points. The two of you will have plenty of time to work out your daddy issues.

  c. -4 points. Wilderness Man: The majority of you most likely chose a wilderness man, but I must now inform you that this is a terrible choice. By nature, a wilderness man is a loner. You need him more than he needs you, and he will ditch you the first chance he gets. In addition, they are notoriously bad conversationalists.

d. -8 points. Plumber: If you picked a plumber, hit yourself upside the head with a lead pipe. This question was supposed to be a gimme, but apparently you managed to fuck it up.

e. -4 points. Prostitute: Unlike if you were to bring a stripper, you will probably get laid frequently with a prostitute companion. While this might seem appealing, you must remember that prostitutes don't fuck for free. You are going to have to take care of this person. That means feeding them, clothing them, and putting up with their bullshit. You will also spend most of your days foraging for medicinal plants to soothe your burning loins.

f. +10 points. Navy SEAL: Navy SEALs might not be as familiar with surviving off the fat of the land as wilderness men, but they are as tough as nails and great improvisers. They also often have a hero complex, so there is a good chance that they will take you under their wing and save your ass from dying a horrible death. This was the correct answer.

g. +5 points. Little Person: This was another correct answer. Little people are great entertainers, and they are small enough that you can carry them around in a backpack. They can also be quite useful—you can send them up trees to steal eagle eggs, into caves to scout for dangers, or even down into small holes in the earth to flush out furry animals. (Unfortunately, the word "midget" has gone the way of the word "Oriental." Midget used to be a socially acceptable way to describe people who were, well, midgets. Now you have to call them "little people" or "vertically challenged" or something crazy like that. I long for the day when I can say the word "midget" again without being judged or called a size-ist.)

6. A good buddy of yours sets you up with a woman who works at his office. You go out on a date, things go well, and at the end of the night you go back to her place. Just before you are about to get it on, she says, "I have to confess something. I have herpes." How do you react?

a. Use a condom.

b. Run from her house, get in your car, and speed away. Even if you are in your own home, leave immediately. No kissing your dog good-bye, no stopping to take a leak. You just hightail it the fuck out of there.

c. Have sex with her, but pour Scope on your genitals afterward to kill whatever you may have picked up.

d. Ask her if she's into blow jobs or anal.

e. Ask if she has a younger sister that doesn't have herpes.

f. Put an arm around her and spend the next four hours listening to her problems, most of which revolve around the fact that she has HERPES.

g. Tell her it is okay because you have syphilis.

ANSWERS

a. -15 points. You are an idiot . . . If you don't know why this is a terrible decision, there is no point in me telling you. Chances are, you will bring a hair dryer into the shower at some point in the very near future.

b. +8 points. Good job, you are not a complete moron. When this happened to me, I think I may have made a few minutes of small talk, but I was out of there pretty damn quick. As you could imagine, I was irate at my friend. In addition to setting me up with a girl who had the gift that keeps on giving, he also set me up with a promoter who wrote me a bad check and a roommate who went completely nuts and called the cops on me. Yeah, I really need to start choosing my friends more wisely. I'm telling you, this chick roommate was a fucking nutcase. I had a girl over one night, and I guess she could hear us laughing and talking and humping. Not sure why that would piss her off, but it did. Instead of asking us to quiet down, she kept turning off the a/c. It was Georgia in the middle of summer, so it was hot as fuck. To avoid my bed turning into a swimming pool, every time she turned it off, I would turn it back on. The next morning, she called the cops on me. They busted into the house like some sort of domestic disturbance was going on. I talked my way out of it, but I had to live with the bitch for another few months. The surprising part is when she moved out, she actually left me money for the bills.

c. -5 points. I actually heard this on one of those sex talk shows. The guy shaved his pubic region, had sex with a prostitute, and then dunked his nuts into a glass of Scope because he was worried about catching something . . . I'm talking Scope, ladies and gentlemen. (As a side note, Bigger John had a friend in college who used to not only wash his junk with alcohol after sex, but also pour it into his pee hole.)

d. -5 points. Although you can't see me, I am shaking my head, thinking about how stupid you are.

e. +5 points. Terribly inconsiderate, but worth a try.

f. +3 points. I am giving you a few points for this because I am really trying to be a better human being.

g. +0 points. Good, you found your soul mate.

7. You're driving home from the gym, and suddenly you realize that you have to take a shit. Not wanting to drop your payload in the Starbucks crapper for fear of getting eighty-sixed for life, you convince yourself that you can make it to your personalized porcelain palace. After ten torturous minutes, you pull into your driveway and breathe a sign of relief. You run into the house and straight for the bathroom, but you quickly realize that it is much more difficult to keep your glutes flexed while running. Your turd stops playing peekaboo and makes a mad dash for freedom. Not wanting to admit to yourself the finality of the situation, you drop your TapouT trunks and leap toward the toilet, realizing this will be a wet one. While in midair, you fire-hose everything in sight. I'm talking the floor, the bathroom curtain, and the fluffy horseshoe toilet mat that your wife adores (I never knew what purpose they served, but now I know). After a few minutes of just kind of looking at the holocaust caused by the in-flight shit storm, you dig deep and begin the cleanup process. You wipe everything down and go through two cans of Lysol, but you still have that damn fluffy toilet mat to deal with. Instead of burning it in the backyard, you toss it into the washing machine. Forty minutes later, it comes out as fluffy and fresh-smelling as the day it was purchased. However, being a stupid man, you're not quite sure if you can put a fluffy toilet mat in the dryer. Wanting to put the whole situation in the past, you toss it on top of the dryer and walk away. An hour later, your wife brings the toilet mat into the living room and demands to know why it is sopping wet. What do you tell her?

a. I couldn't find a sponge, so I used it to wash the car.

b. I have no idea what you are talking about. Didn't know we even had a toilet mat.

c. Oh, the toilet mat. Yeah, I shit on that and tried to clean it up.

d. Is that a new dress? Damn, you look beautiful today.

e. Did you know the capital of Peru is Venezuela?

ANSWERS

a. -5 points. Lying to women about things that transpire in their household is just plain stupid. She might pretend to buy your excuse, but a few minutes later, she will go out and check for clues. If the car is not washed and the driveway is dry, expect another global shit storm. Later that night, when your defenses are down, she will break you. Like a preschooler, you will have to admit that you accidently shit on her fluffy toilet mat.

b. -5 points. Total ignorance can sometimes work. After all, women do not have that much faith in men's intelligence. If you can't remember her birthday, why in the hell would you notice a fluffy toilet mat, right? But be prepared for the topic of the wet, fluffy toilet mat to come up at social gatherings. *Oh, Margaret, I forgot to tell you, the strangest thing happened the other day. I came home and our toilet mat was sitting on top of the dryer, sopping wet.* Chances are, a husband of one of your wife's friends will have shit on a toilet mat at some point in time, and then the cat will be out of the bag.

c. +8 points. This is the correct answer. In my particular case, I was watching TV when my wife came into the room. Without missing a beat, I told her I shit on the toilet mat and then tried to clean it up. She stood there for some time, waiting for further explanation, but I gave her none. I simply began channel-surfing. Of course it led her to say things like, "Forrest, you are a disgusting human being," and "There is no fucking way I am going to take care of you when you get old," but at least I was spared the monthlong inquisition.

d. +5 points. Telling your wife she looks beautiful is an excellent distraction. However, the cause of the soggy toilet mat will eventually pop back up. If you use this time to come up with a more clever excuse, give yourself the five points. If you use the time to drink beer and watch football, you get zilch.

FORTUNE COOKIE WISDOM

This gem of wisdom is designed for my female readers. You all know that
men are inherently disgusting—and I mean *disgusting*. But it is even more
important to realize that as men get older, they get even more disgusting.
More ear hair, more nose hair. In fact, my stepfather actually combs his nose
hair into his mustache. This is true. So, however gross your fella is now,
know that when he's retired, sitting on that porch and watching that sunset,
he will be approximately ten times more disgusting than he is now. In my
case, I keep a rag by the bed to spit luggies in. Do I jerk off and spit luggies
into the same rag? Yes, I fucking do. Is that disgusting? It most certainly is.
But just wait until I get old.

e.   +5 points. If your wife is the argumentative kind, this might actually
     work because of course she will know that Venezuela is a separate
     country, not the capital of Peru. She will take at least ten minutes to
     berate you and tell you what an idiot you are. In the meantime, she
     will forget that she was supposed to be berating and yelling at you
     about the toilet mat. Excellent diversionary tactic. However, if your
     wife is not the argumentative kind, subtract 5 points, as it will only
     piss her off. If you wife is somewhat sane, you must stroke her ego
     or the tactic simply won't work. For future reference, in addition to
     making a remark about her beauty, I will also accept:

     1. You know (sigh), I was thinking about you while you were gone.

     2. I just realized how much care and love you put into decorating the
         house.

     3. I don't know how you do it (dramatic pause). I simply don't know
         how you do it.

8.   **What type of animal do you own?**

     a. Grizzly bear

     b. Tiger

     c. Dog

         1. Standard-size mutt that weighs between fifteen and thirty
             pounds

         2. Tiny rodent that weighs less than fifteen pounds

    3. Big dog that weighs more than thirty pounds

  d. Cat

  e. Hamster

  f. Horse

  g. I do not own an animal.

ANSWERS

a. **+8 points.** We obviously can't all have grizzly bears, but how awesome would that be? If you are one of the select few, you should write your own book on being manly . . . The downside to owning a grizzly bear as a pet is that oftentimes they will kill and eat you. It would be the same as a mouse owning a cat as a pet. Not a smart idea, but still ultramanly.

b. **-5 points.** You would think that having a tiger would be ultramanly, but it's not. Unfortunately, there are a lot of feminine men who have already chosen tigers as pets, especially here in Las Vegas. If you think about it, what real man wants a big pussy? Sorry, buddy, should have picked a grizzly bear.

c. Dogs are pretty standard for guys to own, so we have to break this one down further do decide if you are manly or unmanly in your choice of pet.

  1. **0 points.** If you have an average-size dog, you are pretty much average in every way. Yes, I base your self-worth on the size of your dog.

  2. **-5 points.** Although Chuck Liddell and Mickey Rourke are two of the toughest people I know, they both own small dogs, which costs them points on my manliness scale. If you own a big dog and think that you are manlier than these two individuals, you are wrong. I once watched Chuck jump off a fifteen-foot balcony in a bar in Mexico, just to give a waitress a tip. And Mickey Rourke starred in *9½ Weeks*—can't get any manlier than that. Assuming, of course, you don't watch the last fifteen minutes of the film, where he exposes his weaknesses and cries.

  3. **+5 points.** Before you shoot your wad thinking that you just scored 5 points, there is a catch. If your big dog just sits around at the foot of your chair, farting and chewing on its own limbs, subtract 10 points (do not count the original 5 points I gave you for owning a

big dog). In order to score points with a big dog, it has to be trained to help you out in some way. For example, fetch the paper, kill birds and other dogs, urinate on people you don't like, or play poker.

d. -5 points. I want to make something very clear—I do not own cats; my wife does. I admit that I pet them from time to time, and if her copy of *Cat Fancy* is open on the table, I may read an article or two. But in no way does that mean I own a cat. Sure, I may bring the cats to Starbucks with me and spend exorbitant amounts of money on their vet bills, but I only do that to make my wife happy. I may have even personally picked out one of the cats from the shelter, but that was just to ensure that we got the manliest cat possible. So what I am saying is that if your wife owns a cat, that is totally cool. However, if you personally own a cat, subtract 5 points.

e. -150 points. If you are over the age of seven and own a hamster, you are a very, very disturbed human being. I have taken away so many points that it is impossible for you to pass this test, so you might as well quit and go watch Freckles run laps on his wheel.

Confession: While I may be an adult male with no bizarre sexual proclivities, I do in fact own a hamster (it's name is Marzipan—I know, very nice). However, my hamster was a rescue. That's right, in the Las Vegas valley, people foreclose on their homes all the time, and when they move back to Wisconsin or wherever the fuck they are from, they just leave their pets to fend for themselves. One day, my wife and I saw what looked liked a crazy rat running around my yard. Eventually, it came close enough for us to see, and my wife, being a Good Samaritan, began screaming at me to catch it. I ran upon it, but I didn't realize how fast those little fuckers could move when terrified. After several minutes, I had it cornered up against the house, and I reached out to grab it. Not wanting to get taken, it swiped at my fingers with one of its harmless, microscopic paws, and I literally jumped back five feet, thinking it was going to kill me. Needless to say, it didn't score me any manliness points with the old lady. Anyhow, I ended up catching the eight-ounce hamster, and we nursed it back to health. Now I keep it in my closet, literally and figuratively. Once in a while I set him loose around the house in his little ball to torture the cats. Yeah, I'm pretty much a hero.

f. +8 points. This is another one of those tricky answers. In order to score big points for owning a horse, you must ride it on a regular basis. And I'm not talking about riding up and down the block—you must ride to do manly shit, such as to get across your property to fix a fence or back and forth to work. What kinds of job allow you to commute to work on a horse? A fucking lot of them. You could be a bartender in an Old West saloon, gunfighter, or a border patrolman. All of these are ultramanly jobs. Another stipulation is that you have to wear the proper attire while riding a horse. No biker shorts allowed. You have to wear chaps, a cowboy hat, and boots at all times. However, if you do not wear pants under your chaps, subtract 10 points as this is way too Village People to be manly . . . Come to think of it, I want you to strike the chaps part. They are most definitely a no-go. A certain member of the Village People gave chaps various implications, making them unwearable by the majority of the population. From now on, chaps may only be worn in biker bars that cater to special clientele . . . and by "special clientele" I mean people who are into crazy sex and bondage stuff.

g. -4 points. If you do not own some kind of pet, you are not manly. After all, being a guy is about controlling shit. And since women hate being controlled, you must fulfill this requirement on creatures that don't talk back. The more pets you control, the manlier you become. Unless, of course, you own cats. Please do not be that person who has fifteen cats. That is just kind of sad.

9. When you go to the gymnasium, what is it about you that stands out the most?

a. Your matching clothes.

b. Your body odor.

c. Your perfume or cologne.

d. Your jewelry.

e. Your makeup.

f. Absolutely nothing.

ANSWERS

a. -5 points. Unless you are in the military, do not color coordinate your gymnasium attire. It causes me to laugh and distracts me from my workout.

b. -5 points. I know what you are thinking: "But Forrest, it has been scientifically proven that women like the musky order that emanates from a guy's ripe armpit or crotch." While this might be a hundred percent true, the gym is not a place to pick up women. Real men pick up women at truck stops and on street corners, not gymnasiums (by the way, real men do not train at health centers, fitness clubs, or even gyms. Real men only train at gymnasiums). When working out, I do not want to catch a whiff of your mating scent. PLEASE WEAR CLEAN CLOTHES TO THE GYMNASIUM. I am not opposed to bathing, either.

c. -8 points. I cannot count the number of times I have gagged while doing cardio due to some floozy's perfume or some douche bag's cologne. You're at the gymnasium, not Club Pure.

d. -6 points. This is just hazardous to your health. Not only does it increase your chances of losing an ear or finger in one of the weight machines, but it will also increase your chances of getting mugged in the parking lot . . . By the way, what gymnasium do you work out in? Is the parking lot well lit, and generally what time will I find you there alone?

e. -5 points. Do I really need to explain this one . . . oh, and before I forget, if you can talk on the phone or read a book while doing cardio, you aren't really doing cardio.

f. +8 points. Good, you're a normal human being like the rest of us.

10. You are getting ready to head into the desert again, but this time you get to bring one person of faith with you. Which religious background would you choose?

a. Muslim

b. Scientologist

c. Buddhist

d. Christian

e. Southern Baptist

f. Mormon

g. Hindu

h. Atheist

i. Jewish

j. PENCIL IN YOUR OWN ANSWER HERE. (This choice is reserved for risk takers, as you will either lose or gain major points, depending upon your answer. However, with most people not being nearly as smart as they think they are, I must reserve this option

FORTUNE COOKIE WISDOM

As far as the standard IQ test goes, scoring a 100 means you are about average, scoring under 80 means you are mildly retarded, scoring over 120 means you are intelligent, and scoring over 130 means you are a genius and can join MENSA. If you are wondering what MENSA is, it is a group of socially awkward individuals that are very intelligent, but haven't yet figured out how to use their intelligence in any practical way. Do I say this because I am jealous? Perhaps a little. As I mentioned in my last book, I took a legitimate, sit-down, two-hour IQ test my freshman year in collage, and I was dismayed to learn that my IQ was 84, just five points above being mildly mentally retarded. Remember, this was back in '98 before all this politically correct bullshit, so the sheet of paper that deciphered the scores actually said the word "retarded." Now it says "disabled" or some shit, which probably would have made me feel a little bit better. I remember the people who gave the test tried to give me a pep talk, telling me that it really wasn't that bad, but I was mortally depressed for two days. I mean, I actually tried really hard on the test. So take it from me, never, ever take an IQ test, especially if you are concerned that you might be dumb. Trust me, you are. But as long as you don't take the test, you can always pretend (and just for the record, an IQ test is not that dumb test you download off the internet. A real IQ test takes approximately four hours).

for those who have taken an IQ test and scored over a hundred. If you have taken an IQ test and scored under a hundred [as I did] or never taken an IQ test, you are restricted to picking from one of the choices above.)

ANSWERS

a.   +4 points. Muslim: These guys are headquartered in the desert, so they probably have a good idea on how to survive there. However, if they are fundamentalist Muslims, do your best not to piss them off. For example, do not joke about their faith or use their religion in any type of multiple-choice quiz.

b.   -4 points. Scientologist: From what I gather, most Scientologists live in Hollywood, so they probably know nothing about surviving in the desert. Unless they can call that spaceship down to rescue your ass or you enjoy a good yarn of science fiction, they are terrible traveling companions.

c.   +2 points. Buddhist: There is only one reason to bring a Buddhist—if you want to die a cheery death.

d.   -4 points. Christian: I don't know any Christians that come from the desert, and they always think they are right. They will undoubtedly lead you on a mission to civilize a group of savage squirrels. With that said, I think I might be Christian. I know for a fact my wife is.

e.   -8 points. Southern Baptist: They hate everyone and love guns. You would think this would be ideal, but if are unlike me and actually have melanin in your skin, you will most likely get a decent tan while wandering across the desert, causing the Southern Baptist to lynch you.

f.   -4 points. Mormon: Having a Mormon traveling mate is good because they come from the desert, but it can be very difficult to ride a ten-speed on sand and you will be forced to give 10 percent of your animal skins to the church.

g.   +4 points. Hindu: Not only are they familiar with living on harsh terrain, but they are also used to fasting. Chances are, they will eat very little. Good choice! Just do not murder cows—it tends to really piss them off.

h.   -8 points. Atheist: All the atheists I have ever met have been super negative. In addition to this, they also tend to be super lazy. I mean, if they are too fucking lazy to find themselves a belief system, what makes you think they are going to collect firewood. Terrible choice.

i.   +4 points. Jewish: It is said that Jewish people wandered the desert for forty years, but once they got out, they all went straight to Hollywood. There is a chance that some of that desert survival knowledge got passed on through their genes, but I doubt it. The reason I awarded you with positive points is that they will undoubtedly teach you how to maintain your beard.

j.   PENCIL IN YOUR OWN ANSWER HERE: If you wrote the word "Amish," your risk taking paid off big-time! Go ahead and give yourself 25 points. Amish people are the true survivalists. Having renounced all technology, they have learned how to survive without drilling for oil or making major motion pictures. Give them an ax and a bucket, and they'll make butter, log cabins, and horse-drawn carriages. If you're hanging with one of these guys, no matter what conditions you may find yourself in, you will most likely do all right. Your life will never progress beyond *Little House on the Prairie* and time will probably go pretty fucking slowly, but at least you will live! However, if you penciled in anything other than Amish, the results of your IQ test obviously got mixed up with that of someone much smarter than you. Go ahead and subtract 15 points . . . You might also want to think seriously about taking your own life.

11. What is your favorite magazine?

a. *Fight* magazine

b. *Martha Stewart Living*

c. *Sports Illustrated*

d. *Muscle & Fitness*

e. *GQ*

f. *Playboy*

g. *Hustler* or another hard-core porn mag.

h. *Cat Fancy*

ANSWERS

a. +8 points. A good magazine because I am often in it. Sometimes, they even let me put on my Big Boy pants and write my own articles.

b. -5 points. You've been putting off that gender reassignment operation, but I think it's about time to open that door.

c. +0 points. For the most part, this magazine is reserved for fat has-beens dreaming of their high school football days and living vicariously through some millionaire's numbers. Oh, and by the way, if you collect sports cards, you should burn the cards along with yourself . . . or feed them to your hamster.

d. -5 points. You might not be full-blown gay, but you are definitely peeking over the fence. I mean, even the chicks in this magazine look like dudes.

e. -8 points. Not only have you fallen over the fence, but you've also rolled down a hill, slipped into a creek, washed out to sea, and swallowed by an overly gay whale.

f.   +0 points. You would think that a magazine with a half-naked chick on the cover would be megamanly, but it is not. Once you open it, all you see is articles and stories and advertisements. And in the few naked pictures it does contain, the women are covering most of their junk. If you want to be a real man, you must look at porn mags that actually offend your girlfriend.

g.   +8 points. Now this is what I am talking about.

h.   -4 points. For the second time, I do not subscribe to *Cat Fancy*. My wife does.

ACTUAL RANDOM CONVERSATION IN THE GRIFFIN HOUSE

JAIME: Forrest, for the tenth time, they are never going to put you on the cover of *Cat Fancy*.

FORREST: Sure they will. Don't they have somewhat famous people on the cover from time to time?

JAIME: No, they don't. They just have cats on the cover.

FORREST: But what if I am holding our cat?

12. When does cannibalism become okay?

a.   When you are hungry.

b.   When your buddy Joe actually begins looking like a giant pork chop.

c.   Anytime. Even now, before the apocalypse. Might as well get used to the taste.

d.   Never. You should die before you consume human meat.

ANSWERS

a.   +5 points. I sometimes get hungry between brunch and lunch, so I know how badly it sucks. I will accept this answer.

b.   -5 points. If your buddy starts looking like a giant pork chop, you waited far too long.

c.   -5 points. I am sorry, but I cannot accept this answer. Why eat humans now, when there are so many unwanted dogs and cats?

d.   -8 points. Next thing you'll tell me is that it is "wrong" to piss in the community pool. Go get a job, you fucking hippie.

13. From the last question, you learned that it is perfectly okay to
eat human meat when you are hungry. However, I must now
propose a moral question. At what point is it okay to turn your
traveling mate into food?

  a. The instant he dies of natural causes.

  b. When he is looking kinda sick.

  c. Shortly after you poison him.

  d. When he trips or falls.

  e. When he goes to sleep.

  f. Anytime he turns his back.

ANSWERS

  a. -5 points. Seriously, when have you ever waited for a chicken or cow to
      die of natural causes before you ate that son of a bitch. Personally, I
      have no interest in consuming roadkill. We have butchers for a reason.

  b. -2 points. Although this is a better answer than the last, you still
      probably waited too long. Human meat has an uncanny ability to
      "turn" quickly.

  c. +8 points. This is an excellent answer, but it is extremely important
      not to use a type of poison that will linger in his system. So instead
      of using an actual poison per se, you might want to use some type of
      club or heavy rock.

  d. +5 points. People become very vulnerable when they trip or fall,
      making it an excellent time to turn them into food. If you feel guilty
      about this, just remember that you saved them from having to conjure
      that fake, awkward laugh people always make when they trip or fall.

  e. +5 points. Killing someone in their sleep is the best because they
      don't feel a thing. Or is that when they die naturally? In any case, they
      won't put up much of a fight.

  f. +5 points. All survivors know not to turn their back on someone.
      Chances are, this guy is going to get you killed somewhere down the
      road. Might as well eat him now.

TEST RESULTS

So now I am going to ask you to tally up all your points. If you scored sixty-five points or higher, you are allowed to proceed. Just do so at your own risk. But regardless of score, the following people are not allowed to read my book:

DICKHEAD REPORTER

All reporters are not dicks. As a matter of fact, I owe a lot of my success to this hardworking, underpaid group of people who spread the awareness of my awesomeness to others. However, there are a few reporters who need to cram their head in a blender. A perfect example is the reporter who interviewed me a few days after I defeated Quinton Jackson and received the UFC Light Heavyweight title belt. It was the biggest moment of my life, and I felt on top of the world. In an attempt to sink my ship, he said, "What do you say to the people who think Quinton won, that he got robbed?" I replied, "What do you say to someone who has never tried, never bled, never had the guts to really go for something they really wanted? What do I say to those who sit behind a desk and talk into the microphone and criticize the deeds of others? I say . . ." and I hung up. A second later, I did a victory dance for my wife because it was one of those rare times when I had the perfect comeback. Seriously, I now tell this story with more excitement than I do the one about winning the title belt.

Another time I had a perfect comeback was shortly after I got my ass kicked by Anderson. I was signing autographs at the Olympia, and some muscle head (and I could tell immediately I didn't like him because his shirt was too tight, he had tattoo sleeves on both of his arms, and he had actually shaven his arms so that you could more clearly see the tattoos and the rippling veins in his biceps). He strutted up to me with his chest puffed out and said, "Yeah, bro, I just got to know, why did you run out of the ring after the Anderson fight?"

He was a pretty big guy, so I stood up. "That is a good question," I said, and waved him close as if I were going to tell him a secret. "You see the thing is, your mom—now I'm sure you've heard this—gives the best fucking blow jobs, and she was waiting in the locker room to suck my dick. I was so excited, I just had to get back there and get my dick sucked. I mean, your mom is an absolute pro."

As the words came out of my mouth, I could see him get physically tense. Instead of waiting around for a rebuttal, I walked past him and went over to sign an autograph for a kid. The meathead just stood there for close to a minute, mad-dogging me, and I just smiled at him. As he walked off, he continued to stare at me. I tried to nail him one last time by giving him the universal dick-sucking sign, you know, where you motion your hand toward your mouth and stick your tongue into your cheek, but he had already turned around. Anyway, if you're a douche bag like that reporter or meathead, please do not read my book.

ARMCHAIR QUARTERBACK

On almost a daily basis I have someone on the street come up to me and tell me how to fight. Now I realize that people like to get involved in the sport, and I also realize that there are a lot of fighters out there who are probably better than me, but to have someone who couldn't run twenty meters without vomiting tell me to "keep my hands up" is pretty fucking annoying. It's good advice, but very, very annoying. If you are the type of person who likes to tell other people more knowledgeable than you how to do their job, please do not read my book. I mean, if I walked into McDonald's, I wouldn't tell you how to flip a burger.

INTERNET WARRIOR

This is a message to Fraghead237. Fuck you! I know you thought you were so clever romoshopping me in a tutu and having me dance around a giant dick, but I just wanted to let you know that my private investigator just discovered where you live. I am coming to your house later today to stab you in the neck.

P.S. I am just kidding because I have the strange feeling that you are my target audience. Well, I am not kidding, but you are still my target audience.

PEOPLE YOU SHOULD ENCOURAGE TO READ MY BOOK

LUMBERJACK: There is a reason the Village People didn't include a lumberjack in their soiree—they are simply too manly. In my book, anyone who swings an ax for a living can automatically read my book. This includes serial killers and mohels who use an ax or an axlike instrument to perform their Brith Milahs.

WILDERNESS MAN: Anyone who wears a dead animal on their head is allowed to read my book. The only stipulation is that the animal must have some sort of tail. Personally, I don't think that is too much to ask. You will be hard-pressed to find an animal without a tail. And even if you do find an animal without a tail, you probably won't want to wear it on your head. This includes frogs, apes, sloths, various sea urchins, and, of course, humans.

PIRATE: There are many forms of pirates, but not all of them get an automatic thumbs-up to read my book. If you are a pirate and want to skip all the annoying tests, you must carry a sword . . . and the sword must be constructed from steel. Your flesh sword does not count.

PREPARE NOW, PART I: HOW TO BE TED KACZYNSKI WITHOUT ALL THAT UNABOMBER CRAP

As you may have learned from my first book, I was once a Webelo—that's right, not a Boy Scout, but a Webelo. Pretty low on the survival skills totem pole, but at least it was a step up from the Cub Scouts. Anyhow, before I was ejected from this society for chucking a can of soda at my scoutmaster's head, we went on a few camping trips. These consisted of about twenty of us kids, and five or six parents, all of whom were stupid enough to get duped into taking care of twenty boys in the wilderness. I would like to say that I learned all sorts of practical knowledge on these outings that I could pass on to you, but of course the parents ended up putting up the tent and doing all the merit-badge-worthy tasks we kids were supposed to do. However, I did learn a few lessons from these experiences, the most important being that the wilderness sucks. If you have a house with hot water, you should probably stay there because the wild will do everything in its power to make you absolutely miserable.

On the second day of one of these little adventures into the great unknown, the parents gathered up all the kids, brought us down to a luke-warm creek, and expected us to bathe. That's right, twenty half-naked kids, five adults (also half naked), bathing in a creek with bars of soap. Did I mention that it was in a fucking creek? I immediately felt molested. The only cool thing to come out of the mass bathing ritual was that my step-father, Abe, taught all the kids how to change in nature using a towel. We thought it was the coolest thing, and for the next few days every kid spent at least two hours a day changing and rechanging their shorts (kids are fucking weird).

The absolute worst part about camping was taking a dump. I was excited when we first got there because there were outhouses, which meant I didn't have to dig a hole, but when I ventured into one of these portable shit houses, I learned that the words "cleanliness" and "wilder-ness" do not go together. I made the mistake of looking down into the hole, and it looked like a shit monster had been murdered in there. There was shit everywhere—I mean, how do you get shit on a wall? There was a toilet seat, yet shit somehow ended up on the wall. It was just like that scene from *Slumdog Millionaire* where they shit off the piers.

Fearful of getting consumed by the shit monster, most of us kids resorted to pooping in the woods, and with all kids being inherently lazy, we didn't bother to dig holes. We just shit on the ground and then ran off. So by the end of the three days, everyone had spent seventy-two hours tra-versing a shit field, and we all stunk like walking death. The entire expe-rience made me realize one thing—I fucking hate the wilderness. If you are like me and spend a good portion of your life trying to avoid all things outdoors, this book will do you well, because, when doomsday comes, the outdoors will be your new home.

Before I tell you how the world will end, there are some things that you need to do to prepare yourself. Since you are currently reading a book on the apocalypse written by a professional fighter who's suffered some pretty serious head trauma, I'm assuming that you have some mental impair-ments of your own. You're not a full-blown moron, but you have trouble with simple things like walking without tripping, wiping your butt, counting, and, most importantly, reading. I will not judge you because I am well versed in moron, and we're in this together. However, it is quite possible that it will take you several years to read this book from start to finish, making it important that we start your training before I supply you with the various end-of-the-world scenarios and tell you what to expect. Just trust me that all this stuff will come in handy.

IS THAT AN ASSAULT RIFLE IN YOUR PANTS? (WELL, IT SHOULD BE)

Learning how to defend yourself is not something that happens overnight. It takes a lot of practice, which means you must start your training now. While numerous accountants, stockbrokers, housewives, and other regular people will survive the apocalypse by blind luck, the majority of those who dodge death's bullet will be survivalists who predicted the coming-of-the-end and received the proper training. These people will have at least basic knowledge on how to shoot and kill with their hands, and unless you are on a level playing field, there is a good chance that you will become their future food source.

To avoid such an outcome, I've included some very basic knowledge on how to defend yourself. You don't have to become an expert marksman or a professional fighter, but at the very least, you must be able to shoot a

DICK IN A BOX BY BIGGER JOHN

Both Forrest and I are firm believers in being armed at all times. Back before I got replaced by a bunch of Vegas douche bags, I used to corner Forrest for his fights. When he went to Sacramento to fight Tito the first time, I went with him. We were hanging outside with all the fighters, and suddenly Tim Sylvia comes up to us and starts making fun of Forrest for the thick leather coat he had on.

"Dude, what the fuck you wearing that huge jacket for?" he said. "Are you a moron? It's eighty-five degrees out here."

Without batting an eye, Forrest said, "It's not a jacket, it's a holster."

"Excuse me?"

"I said it's not a jacket, it's a holster." And with one quick movement, Forrest pulled the Glock 40 from the inside pocket.

Now I am not trying to call Tim a pussy or anything, because I honestly think he is one of the toughest heavyweights we've seen in the sport of MMA, but you should have seen the look in his eyes when Forrest pulled that gun. Instantly he knew he was dealing with someone on a whole different level of crazy.

Hating to get left out of anything, I decided to add to the effect and pulled the Glock 40 I had in my belt holster underneath my shirt. Tim immediately tried to grow back his balls by talking about his favorite guns, but I will never forget the look on his face. It was priceless . . . Anyhow, I guess the moral to this story is that you should always remain strapped, even if it requires you to wear a thick leather jacket in eighty-five-degree weather.

target at close range and understand how to properly apply a choke hold. Note from the HarperCollins legal team: Keep in mind that the apocalypse hasn't hit yet. Every state has its own laws about who can legally acquire a gun and how that gun must be carried. I'm not saying you should break any of those laws so that you can buy or use guns, and if you're not eighteen (or twenty-one in some states), then this section doesn't even apply to you.

HOW TO STAND WHEN FIRING YOUR GUN IN AN INCREDIBLY SAFE AND RESPONSIBLE WAY

There is no such thing as a proper shooting stance. It is important that your stance is balanced and stable, but the exact foot positioning is entirely up to you. Some people like to stagger their feet, while others prefer to keep their feet square. My only suggestion is to establish a shooting stance that feels comfortable and familiar. For example, I shoot from my fighting stance, which involves placing my left foot forward and my right foot back. I could just as easily shoot from a square stance, but being a professional fighter, my fighting stance feels very comfortable and natural. If Lyoto Machida shot guns, I am sure he would shoot from a karate horse stance. And if Royce Gracie shot guns, he would shoot from a butt-scoot stance. See what I am getting at? If you choose a shooting stance that is not familiar, it can take you a moment to establish it when shit goes down, and the last thing you want to be focusing on in a shoot-out is the positioning of your feet.

To learn what feels most comfortable, practice drawing your gun and aiming. This can be done on the firing range, or, if you're like me, while traversing the desert in your underwear. Whatever position your feet naturally gravitate to, adopt that as your shooting stance. Once you've got your feet positioning down, make sure to square your shoulders, put a slight bend in your arms, and keep your head up and straight.

Quick Draw

The Old West quick draw is fun to practice in abandoned warehouses on unsuspecting vermin (and by *vermin* I mean rats, not homeless people).

To assume my shooting stance, I step my left foot back and my right foot forward. With my feet spread roughly shoulders' width apart, I bend my arms and keep my head up. It is very important to notice that I am not leaning backward away from the gun, which is a mistake a lot of people make when first learning how to shoot.

While creeping around an abandoned warehouse, I am surprised by a very large rat. Immediately I spread my feet apart and grab the grip of my gun.

I place my left hand on my abdomen to ensure I do not shoot my fingers off.

I quickly jerk my gun from my holster. Instead of extending my arm straight, which would take too much time, I keep my elbow back and simply level the barrel with the ground. This last step is very important—if your gun is not level, there is a good chance that you will shoot yourself in the foot. Note: To state the obvious, do not actually shoot the vermin.

GET A FUCKING GRIP (OR WHY RAP VIDEOS ARE NOT A GOOD WAY TO LEARN ABOUT GUNS)

Back when I was playing high school football in Georgia, a few idiots on my team unfortunately decided to do a drive-by shooting one night. As they crept by the house, both the driver and the passenger opened up. Being a complete genius, the driver extended his arm out his window, turned his gun sideways, and attempted to shoot over the top of the vehicle. Instead of riddling the house with bullets, he shot though the roof of the car. A bullet entered the back of the passenger, which prompted him to turn his gun on the driver. A shouting match ensued. A few hours later at the hospital, the police showed up and rightfully arrested both of them. Please, attend to this lesson and learn how to shoot like a normal human being.

How you grip a gun is another matter of debate, but there are a few general rules everyone can agree upon. First off, you want to establish a two-handed grip. If one of your hands is injured or holding something of importance, it's possible to establish a single-handed grip and still aim accurately, but a two-handed grip will give you far better results. In the illustrations below, I demonstrate a single-handed grip, as well as the two-handed grip that I always use.

FORTUNE COOKIE WISDOM

If you talk too passionately and too much about guns, it may lead people to believe you have a tiny penis.

Single-Handed Grip

To establish a single-handed grip on my gun, I grab the grip with my right hand. If you are left-handed, you want to grab it with your left hand. Notice how the web between my thumb and index finger is positioned as high up on the grip as possible, my thumb is positioned by the safety, and my finger is not on the trigger. The only time you want to actually place your finger on the trigger is when you are about to shoot. If you are running or walking with your gun drawn, always keep your finger off the trigger to prevent an accidental discharge. All law enforcement officers are taught this during training, but apparently no one mentioned it to Kiefer Sutherland. In the few episodes of *24* that I have seen, he is always running with his finger on the trigger. Although I find this extremely annoying, I keep praying that he will accidently shoot that sniveling computer cunt Chloe O'Brian.

Double-Handed Grip (Not to Be Confused with the Similarly Worded Masturbation Technique)

This method of gripping a gun is often employed by law enforcement officers and competitive shooters. To begin, I grip the gun with my right hand just as I did when performing the single-handed grip, except now I run my right thumb down the length of the barrel just below the slide. Next, I wrap my left hand around my right hand, and then run my left thumb down the barrel just beneath the slide. This grip, I assume, gives me optimal control of the gun and allows me to quickly shift from one target to the next. In addition to this, the forward positioning of my thumbs helps me quickly line up my sights on new targets.

The Gangster Grip

If you feel the best way to hold a gun is sideways, you're either an idiot or a wannabe gangster. The only reason you should ever hold a gun sideways is if you have a severe shoulder injury that prevents you from holding a gun straight. *But it looks super cool*, you say. No, it doesn't. In addition to making you look like a complete retard, it will be next to impossible to hit the broad side of a barn.

IT'S NOT JUST POINT AND CLICK

Most guns have two sights, one on the front of the gun and one at the back. If you are shooting at something more than fifteen feet away, it is in your best interest to line up both sights on your target. However, this process can take a few seconds, which can get you killed when in a close-range shoot-out. If an aggressor is within fifteen feet, hold your gun level and place your front sight on the center mass of your target. Unless your gun is cocked upward or downward, there is a good chance that you will hit what you are aiming for. Then again, Bruce Willis and Arnold Schwarzenegger never do this, and they seem to hit people from twenty or thirty meters away, which is amazing accuracy. So maybe you should stop reading this book and start watching more action movies. As a matter of fact, I think you can get a lot out of a movie if you watch it fifty thousand times, which is what I did with *Good Will Hunting* when I was living in that shitty one-room apartment back in my college days. Unfortunately, instead of learning how to shoot a gun, I learned how to freak out my family members by having imaginary conversations with the characters in the movie and referring to them as my friends.

When firing, do not pull the trigger: squeeze the trigger. The smaller the squeeze, the more fluid you will become at shooting your gun. And once you have shot a round, slowly release your pressure on the trigger. Although this might seem simple, it is very difficult to accomplish, especially when someone is shooting back at you. To avoid this rookie mistake, learn to steady your nerves by shooting as often as possible.

WHEN YOUR GUN GOES LIMP

There are three types of malfunctions that can prevent your gun from firing. Having a gun is great, but having a gun that doesn't fire sucks. To avoid having to use your gun as a boomerang, I recommend practicing how to deal with all three types of malfunctions.

TYPE ONE: This malfunction is usually caused by not properly seating the magazine into the well. You'll know when it happens because as you attempt to fire a round, you hear your gun click but no shot is fired. To solve the issue, you remove your finger from the trigger, release your support hand from the gun, smack the bottom of the magazine with your palm, tilt the gun to the side, rack the slide back with your free hand, and then reestablish your two-handed grip on the gun and again squeeze the trigger. To simplify, TAP, RACK, ROLL.

TYPE TWO: This type of malfunction is often referred to as a "Brass High" or "Stovepipe" because it is caused by a shell casing getting stuck in the ejection port, which locks the slide into the back position and prevents you from firing off any more rounds. While this is different from a type-one malfunction, it is remedied in the exact same way: TAP, RACK, ROLL.

TYPE THREE: A type-three malfunction is often referred to as a "Feedway Stoppage" because you have two rounds competing for the same space in either the chamber or receiver. To remedy this issue, use the steps below.

1. Remove your finger from the trigger (pretty fucking obvious, but you would be surprised).

2. Release your support hand from the gun and then use it to pull the slide back until it locks.

3. Release the magazine, grab the slide again with your free hand, and rack it three times. If the magazine doesn't eject, you might have to pull it free.

4. Insert a new magazine.

5. Reestablish your two-handed grip on the gun and begin firing.

It is important to mention that this type of malfunction takes considerably longer to fix than the previous two. If you are in a gunfight when a type-three malfunction occurs, there is a good chance that you will get shot if you remain out in the open. To prevent this, move for cover as you fix your weapon or beg for mercy.

If you choose the latter, here are some of the things you might want to say:

a. I was just kidding; my gun wasn't even loaded.

b. Hey man, these aren't even real bullets.

c. I thought we was just playing, dog.

d. Don't shoot! I'm pregnant!

WHAT TO DO WHEN BEING CHASED BY TINA TURNER

During the apocalypse, a lot of shoot-outs are going to occur on the road as you are attempting to go from point A to point B.[6] Sometimes these will occur while you're driving a semi loaded with gas and being chased by Tina Turner wearing earmuffs. Obviously, while driving, it is a good idea

---

[6] It's good to be prepared for this type of encounter, but as of yet, I have not found a firing range that allows you to shoot out of a moving vehicle. Occasionally I do this in the desert, and I've found that my aim is absolutely horrible. But I haven't given up hope because they make it look pretty easy in the movies.

to wear your seat belt at all times. In addition to there being numerous obstacles in the road, a lot of people will use their vehicles as battering rams in an attempt to disable your vehicle.

However, anytime you are parked, you want to remove your seat belt, which is something I learned while in the police academy. If you're right-handed like most people, you will most likely wear your gun on your right hip. This is the exact location where your seat belt locks, and it can make it very difficult to get to your gun. Not wearing your seat belt will help you get to your gun quicker, but if you're a douche bag like me and habitually lock your seat belt every time you get in the car, it is good to get into the habit of removing your gun and placing it underneath your left thigh.

Another reason not to wear your seat belt while your car is parked is that it makes it too difficult to exit your vehicle when shit hits the fan. In most cases, attempting to start your car and drive away takes too much time. By the time you put your vehicle into drive, your aggressors will have already showered it with bullets. A much better option is to quickly bail out of your car and use it as cover.

DICK IN A BOX: MR. & MRS. GRIFFIN BY JAIME

One night not long ago I woke up at two or three in the morning, and I noticed that Forrest was not in bed next to me. I figured he was either jerking it on the Internet downstairs or he had gone to the store to get some sweets. I called his name, and when I didn't get an answer, I went downstairs to check on him.

I couldn't find him anywhere, so I went into the garage. I was horrified by what I found. The car was gone, the garage was wide open, and the door leading into the house was unlocked. I instantly lost my mind. I thought, "This motherfucker left me here by myself, and someone could have murdered me." I was shaking mad, and so I decided to get a little revenge by faking a crime scene. I dumped the contents of my purse onto the floor and knocked everything off the tables. Once the setting was perfect, I hid behind a cabinet in the living room. In case someone broke in before Forrest returned, I armed myself with my .38.

Ten minutes later I heard Forrest come in. I almost let out a laugh, but then I heard his grocery bags drop to the floor and the familiar sound of him chambering his Glock 40. It was at this point that I realized faking a crime scene might not have been the smartest move. Not wanting to say anything for fear of startling him, I remained utterly quiet. I heard him creep up the stairs, and then I heard him slowly open each of the upstairs doors. He never yelled, never gave up his location. He moved in and out of each room, clearing them like an assassin.

Suddenly I heard his footsteps back downstairs, moving toward me, and that's when I shouted, "I am right here, I am right here." I came out of hiding with my .38, and he came into the room with his Glock 40. It was like a scene straight out of *Mr. & Mrs. Smith*. Needless to say, he was not thrilled by my antics, but eventually he realized that he was in the wrong and apologized.

Luke Rebuttal

Jaime told me that story shortly after it happened, and her tone was quite different. It was almost gleeful. When Forrest cleared the house like a trained killer, it actually turned her on. Forrest was just as aroused. Although I wasn't there, I know for a fact that he was excited about the fact of possibly getting to shoot an intruder. I wouldn't be surprised if later that night, they had the best sex of their lives.

Never have I met two people more paranoid or heavily armed. Between the two of them, they must have more than fifteen guns in their house. And they are not just handguns. Forrest has a .22 rifle with a built-in silencer, as well as an AR-15. That's fucked up. Who needs an automatic weapon for home protection? In addition to having his own personal armory, he is always going on and on about reactionary gaps. For example, the gate that surrounds his neighborhood is a reactionary gap because it gives him time to arm himself against a possible intruder. The wrought-iron bars on his windows are a reactionary gap, the four locks on his front door are a reactionary gap, his state-of-the-art alarm system is a reactionary gap, and the key lock he has on his bedroom door is a reactionary gap. I don't know how much time

Forrest needs to reach his guns—there is one in every room, for Pete's sake—but I guess the guy likes to be prepared.

I'm not quite sure what's wrong with them. Jaime grew up in a small town in Arizona, and Forrest and I grew up in a suburban neighborhood in Georgia where you left your doors unlocked at night. Neither one of them has ever been held at gunpoint, but both seem convinced that it is only a matter of time until the shit hits the fan. Think I am blowing their paranoia out of proportion? Most fighters are sponsored by companies like Muscle Milk and Condom Depot. Forrest is sponsored by Advanced Armament, which is a company that builds silencers for all types of guns. Instead of getting free protein shakes in the mail, Forrest receives free silencers.

I'm telling you, Jaime and Forrest are meant to be together. Like most couples, they have date night, but instead of going ice skating or to Applebee's, they go to the firing range. They also go to the firing range every Sunday after church. So if you are thinking about trying to break into Forrest's house or carjack him because you found this book repulsive, you are going to get hurt. And Jaime won't be one of those girls who cries after she kills you. As she etches another notch into her belt, you'll hear her whisper, "Fucker, you shouldn't have tried to break in." In fact, that will be the last thing you ever hear because according to Forrest, if Jaime has to shoot a home invader, she will do everything in her power to ensure he is dead to prevent him from plotting any type of revenge. Never have I met two people more perfect for each other. Guns are what tie them together—that and the violent sex they have.

NEWSFLASH: GUNS ARE USELESS WITHOUT BULLETS

Having guns and knowing how to use them is all well and good, but you're not going be able to do shit with them if you don't have bullets to put in them. If you're truly serious about getting ready for our impending destruction, you need to start buying bullets. Now. Seriously, go this second. I'll be waiting right here when you get back. Go now, jackass. Oh, so you think you don't need to go this instant? Now you're too good for this book?

Let's see you try and use your Glock when the only stashes of bullets are in the hands of powerful, tribe-leading overlords with nicknames like "Zeus" and "The Professor."

Go buy bullets now and bury them in your backyard under the old oak tree. And don't tell anyone where they are. Especially not me.

FIGHT, FLIGHT, AND WHAT TO DO WHEN PISSING YOUR PANTS ISN'T AN OPTION

I imagine that cavemen were pretty in tune with their fight-or-flight instinct. If a caveman headed out into a field to pick some berries (not sure if cavemen picked berries or not, but it seems like a very cavemanish sort of thing to do), and suddenly a woolly mammoth came charging out of the bushes, his mind would instantly assess the situation and decide which option would give him a better chance of survival. In the amount of time it takes you or me to step on the brakes at a red light, the caveman would either chuck a spear at the advancing beast or begin running his fucking tits off toward the nearest tree. Although the life of the caveman sucked in pretty much every way imaginable, especially when it came to mating, he had a serious leg up on modern man when it came to interpreting his instincts.

Most of us still have the fight-or-flight instinct buried deep in our brains; we just struggle with its interpretation, which is what leads to panic or making the wrong choice. Luckily, in the civilized world in which we currently reside, we often get a second chance when we fail to interpret our instinctual signals correctly. However, the apocalypse will be the caveman days all over again, so it is in your best interest to start getting acquainted with what your mind is trying to tell you in times of stress.

This can be accomplished by putting yourself in extremely dangerous situations where the only hope of survival is to make the right choice. For example, you can jump out in front of a moving bus. Your brain will undoubtedly send you a shit load of terrifying signals, but you must learn to interpret them correctly. If your instincts tell you to stand your ground and fight the bus, you are probably not making the right assessment. In such a situation, your only chance to live another day is flight.

WHY YES, YOU CAN KILL SOMEONE WITH A PENCIL: WEAPONS OF OPPORTUNITY

A weapon of opportunity is anything around you that you can use as a weapon (no, it couldn't more self-explanatory). For example, as I sit here writing this, I can see several weapons of opportunity. I can use the pen sitting on the table to stab you in the eye, I can use the strap-on lying over in the corner to bludgeon you over the head, and I can even use the hot cup of coffee in my hand (yes, I only type with one hand) to blind you. However, if the cup of coffee in your hand happens to be an iced latte, not only would it be a terrible weapon of opportunity, but it would also make me question your manhood. If you threw that into my face, it would just piss me off. Another terrible weapon of opportunity would be a banana. You starting to see what I am getting at? I would love to have had this idea all on my own, but when I did a seminar at a Marine base, that is what they preached—weapons of opportunity. If you're in a position where you need a weapon, a household object will do. If there is a knife, a vase, a shoehorn around you, turn it into a weapon. Remember, you never want to be in a fair fight if an unfair fight is an option (that line was all mine, I swear!).

Obviously, this type of training will increase your chances of dying a horrible death and never making it to the apocalypse, but if all goes well and you hone your instincts, you will be well prepared for the end of the world. (Just kidding, of course, I don't want you to jump in front of a bus. Besides, there is no way to hone your instincts—that is why they are called instincts.)

To give you an idea of how to properly and improperly read your instincts, I will share a story with you from my drunken college days. I believe I was nineteen or twenty at the time, and I was hanging out in a bar that was notorious for serving minors. After a few beverages, the front doors flew open and cops stormed in, shouting about how they were conducting a raid for underage drinkers. My fight-or-flight instinct kicked in, and luckily I made the right choice. Instead of taking a swing at an officer of the law, I ran toward the emergency exit, kicked it open, and bolted out into the night.

Two cops were standing there, ready to catch anyone who decided to skip out, and I was again presented with a fight-or-flight choice. I could have chosen to tackle one of them, which would have led to me getting beaten with clubs, Maced, kicked, and handcuffed, but again I read my instincts correctly. With a little shuffle of my feet, I avoided their reaching arms and then sprinted down the street with all my strength.

After about four minutes sprinting at full velocity (that was drunk time, so it was probably more like twenty seconds) I was gassed out of my mind. Certain that a full-scale manhunt had been launched to find me (yes, I was drunk *and* paranoid), I began searching for a place to hide. The first location that jumped out was a fraternity house. Figuring that if anyone could sympathize with my predicament, it was a group of drunken ass-holes, I headed toward it. Huffing and dripping sweat, I opened the front door without knocking, ran into the living room, and then knelt down by the window so I could peer out at the street for cops.

While I was huddled there, three frat brothers walked into the room, each with a plastic cup filled with beer. They looked at me for a second, I looked at them, and then I returned my eyes to the street.

"What the fuck you doing in our house?" one of them shouted.

"Don't worry about it," I returned without even turning around.

"Dude, I said what the fuck are you doing in our house?"

"Your mother will explain it to you when you're a big boy," I said, slightly perturbed.

I heard a cup of beer drop and feet rapidly approaching me. By the time I stood up, all three of them were in my personal space, shouting at me. For the third time that night, I found myself in a fight-or-flight scenario. Outnumbered three to one, my reptile brain was sending me all sorts of messages. I probably should have interpreted the signals the same as I did on the previous two occasions, but for some reason I thought my brain was saying, "Hey bro, fuck this running shit. You need to fight these bitches. You got 'em, bro. Ain't no tang." Apparently, my reptile brain really likes clichés and is a frat-boy douche bag at heart.

There were three of them lined up in front of me, and not knowing their names, I will refer to them as Dickhead one through three. Well, I saw Dickhead One pulling his fist back to hit me, and for some reason my

drunken mind gave me the instruction to hit Dickhead One. So, that is
what I did. About half a second after my fist bounced off his face, Dickhead Two crashed his knuckles into my cheek. Pissed off that I had just
gotten punched, I socked Dickhead Two in retaliation. Immediately after
my fist landed, Dickhead Three belted me one. Again, this angered me, so
I punched Dickhead Three. A split second later, Dickhead One tagged me,
and the vicious cycle began again. I hit Dickhead One, which prompted
Dickhead Two to land his second shot. After I hit Dickhead Two, Dickhead
Three hit me.

Believe it or not, we went down the line like this for more than four
minutes (again, drunk time—I have no idea how long it was in real time).
With there only being one of me and three of them, I obviously got the
worst end of the deal. It was kind of like I was playing a game of charley
horse, except instead of playing with one guy I was playing with three. And
instead of slugging each other in the arm, we were slugging each other in
the face. Luckily, everyone sort of got tired at about the exact same moment
and we stopped hitting each other. Realizing that it was only a matter of
time before we all recuperated and the hitting began again, I reassessed
my previous interpretation and ran. I bolted straight out the front door
and sprinted my way home. Apparently, I didn't learn much from this lesson because twelve years later when I stepped into the cage with Anderson Silva, my reptile brain told me to actually fight him. It wasn't until I
regained consciousness that I realized the correct response should have
been flight, at which point I fled. It was obviously too late by that point.

The moral here is that when your mind is sending you mixed messages
in a dangerous situation, running is probably the safe choice to make. The
only time you actually want to fight is when you are matched up with a
much weaker opponent and actually have something to gain. For example,
either fighting a mentally handicapped person in order to impress your
girlfriend or fighting a child to acquire his satchel of sweets is acceptable.
But other than these two scenarios, you pretty much want to run.

LUKE

Forrest is one of the few fighters who doesn't have a nickname. But if he did, it would undoubtedly be "Tackleberry." If you don't understand this reference, go rent *Police Academy*.

THE WILDERNESS IS JUST LIKE THE OCTAGON BUT WITH TREES

You never want to bring your fists to a gunfight, but there will come a time during the apocalypse when the majority of ammunition gets exhausted. Granted that might take a long fucking time, but it is important to prepare for it nonetheless. If your goal is to become a badass fighter, there are dozens of exceptional MMA instructional books on the market, all of which are produced by Victory Belt Publishing (Erich is fucking shameless, plugging his own company . . . what a douche). However, the chance that you will encounter a professional fighter during the apocalypse is slim.

The majority of people you have to contend with will most likely be tough sons of bitches—after all, they somehow found a way to live long enough to see all the ammunition dry up—but they probably won't be super dangerous in the hand-to-hand combat department. Although learning how to throw proper strikes and apply fancy submissions will not hurt you in any way, it is not high on your apocalypse-preparation to-do list. When it comes to fighting during the apocalypse, you want to focus on choke holds because they are the only techniques that allow you to turn your aggressor's lights out, permanently.

Below I have included two of the more effective choke holds that can be applied from the standing position. My suggestion is to practice these techniques as often as possible. Simply learning how to apply these choke holds is not enough—you must train them ritualistically. When they are applied improperly, you will fail to sever blood flow to your opponent's brain and quickly gas out your arms, which puts you in danger. Personally, I recommend practicing them on drunk people in your local bar, and once you have them down, work up to moderately sober people. Trust me, applying an effective choke hold is not as easy as Sayid makes it seem on *Lost*.

Standing Rear Naked Choke from Behind

I sneak up behind Erich and wrap my left arm around his neck. If your opponent tucks his chin to his chest in an attempt to prevent you from cutting off the blood supply to his brain, which is probably a good tactic on his part, you can pull his head upward using your opposite hand.

To apply the rear naked choke, I grab my right biceps with my left hand and then position the back of my right hand behind Erich's head. To sever blood flow to his brain and give myself an immense amount of pleasure in getting back at him for constantly editing the shit I say in this book, I squeeze my arms tight.

Guillotine Choke
Off the Tackle

Erich attempts the old-school football tackle, and being a good deal taller than him, I simply place my hand on his head. In addition to stopping his forward momentum, it is quite demeaning.

Before Erich can elevate his head, I step forward and wrap the blade of my left arm across the front of his neck.

To apply the standing guillotine choke, I clasp my hands together, drive his head downward using my chest, and pull my left forearm up into his neck using my right hand.

FORREST FACTOID

Ages ago I was in a friend's bar in Georgia and some dickhead out in the street decided to chuck a beer bottle into the air. Being slightly drunk myself, I charged out there, took the guy down, and mounted him. I had no intention of busting him up—I simply wanted to prevent him from getting more out of hand and wrecking my buddy's bar. After he calmed down, I walked back into the bar like a big hero. The encounter couldn't even be described as a scuffle, but when I looked down, I noticed that I was gushing blood out of my foot. I was covered in blood, and everyone began looking at me like I just got my ass handed to me out in the parking lot. Apparently when we were on the ground, my foot rolled over the beer bottle he had broken.

Learn from my mistake and pain. If you want to be an MMA fighter, you absolutely must learn how to grapple, but taking your opponent down shouldn't be your first choice in an apocalyptic street fight. Unless the natural disaster that eliminated the majority of humanity somehow covered the surface of the earth with soft feathers, I would recommend doing everything in your power to keep a fight standing. Just think about all the rusty nails and jagged pieces of scrap metal that will be littered about. Do you really want to end up with that shit embedded in your backside? I didn't think so.

NOTE: As far as the guillotine choke goes, realize that you have just crammed your assailant's head down toward your legs, and he still has two free hands to completely annihilate your groin with, which is most likely what he will do when he realizes he can no longer breathe and begins panicking. But don't worry, you don't need your groin—there will not be that many women around during the apocalypse anyway. And besides, pee tubes are not that bad.

THE MAN CAVE

Note: The "Man Cave," in today's society, is a stupid term for the room in which you keep your foosball table. During the apocalypse, the Man Cave will actually be a cave you live in. It will protect you from the elements and keep you safe from predators.

When a fifty-kiloton nuclear bomb goes off, everything within a several-mile radius gets completely annihilated. If you are outside the immediate blast zone and you have built a fallout shelter in your backyard, your survival will depend upon your ability to quickly take refuge in it. If you are located ten miles from ground zero, you will generally have about thirty minutes before radioactive fallout reaches your area. If you are fifty miles out, you have about three hours. And if you live a hundred miles out, you have approximately six hours. The good news is if you are quickly alerted to the fact that a nuke went off, and you manage to speedily make it to your shelter, you only have about two weeks until the radiation drops to a surviv-able level. Granted it will be a frustrating two weeks—most fallout shelters do not have Internet access, which means no porn—but making do with just the bare necessities for a spell is better than dying an agonizing death.

In addition to preventing you from sucking up large doses of radiation and growing a set of hairy eyeballs on the back of your head, a well-con-structed fallout shelter will protect you from hurricanes, tornadoes, viral outbreaks, police search warrants, and alien invasions. Sure, most neigh-borhoods have community fallout shelters, but I highly recommend steer-ing clear of these. There is always that guy who at the last minute begins banging on the door, wanting to get let in. And there is always that old woman who wants to obey said fuck-nut's demand, jeopardizing everyone who was smart enough to show up early. Another problem with commu-nity fallout shelters is the smell. While the stench of your own farts doesn't bother you too bad, other people's farts smell horrible, and when you are in a confined space, they can make you physically sick. Personally, I've experienced farts so bad that I would have rather gone out into nuclear radiation than suffer through them. When you add crying babies into the mix, it simply isn't worth it. Just imagine spending two weeks at your local DMV—that is what surviving in a fallout shelter is like. You will be much better off constructing your own shelter.

The first rule with building a fallout shelter is not to tell anyone about your fallout shelter. If you go around running off at the mouth, every neighborhood shit bag will flee to your backyard when shit hits the fan. As a matter of fact, you don't even want to tell all of your so-called friends. Douche-bag friends are like herpes—they tend to follow you around and ruin an otherwise glorious day. Even if they are not colossal douche bags, you still won't have enough supplies to feed all of them. To ensure your own survival, you want to limit yourself to two, maybe three, other people. If you have a lot of children, you only want to take your favorite ones, or at least the ones that you think will have the best chance of helping you survive. However, keeping your fallout shelter a secret during the construction phase poses a problem. To solve this dilemma, I suggest taking everyone camping. Shortly after you get to the campgrounds (before you have to visit the awful outhouse and shit monster), disable their vehicles and leave. While they are out there trying to figure out how to get their vehicles going, race home and build your fallout shelter. As an added bonus, some of your friends or family members might die during their long trek back to civilization, which means fewer mouths to feed.

However, if you do decide to prohibit some of your friends and family members from entering your shelter when shit hits the fan, it is very important to bring some type of radio or noisemaker to drown out their screaming and begging and banging as they perish from radiation poisoning and starve to death. Listening to their whimpering is horribly uncomfortable, and we don't want any of that.

Before building your shelter, you are going to want to purchase plans from a qualified professional. I could have offered you step-by-step instructions, but they would have undoubtedly led to your demise. However, I can offer a few tips in this area. The majority of fallout shelters should be built underground, and with limited space in your backyard, deciding upon its location involves some careful consideration. Obviously, you do not want to disturb your workshop, horseshoe pit, barbecue area, or the dirt patch where you and your buddies swill beer, so you will most likely want to backhoe your wife's rosebushes and tulip garden. In addition to this, you will want to build at least two rooms. The first room will be your general living area, and the second room will be the "jail" or "time-out" room where you lock annoying family members. The spare room will also serve as the toilet.

THE LIGHTS JUST WENT ON AT THE STRIP CLUB . . . YOU AIN'T GOTTA GO HOME, BUT YOU CAN'T STAY HERE (AKA GET THE HELL OUT OF DODGE)

Having a fallout shelter in your backyard can save you from dying from radiation poisoning or a rapidly spreading virus, but it will do very little to help you survive for the long term. After the initial shit storm passes, you'll want to be prepared to get as far away from metropolitan areas as humanly possible. Sure, large cities are packed with food, ammunition, and every other luxury you could ever want, but if you survived, chances are others did too, and it will quickly become a battle of "who can get what first."

People will undoubtedly band together to form militant groups, and if the government is still around, there is a high probability the lawmakers will declare martial law. Every day you spend mulling around town, your chances of getting attacked increase. I'm not saying that you should bug out if a storm passes through your area, but if you're listening to your portable radio in your shelter and you hear chatter about how entire cities have been laid waste, your best chance of survival is to find an isolated area in which to lay low (much like you do when a girl you "know" is pregnant). It is much easier to get out of town during times of chaos than waiting for a lockdown or full-blown revolution to occur.

If you live in a town that has just a few hundred inhabitants, remaining in your home can be a lot safer. But even then it can be beneficial not to actually stay indoors. Remember, there will be a lot of people on the move, and when traveling through your area, they are going to need supplies. They will raid the stores first, but when all resources have been depleted, they will begin to go from door to door. With this, I give the same advice I do to upcoming fighters: Be First! Don't sit around and wait to get looted. Get out there and be first by looting your neighbors.

WHERE YOU RUNNIN' TO, BOY?

The first step is to find a safe zone not far from where you live. It could be a national park, a wooded area on the outskirts of your city, or a cabin up in the mountains. Basically, you need to find an unpopulated area that holds no real interest to anyone. The only requirement is that the safe zone has some type of running water, whether it be a stream, a well, or a natural spring. In the case of a nuclear or biological attack, there is a good chance that the water will be contaminated for some time, but this can be remedied by ensuring you have a water filter in your Go Bag, which I will touch upon later (unless I forget).

THE ONLY SHOPPING TRIP THAT WILL EVER MATTER (OR BE EVEN REMOTELY FUN)

Once you have found an isolated spot, the next step is to prep it for a prolonged stay. Personally, I recommend digging a fairly large ditch, lining it with thick plastic, and then filling it with your supplies. Deciding on the amount of supplies you'll need depends on the type of apocalypse that has occurred. With some disasters, it could take as much as six months for things to begin to settle down, so I would recommend being on the safe side and packing as much shit as possible. It seems obvious to me what

LIVE LIKE A LESS-ANNOYING EWOK

If digging a ditch to stash your supplies seems like too much trouble, build a tree house like you did when you were twelve. Although it will be super difficult to haul all your shit up there, it will allow you to play "pirate" and supply you with hours of self-entertainment. It will also give you enhanced visibility of your surroundings. The only catch is that the tree fort must be in the wild. If you can see the roof of your home from your tree fort, your safe zone is not located deep enough in the wilderness. Personally, I like the tree-fort option because I grew up in an urban area, and there was no space for that kind of shit. In fact, I wanted one so bad as a child, I made my mom go out and buy me one of those bed tents, which is basically a tent that fits over your mattress. They are pretty pathetic, but realizing the alternative was no tent at all, I kept mine until I was fifteen. I would have kept it longer, but one day when I invited my friends over, they all began making fun of me. I reluctantly disposed of the tent, and now I can no longer find them on the market. If I could, you bet your ass my wife and I would be sleeping in one.

type of shit you should be stuffing in the hole, but then again, I'm writing this book and you're reading it, so it might not be obvious to you. Here are the essentials:

1. **CANNED FOOD:** I recommend bringing a lot of it. Unless you are morbidly obese, you should be able to survive just fine off three cans of food per day. Multiply that by six months, and you have 720 cans of food. I know the economy might currently be tight, but this is not an area in which you want to skimp. Trust me when I say that you don't want to resort to eating squirrel. Just trust me. And it is very important to have some variety. I know you might love canned peaches, but they'll get pretty fucking gross after eating them for a month straight.

2. **TENT:** As I will cover later, your Go Bag does not include a tent, so it is important that you stash one at your safe zone. There are a lot of tents on the market, but most of them are designed

for weight rather than durability. Seeing that you won't need to carry your tent out of your safe zone, I recommend purchasing one from a military surplus store. Although they tend to weigh more than expedition tents, they are a lot more rugged, and they are also usually camouflage color, which will do wonders to conceal your whereabouts.

3. **SLEEPING BAG**: You're going to want to get a minus-twenty-degree sleeping bag. It might be hot as hell in the summer months, but you will be glad you have it should a nuclear winter set in. To ensure you are warm enough, I would also include several wool blankets (wool retains heat more than most other fabrics when wet).

4. **PROPANE STOVE**: Cooking on a propane stove is a smart move because it gives off very little light and almost no smell. To ensure you don't run out of gas the first week, I recommend bringing at least two five-gallon canisters.

5. **GUNS**: Although your bug-out bag should contain a gun and a healthy amount of ammunition, you can never be too safe. I recommend burying a shotgun or automatic weapon, both of which are burdensome to carry while on the move.

6. **MATCHES**: You should include at least a dozen large boxes of matches, all individually wrapped in plastic. The waterproof kind is mandatory.

7. **BOOKS ON NATIVE PLANTS**: Although you're probably not going to take the time to read up on the local flora and fauna pre-apocalypse, you will have nothing but time on your hands while chilling in your safe zone. This book could save your life should you be forced to remain in the wild longer than you thought.

8. **FIRST-AID KIT**: This should not be your standard first-aid kit containing a few Band-Aids and antiseptic. You want to include gauze, bandages, antibiotics, needle and thread, the whole nine yards.

9. **SHOVEL AND PICK:** These will come in handy for all sorts of things, including making various pitfalls for intruders to fall into.

10. **AX:** Needs no explanation.

11. **FISHING LINE:** In addition to allowing you to catch fish, fishing line is also excellent for setting traps. These traps might not hurt an intruder, but they can be rigged as an alarm system to let you know people are near your camp.

12. **SEVERAL PAIRS OF BOOTS:** Your feet are more precious than you know. You have to take care of them. As far as the type of boot, you want to go with something fashionable. Think *Outlaw Josey Wales* boots. If you are a real man, you can run in cowboy boots with no problem. They will serve no purpose in the apocalypse because I am pretty sure horses will be the first creature to go, but man, they look cool.

13. **A GARGANTUAN SUPPLY OF CREAM PUFFS AND HONEY:** These are among the few foods that never go bad. If you do not like cream puffs, you can substitute anything made by Little Debbie. Although Little Debbie products don't taste the best, no matter what biological conditions should occur, they can never taste any worse. They are so heavily preserved, they already taste nuked.

Once you have filled your hole with all these goodies and any personal items you might desire while living alone in the wild for months and months, fill it in with dirt, cover it with leaves and twigs, and then leave some sort of marking so you can find it again. Personally, I recommend using a large obsidian rock, one which has "no right being in that type of field." And yes, I stole that from *The Shawshank Redemption*.

WHEN THE SHIT HITS THE FAN, YOU'D BETTER HAVE A PLAN: CREATING YOUR ESCAPE ROUTE

The subject of this section is very similar to what your mom explained to you about getting out of the house in case of a fire. I'm basically telling you how to get out of Dodge when the shit goes down. However, creating an escape plan in order to reach your safe zone is not as easy as it sounds. You have to assume that shit is going to be fucked up big-time, which means that the roadways will either be packed with other fleeing people or choked with abandoned and ruined vehicles. In addition to not being able to speedily traverse major thoroughfares such as freeways and even byways, roads will also be very dangerous. These usual transportation arteries will be patrolled by law enforcement, military, bandit groups, and escapees from Jenny Craig Twinkie Rehab Centers. If you disregard my advice and begin humping it down the highway, you're asking for trouble.

To avoid becoming an easy target, you want to chart out a drivable escape route using back roads. Purchase a topographic map of your area, and then simply begin connecting residential streets with power-line access roads to scenic byways. Get creative. Railroad tracks, dry riverbeds, and some hiking trails are often drivable. However, it is extremely important that you practice this route every four or five months in your four-wheel-drive vehicle. The first time is just to see if it is doable, and the follow-up times are to make sure nothing has changed. If you chose a dirt access road as part of your escape plan, and a tree has fallen across that road, it can stop you dead in your tracks. You also want to avoid traveling under any man-made structures such as bridges and tunnels, as these may be purposely destroyed by the military in times of martial law to ensure the containment of specific areas. Also, I would not recommend using any routes that require you to physically swim or immerse yourself in a body of water because many disasters will contaminate the water supply.

AN EXPLANATION

Before we get too far into talking about the apocalypse and all that, I need to clear something up. In my previous book, *Got Fight?*, I had a few of my childhood friends offer some background knowledge on me. Thinking that they would all talk about how great I was, I told them ahead of time that I would not alter or edit their writing. As it turned out, my friends do not view me in the same light as I view myself. In other words, they said some pretty horrible shit.

Thinking that the book would sell five copies, I held true to my promise and included their insights unedited. I did, however, say some pretty horrible stuff in return, especially about my psychopathic friend "Big John." Having only spent an hour and a half working on the entire book, it did not occur to me that people would automatically assume that I was talking about Big John McCarthy, the world-famous MMA referee. I overlooked this fact, and as a result, everyone who read my book now thinks Big John McCarthy is a total nut-bag degenerate. This is not true. McCarthy is actually a very nice person who cares about the well-being of others. Big John my friend cares only about himself and combs the neighborhood in which he lives looking for unwanted puppies to drown. To save McCarthy from this terrible association he has had to endure for the past year, I have included descriptions of both men. In addition to this, I will now refer to my childhood friend as Bigger John.

This is the picture Bigger John sent for the book. Looking huge, am I right?

If you think I was too harsh on my childhood friend Bigger John in my previous book, let me explain the type of person we're dealing with. When I told him about this apocalyptic book, he wanted to include a section titled "When Killing a Man Just Isn't Enough." In John's world, revenge is everything. For example, if someone were to kill his family, simply killing that person would not be enough. He would want to make him suffer, and how would he achieve that? Yep, you guessed it:

by raping him. (When Bigger John read this, he wanted to make sure that the reader knew the difference between man-rape and homosexual sex. Man-rape is all about humiliation and dominance. Homosexual sex is about being gay. His words: "You can fuck a man, and depending on your reasoning for doing it, you can still be a real man.") I thought about including the section because I didn't want to anger him, which might provoke him to use his step-by-step instructions on me, but in the end I just couldn't do it. As a result, I have taken to hiding, so you might not see me for a while. Anyway, be on the lookout for the man in the photos, and if you ever see him, by all means, never turn your back on him.

Now as for Big John McCarthy, he was one of the first MMA referees, and he did an insane amount to promote and legalize the sport in the early years. I respect him as a person—not so much can be said about the man on the previous page.

The next step is to develop an escape route on foot. Hoofing it out of the chaos is not optimal, but with many disasters, it will be your only choice. Although you still want to avoid major roads when mapping out this route, you also want to choose the straightest possible line to your safe zone. If the path you choose involves hiking through remote parts of the forest, you may want to stash alternate methods of travel such as bicycles, off-road vehicles, or even a rubber raft to cross a river. However, a word of caution: Do not attempt to use a super-spring pogo stick to make your escape. As practical as this might sound, the pogo stick offers far more danger than it does value. Trying to pogo-stick down a steep embankment of volcanic rock will seldom end in success. Don't feel badly if you already purchased one—I was a rookie once myself.

You can never be too safe. Once you have mapped out both escapes, learn all the ins and outs of your path to freedom. Get to know both routes like the back of your girlfriend's head. This involves traveling them with nothing but the supplies you will have with you, as well as at various times of the year, in order to learn how the terrain and climate will affect you. Although this might arouse suspicion from law enforcement, especially if your route takes you through people's backyards, getting chased will only benefit your training. Find possible sources of fresh water along the way, and search out hiding places and defensible positions.

When I was a child, I loved hiding places, but living in an urban environment, I often had to create my own. I remember for one of my birthdays my mom bought me a shovel (yeah, strange present, I know). The only place to dig was a small dirt patch in the backyard, so that is where I took to digging a hole. In a matter of days, I had dug a ditch well over my little head. The coolest part about it was that I had to maneuver around several water pipes, which I used as a ladder and to store stuff on. I even covered the thing with a piece of plywood that had fallen off my neighbor's fence. It was fucking epic, but needless to say, my mother made me cover it up once we began having plumbing issues. I guess my reason for bringing up this story is that holes are excellent hiding places.

In any case, both of the routes you create should be segmented into several key checkpoints that will allow you to regroup and hunker down for a few days if need be. If the route to your safe zone is more than a few miles, you might also want to stash weapons and supplies along the way.

As with your shelter, tell no one about your escape routes. People have a way of talking, even if it is just to tell others how crazy you are. Keep your mouth shut, plan in secret, and do not leave any maps or traceable evidence behind. Think I am being overly paranoid? Let me tell you a story. At eighteen, I was still living at home with my mom. Shortly after I broke up with my longtime girlfriend, I brought a new girl over to the house. My mom had always told me that I could tell her anything, and so when she asked me how things were going with this new girl, I said, "Great, we had sex on the patio furniture by the pool." I quickly realized by the look on her face that she was not as "cool" as she reported herself to be. She was absolutely not cool with me having sex with random chicks on the patio furniture.

In addition to telling no one about your escape plan, when the piss hits the wind, be very selective about who you bring with you. Personally, I recommend traveling alone, but if you absolutely have to bring that special somebody, make sure he or she is capable of handling themselves in stressful situations. And once you are on the move, do not pick up stragglers. At the onset of the apocalypse, people will be freaked out and desperate. The last thing you need is some desperate cling-on waving down the National Guard when you're almost home free. However, I am sure my sweet, seventysomething-year-old grandma Ruth would disagree with me on this point. She picks up scraggly, obvious-serial-killer hitchhikers on the freeway every chance she can get. Seriously, I have no clue how she hasn't yet been killed.

SURVIVAL IN A BAG (YOUR GO BAG)

Your Go Bag should contain everything you need to get from your house to your safe zone. Remember, you're not going on a two-week camping trip: You're running to save your fucking life. As a result, you only want the bare essentials. If your Go Bag ends up weighing seventy-five pounds, you will need a Sherpa. And a Sherpa will not only slow you down, which makes you vulnerable to anyone chasing you, but he will also have a very difficult time getting over fences and other obstacles (might have something to do with them being very squat people, much like my coauthor Erich, who, by the way, I make carry all my shit). Personally, my Go Bag weighs less than thirty pounds. Here is what it includes:

- **GLOCK .45:** Small, light, and effective.
- **AMMUNITION:** Fifty rounds. While people like Bigger John would suggest including a lot more than fifty rounds, ammunition gets heavy really quickly. The goal is to reach your safe zone as fast as possible, not to see how many shoot-outs you can get into.
- **MULTIPURPOSE TOOL:** Personally, I like Leatherman and Gerber (or anything a manufacturer will send me for free . . . hint, hint). Whichever tool you decide upon, it should come equipped with a knife, a screwdriver, some type of sexual aid, and a pair of pliers, which will come in handy in case you need to hot-wire a car (see chapter 4).
- **MRES:** This stands for "Meal, Ready-to-Eat," and they are light-weight, self-contained, filed rations that you can eat while on the journey to your safe zone. Deciding how many to include should be based upon how long it takes to reach your safe zone. I would recommend planning on three per day, and then adding a couple of extra on top just in case you encounter some unseen obstacle.

Chances are you are either going to be running or walking at a very fast pace along your escape route, and it is very important to keep your energy high.

- **PEANUT BUTTER**—It is high in calories and protein and doesn't spoil. And if I see you dehydrated on the side of some trail with a mouth full of peanut butter, in utter and complete agony, it will provide me with a good belly laugh.

- **WATER:** How much water to bring should be based upon the time it takes to reach your safe zone, as well as if there are any water sources along the journey. In either case, I would bring at least three sixteen-ounce bottles for each day you will be traveling, even if there are available water sources. Water adds serious weight to your Go Bag, but it is something that you absolutely cannot live without.

- **WATER PURIFIER:** These days, water purifiers are small, light, and easy to use. Even though a water source may appear clean, in the wake of a natural disaster or viral outbreak, you can never be too careful.

- **MAP:** Packing that topographic map you bought, which charts out your escape route to your safe zone, is extremely important because you might need to take a detour due to an unseen occurrence. Later in the book, I teach you how to read topographic maps, because trust me, you won't be able to figure it out on your own.

- **COMPASS:** Just like having a topographic map, this navigational tool might very well save you from getting lost and dying a horrible death in the wilderness.

- **WATERPROOF MATCHES:** Fires should be avoided when possible because they can give away your location. However, a small fire could save your life should the weather turn bad. Waterproof matches are just awesome. In fact, why wait until the apocalypse to start carrying them!

- **GOGGLES:** They seem like a very postapocalyptic thing to have, so I threw them in my bag just in case.

FORTUNE COOKIE WISDOM

Bar fighting makes you tough, without a doubt. Even if you win, you are often carted off to jail, where you are usually required to participate in more fighting. And if you really mess a guy up in a bar fight, you get to go to prison, which makes you super tough because you have to spend all your time trying not to get raped . . . As a side note, I am not down with that saying "Anything that doesn't kill you makes you stronger." I am pretty sure getting raped in prison makes you and your bowels a little weaker.

- **GLOVES**: Gloves are an absolute necessity when navigating through a postapocalyptic wasteland. However, they should not be so bulky that you have a difficult time holding and firing your weapon.
- **WOOL SOCKS**: If your feet are fucked, you're fucked. I recommend bringing five pairs of wool socks and putting on a fresh pair every eight hours. If the weather is warm, strap your wet socks to the back of your backpack so they can dry.
- **BOOTS**: The reason I included a pair of boots in your Go Bag is that you might not have enough time to put them on before fleeing your home. The first step is to always get the hell out of Dodge—when you reach a place that is somewhat safe, remove the shoes you are wearing and put on your boots.
- **WOOL BLANKET**: If at all possible, you do not want to stop and sleep while making your escape to your safe zone. However, if the terrain is too dangerous to traverse at night, you might need to bed down for a few hours. While there are some excellent sleeping bags currently on the market, nothing retains heat in wet conditions better than, or is as durable as, a wool blanket.
- **FLASHLIGHT**: You don't need to go crazy and stash a floodlight in your Go Bag. You just need something that is bright enough to show you where you are going. If you find a flashlight that doesn't suck through its batteries in twelve minutes, e-mail me the name of the brand.

- **TOOTHPASTE:** If you have never heard of this handy little device, you are a filthy fuck mongrel. For those of you who have been using a toothbrush your entire life, I just want to reiterate the importance of taking care of your teeth. Later in the book I give instructions on how to pull a rotten tooth, but you want to avoid this at all cost. Granted, a few days without brushing won't do you any harm, but if you are unable to reach your safe zone for whatever reason, you will be very glad you brought some toothpaste.

GET INTO SHAPE, YOU FAT SLOB

As you're fleeing from the apocalypse you're almost certainly going to need to be on foot for some of the time; therefore, it's crucial that you're in Armageddon-ready shape at all times. There are two ways you can get in shape to survive the apocalypse. You could be like me and train in a climate-controlled gym on a treadmill, which is obviously the pussy way out. The only reason I do this is that this type of preparation actually helps speed up the arrival of the apocalypse. Here is my routine: I overconsume food, and then go to the gym to burn off that food on an electric treadmill in an air-conditioned room. I figure that if enough people follow this layout, the apocalypse will be here before you know it, which is a good thing.

However, if you want a more manly approach, simply walk out into the woods and see how far you can go in any direction. You could buy a weight vest to increase resistance, but again, that is pussy. A much better approach would be to simply gather all the shit you would need in a real survival scenario and haul that shit instead. Remember, there will be no CrossFit during the apocalypse. There will also be no trendy diet-and-exercise programs. Having the ability to hike long distances and sprint really fast will be the most important attributes you can possess. Being a good hiker will allow you to travel for long distances to reach sources of food and water, and being able to sprint really fast will allow you to outrun predators. When it comes to jump squats, Thai kicks, and all that nonsense, leave it in civilization.

VEHICLE OF DEATH

While being in shape is good, your own two feet will only get you so far. Remember how I was telling you to chart a drivable escape route to your safe zone? Well, if shit hits the fan big-time, chances are you won't be able to make that drive in your family sedan. In order to make it out of your driveway and over the rubble, you are going to need to build a *Vehicle of Destruction* (VOD). I toyed with the idea of coming up with my own step-by-step instructions on how to build this monster, but realizing I should probably give you something you might actually be able to use, I decided to bring in an expert. Trying to find the perfect expert could have been rough. In addition to his being knowledgeable about automobiles, I also wanted him to be a dirty, mean fucker. You know, the kind of guy who lives out in the mountains like Gargamel and spends all his waking hours dreaming up sinister ways to exterminate his enemies. A guy kind of like me, except he knows a thing or two about cars. Luckily, I knew the perfect man for the job.

Let me tell you about this fucking guy. Certain that it was only a matter of time before the world as we know it crumbled and fell into the fiery pits of hell, he purchased his own mountaintop outside of Los Angeles, on which he built a bunker and a recording studio. The bunker is so him and his family can survive the end of days, and the recording studio is so he can compose the dark symphony of the apocalypse, which will inspire people like you and me to press on. I have never seen this guy's parents, but I am pretty certain one is a Hell's Angel and the other is Thor, god of thunder. The guy is six two, 235 pounds, and one terrifying son of a bitch. I mean, his beard alone is enough to make children cry. It looks like something a plumber would remove from a clogged drain in a crack house.

Seriously, how this guy gets his beautiful wife to mate with him is beyond me, but he's got three kids that resemble him enough to convince me that it wasn't the milkman. Anyway, after reading the lyrics to his songs "Destruction Overdrive" and "The Blessed Hellride," and hearing rumors that he themed a room in his bunker after the movie *The Exorcist*,

I put a silver cross around my neck, armed myself with a Bible and some garlic, and approached him about giving my readership some pointers on constructing a VOD. Who is this mechanical visionary I have brought into our friendly picnic? None other than Zakk Wylde, Ozzy Osbourne's lead guitarist for the past twenty-five years and front man for Black Label Society, the kind of band your mother warned you about. So put on your thinking caps, I am now going to turn you over to the modern-day Viking.

ZAKK WYLDE'S DO-IT-YOURSELF DEATHCORE WARMACHINE

What's going on, brothers and sisters of the Berserker Nation? Here's the situation: You've never been through a catastrophic disaster and you need some advice for gettin' yourself from point A to point B without some *Mad Max* motherfucker hunting your ass down and then killin' and grillin' you like it's the fucking Fourth of July at the Dahmer's house. Don't want your organs to become a shish kebab? Well, you've come to the right place. Before Mr. Dahmer gets hold of your loins, Father Zakk here is gonna open up the Black Label Garage and explain how to build the ultimate postapocalyptic, land survival vehicle, or as I like to call it, **the Deathcore Warmachine** (DW).

Since I brought up *Mad Max*, remember Mel Gibson's black-on-black "Interceptor" from the movie? It was the makeshift car he drove around through the decimated terrain of Australia. His base vehicle was a 1973 Ford Falcon XB GT hardtop coupe with a 351-cubic-inch V8 that was supercharged and modified to put out six hundred horsepower. Cool car, am I right? Wrong. The only part of *that* ride we have any use for in our design is the paint job; at least Mel got the colors right. Nothin' for nothin', the Deathcore Warmachine will run Mel's car right-the-fuck over.

I'm using the exact truck I drive today for our base vehicle, a black Ford F-350 Super Duty. Yes, I suggest you start saving your pennies now so you can go out and buy one.

The F-350 has a 6.4L Power Stroke turbo diesel engine that runs stock at 362 horsepower and delivers 650 pounds of torque. It has a towing capacity of 25,000 pounds and can haul over 6,000 pounds in the bed. Although this is a pretty powerful monster, you are going to want to do some modifications to get it outfitted for Judgment Day.

In order to begin the transformation of your DW, you want to get a turbo supercharger under the hood, increase the intake and exhaust velocities, and install a superchip specifically fine-tuned for increasing the horsepower and torque of your ride. My DW already came with a turbocharger, but we needed a better one. The upgrade kits they make, with all the specialty hardware and fittings, can be installed at your local performance shop (not the oil-change place guys). If you consider yourself a gear head and want to save a few bucks, you can order most of this stuff online and do it yourself. All you have to do is pick up a copy of an auto performance magazine next time you're gazing at porn mags at the liquor store—the performance magazines have tons of ads in the back selling this shit. (While you're at it, you might as well check out the ads in the back of the porno mags, as they also contain some pretty cool gadgets.)

Once all these modifications are complete, take your ride into a performance shop and have a superchip installed. The guys there will check the tuning and program the chip to optimize all the modifications you've made. I know what you are thinking: "This sounds fucking expensive!" Well, it is. All of the modifications will cost you between $7,500 and $12,000, depending on how much of the work you do yourself. But you can't really put a price tag on power.

Why do you need so much power? Suppose you, Forrest, and I are out in the DW hunting down something to eat and we come upon a roadblock caused by a fallen tree or some giant boulders. Instead of Forrest getting out and moving that shit off the road himself, we wrap the DW's heavy-duty winch and cable around that motherfucker (the *tree*, not Forrest), and tow it out of our way. Five minutes later, we're all back to hunting caribou.

Seeing that I'm already talking about killing shit, let's talk about the next round of modifications. Since most living things on the planet will be dead, it will probably take you quite a long fucking time to hunt down a food source. So it is important that your DW is capable of traveling for long distances without having to refuel. To ensure this, you want to install two fifty-five-gallon, heavy-duty drums on the bed of the truck. One drum will serve as your water supply, and since you don't want to drink toxic waste or some bacteria that cause you to shit yourself for a month, I suggest you purchase a filtration kit at your local camping store. Next, you want to install that filter directly to the drum, so you will also need to pick up the proper fittings, a pump, and the appropriate length of half-inch polyurethane tubing, all of which you can find at a pool supply store, or if you are on a budget, you can simply steal them from the next koi pond you come across. I recommend the pool store, though. Those goldfish do some crazy shit.

If you think water is for pussies and prefer beer instead, you'll want to ignore what I wrote in the previous paragraph and turn that first drum into a fermentation tank so you can brew your own beer, which will be great when there's not a bar left on the planet. Just remember, the goal is not to make a nice-tasting beer, but rather a beer that will get you fucking plastered. Luckily, beer is the easiest thing to make on the planet. I mean, you can even make that shit in a plastic bag in prison. There are four ingredients that you need, and these can be purchased online or stolen from microbreweries across the globe:

INGREDIENTS

> Specialty grains
> Malt extract
> Hops
> Yeast

Here's what you do:

1. Put the specialty grains into a large grain bag (like a giant tea bag) and boil it in a pot for thirty minutes to an hour at 150 degrees.

2. Add the malt extract before the boil and add the hops just after, creating a subtle, yet vibrantly bitter taste. Ahhhh yes!!!

3. Next, cool the boiled mix down to about eighty degrees, at which point it is ready to transfer into the tank.

4. Stir in the yeast while the mix is still warm in order to start fermentation. Once you have agitated the mix, you'll need to cap off the container so it is airtight, and then let it sit for about a week.

The second drum you install on the back of the DW will serve as a mixing tank for biodiesel, a clean-burning fuel derived from a hundred percent renewable resources. I strongly recommend this modification because our current fuel reserves won't last forever, and the DW won't do you jackshit if runs out of gas in the middle of the fucking desert.

With the fuel situation sorted out, the next step is to battleproof the DW. I recommend a full metal jacket made from depleted uranium plate metal like they use on the M1A1 Abrams Main Battle Tanks. If you can't get your hands on some of that stuff, any heavy-gauge sheet metal from your local metal shop will suffice. Ideally, you want to reinforce the hood, front wheel wells, and sides of the truck. You will also want to add a firewall between the cab and the truck bed to protect your ass from explosions or impacts from the rear. Next, on the front of the DW you want to install a heavy-duty plow so you can charge and knock shit over. A variety of plows can be purchased for trucks—a grand will get you one of the basic models, and $4,500 will get you a badass plow with a robotic arm and joystick controller for the cab. I recommend going with the joystick plow, as tearing shit out of the earth will be the closest you get to video games in the apocalypse.

Now let's talk about hardware. Not that geeky computer intra-Web shit all those iPhone-carrying twittering twats run around with in their sophisticated world of nonfat soy lattes and Bluetooth wireless whatever-the-fucks. Remember, it's fucking D-Day and all that shit is out the fucking window. I'm talking about the arsenal of weapons we're gonna outfit this motherfucker with in order to keep your heart beating another day.

In addition to stocking your cab with the guns Forrest and friends explained earlier, you want to mount the tripod of a 7.62-millimeter, multibarrel machine gun to the center of the truck bed. This piece of hardware has Gatling-style rotating barrels, and is electronically driven by the small generator running off biodisel fuel. Not sure where to get one? Try the same *Soldier of Fortune* magazine that you used as a kid to buy ninja stars and nunchucks. In fact, get some of those too. You never know when it's gonna come down to hand-to-hand combat.

Once your vehicle is equipped with all the essentials, the last item of importance is the rear seat. While this could serve as another area to store food, equipment, and weapons, you are going to need a place to shag your old lady. Remember, it's all about survival, and without a good spot to bang one out with your girl, your seed-spreading days are over, end of story. To make sure your gene pool survives, install a long, spring-cushioned seat in the back, without any obstacles that will jab you in the nuts or become uncomfortable while taking the skin boat to tuna town. Make sure you have proper height in the back area as well. This can be accomplished by standing on your knees and then measuring the distance from the cushion up to about two inches above your head. With the proper room, you can not only bang your girl doggie style, but also have the space needed to easily get a thumb in her ass and then reach up and give her one of those Dirty Sanchez mustaches. Hey, if it's the end of the world, you ought to be able to stuff her like she's a Thanksgiving turkey and have some fun with it.

Anyhow, that is what I got on the subject. I'm fucking out of here. God Bless.

Strength – Determination – Merciless – Forever

PREPARE NOW, PART II: DON'T FORGET TO PACK YOUR TOOTHBRUSH

Being prepared for the apocalypse is about a lot more than just having the right gear and knowing how to use a compass. You need to get mentally ready, because you're going to have to sacrifice a lot of things that were essential not that long ago if you want to survive. And when I say "essential" I'm not talking about your Xbox 360 or Internet porn subscriptions. I'm talking about your family and friends (though if you're reading this book, video games and porn probably are your family and friends).

Supposing you have an actual family and/or friends, you're going to have to prepare yourself before the shit goes down to make some tough decisions after the sky has started falling. These decisions are not going to be easy; therefore, it's important to get ready now.

NOTE: I like this saying—If you are going to be dumb, you better be tough. And trust me, buddy, you are fucking dumb. But I like you, and I don't want you to suffer, so heed my words well in this section, and you will be as mentally tough as a washed-up porn star's meat-clam.

LOVE, THE GREAT ARCH-NEMESIS

If you're a decent human being, chances are your kids, parents, significant other, and household pet "Scraggels" have grown somewhat attached to you. This is no good because "love" is the arch-nemesis of the apocalyptic survivor.

In every apocalyptic movie I have ever seen, people are always trying to find someone they love, which introduces them to all sorts of unnecessary dangers. If you happen to be away from your family when the shit goes down, the last thing you want is for one of them to set out on a heroic cross-country journey to find your ugly ass. Since you prevented all members of your family from reading this book (and rightly so), *you* will be much more prepared to find *them*. It can help to inform them to stay put in case of a disaster, but once fear sets in, people do crazy things. Unfortunately, the only real way to prevent your family from searching for you postapocalypse is to get them to dislike you now using the tactics below. Although some of these might sound a bit cruel, adopting them may very well save the ones you love from doing something stupid when civilization falls.

1. Stop leaving notes when you go places. Notes attach you to people when you are far apart. It is your way of saying, "Even though I am not with you, I was thoughtful enough to tell you where I was going and when I would be back." For many of you men out there, this will not be a problem because you are already completely inconsiderate. For women, this might be as difficult as trying to quit smoking, but it is an essential part of the distancing process.

2. Purchase your loved ones generic cards for special occasions such as birthdays, Christmas, and Valentine's Day, but purchase

the wrong card for the occasion. For example, if it is your son's birthday, purchase him a Christmas card. If it is Valentine's Day, purchase your wife a "get well soon" card (personally, I bought my wife a "condolences" card, as I find myself deeply sorry for having brought her into my twisted existence). Giving family

members these cards will tell them that you put absolutely no thought into the gesture. In addition to causing them to love you less, it will fuel animosity between you. Build enough animosity, and they'll be glad when you "go missing." This is the best-case scenario.

3. Make your significant other think you are cheating. This can be accomplished by:

a. **IF YOU ARE A MAN:** Steal strands of long blond hair from a beauty salon and strategically plant it in your underwear. To ensure she finds them, you might want to tie a few into a bow around your junk.
   IF YOU ARE A WOMAN: Start going to the gym.

b. **IF YOU ARE A MAN:** Spray various types of perfume on your suit while at the mall.
   IF YOU ARE A WOMAN: Soak your panties in Jack Daniel's.

c. **IF YOU ARE A MAN:** Leave used condoms EVERYWHERE.
   IF YOU ARE A WOMAN: Purchase a box of Magnum XL condoms, and then hand one to your man the next time you have sex. He will quickly realize that this raincoat is not his. However, if Magnum XL is his regular size, you'll probably want to bake him a cake to ensure he sticks around. A man that large has options.

d. **IF YOU ARE A MAN:** Sprinkle stripper glitter on all your clothes.

IF YOU ARE A WOMAN: Sprinkle stripper glitter on all your clothes.

e. **IF YOU ARE A MAN:** Sleep with other women.

   IF YOU ARE A WOMAN: Sleep with other ~~women~~ men.

f. **IF YOU ARE A MAN:** Purposely leave the toilet seat up, the cap off the toothpaste, dishes in the sink, and your dirty underwear on all door handles in the house. I know these are little things, but they add up. Just ask my wife. After several years living with me, she cares not if I live or die.

   IF YOU ARE A WOMAN: Leave used feminine hygiene products in plain view in the trash, call your man every fifteen minutes to ask him how he feels, ask to snuggle after sex, replace all his meat with soy burgers, and never wash your feet.

If you followed my advice above, your significant other has most likely left, your kids hate you, and you're currently in your new, one-bedroom apartment, sleeping in a twin bed and weeping into a bottle of Southern Comfort. On the upside, your family will most certainly not come looking for you when the shit goes down. And that was the goal, so consider the whole deal a triumphant success. If you are starting to think that perhaps that's not what you wanted, next time you might not want to take advice from a guy who punches people in the face for a living. Just a thought.

THE POSTAPOCALYPTIC FAMILY UNIT

If you are lucky enough to be with your family when the apocalypse occurs, and all of you somehow survive, consider yourself blessed. However, men, women, and children in our society have inherent weaknesses. Some of these weaknesses will have a negative impact on the family unit during the apocalypse, so it is important that you begin eradicating these now.

FACT: Men Think They Know It All

Men are constantly getting their families into trouble because they are too prideful to admit when they don't know something. While we men secretly realize that there are certain times when it's in everyone's best interest to hand the reins over to our smarter half, we will never do this willingly. It is up to the women to force this transformation. Below I have included some examples of ways to shatter a man's know-it-all attitude:

1. Every time your man listens to your advice, immediately start blowing him.

2. Make sure that your man's beer is chilled at all times. Men tend to listen to the one bearing the coldest beer. This is the only reason we pay attention to Hooters waitresses, I swear.

3. Every time your man admits he does not know something, reward him with a little backdoor action.

4. Every time your man ignores your directions while driving and ends up getting lost, give him " the shocker for men" the next time you have sex. The shocker is the number one way to teach a man a lesson. What is the shocker? It involves your pinkie, a hole, and a whole lot of discomfort. If your man is a real idiot, use your thumb. (Seriously, men are so misguided and ignorant, they actually think they are good in bed. They think this simply because women, not wanting to crush their egos, have told them they weren't horrible. Personally, I just don't ask.)

5. Promise your man sex if he can assemble the IKEA computer desk without any leftover pieces. Trust me, you won't have to deliver. Next time, he will hire a qualified craftsman. Note: Let him know ahead of time that taping the missing pieces to the legs or base does not count. Remember, men will cheat whenever possible, especially when sex is the reward for victory. Note II: I am not trying to come down on other men for being retarded at putting shit together because I am no better in this department. Before I made it in fighting, I was living with my friends John and Amber. I bought a bookshelf, put the four walls of the thing together, and then decided to postpone the rest until a later date. Three weeks later, I came home and learned that Amber had finished its construction herself. I guess she got tired of looking

at it. Note III: Leave shit half finished, and women will usually do the man's work for you. Note IV: Scratch that last note—I forgot this section was supposed to be for women.

FACT: Women Panic

In every household around the planet, a woman jumps on top of a table at least once a day while the man of the household must vanquish the creature that startled her. While coming to the rescue might make you feel manlier pre-apocalypse, it is a good way to get yourself killed post-apocalypse. Don't believe me? Let's take a look. Below is the phrase that currently inspires you to stop looking at porn and come charging out of your office with a broom. However, instead of putting "mouse" into the sentence, we will replace it with something that you will more commonly find postapocalypse. Let's see how large your stones are now.

PHRASE: Eeeek! . . . Honey, I just saw a _____. You must come out here and kill it!

WORD SUBSTITUTION:

- Ravenous motorcycle gang
- Lion
- Crazed chimpanzee
- Nuclear explosion
- Pack of hungry wolves
- Global superstorm
- Volcanic eruption

As you can see, a woman's inclination to panic is a great way to get yourself eaten or killed or both. If you want your family to survive, you must break her panicking habits NOW.

The best way to do this is to get her familiar with the things that cause her panic. Here are some suggestions:

a.　Place fake spiders around the house so she gets used to insects.

b.　Nail all the doors and windows shut, crack a couple of smoke grenades, and scream "Fire!" Note: Stink bombs and smoke grenades are two different things.

c. Lock her in a closet with a harmless rat and scream, "Two enter, but only one shall leave!"

d. Blow horns at odd hours of the day.

e. When your wife falls asleep in the car, park your front bumper up against a brick wall, scream as loud as you can, and slam your fist into the horn.

f. Leave a pile of cut-up credit cards on the kitchen table and tell her that they are hers. Note: To avoid losing an eye or testicle, wear protective gear.

If your wife survives these little tests, and she doesn't make you sign divorce papers, she will be one step closer to being ready for the End of Days. Consider yourself a wonderful husband and treat yourself to an all-night drinking binge down at the tavern.

FACT: Children Are Lazy

Remember when there was only one fat kid in every group of children. He was always the jolly sidekick who never got to dance with the hot chicks, so he ended up going gay and being the "IT" guy with the ponytail. Well, not anymore. These days, most kids in the group are fat. They shovel burritos, pizza, burgers, and nachos into their increasingly fat faces, and then huff around the school yard complaining. Why are they complaining? I have no idea. Their parents maxed out all the family credit cards to purchase their precious little muschbags every video game they ever wanted, as well as all the Snackdoos and Tootsie Shit-Pops they could suck down while playing said video games.

I have a perfect example. Back when my little brother Lief was twelve, I cooked him some bacon on the stove. I fed him his meal and then went to take a shower because I'd gotten grease on my arm (yes, grease splatters require a shower). Well, it turns out that I forgot to turn off the stove, and about ten minutes into my shower, Lief walks into the bathroom and tells me that the kitchen is on fire. The expression on his face was not alarm, but rather annoyance. I guess he had sat there for several minutes, smelling smoke, and finally found the energy to come down the hall to tell me.

I went sprinting out of the bathroom naked, and by the time I got to the kitchen, the wall was actually on fire.

You can't really blame kids for being disgusting. When I was young, I would have continued to shit in a diaper and have it magically cleaned if I'd had a say in the matter. It's the parents. If your goal is to survive the apocalypse, you are going to have to transform your child into a survivor. I'm not talking about going nuts with it like Sarah Connor, but you are going to have to get your kid into good enough shape that he can run at least a few laps around the track without having an asthma attack.

Here are some suggestions:

1. Have them make their own food, and I'm not talking about making their own PB&Js. I'm talking about forcing them to kill and skin the animals they eat. If they have no problem killing forty thousand people in Call of Duty: Modern Warfare, they should have no problem skinning a chicken. At the very least, it will teach them the value of life.

2. Cancel their Internet. Notice how I said "their" Internet and not "the" Internet. Porn is one of those things that will vanish in the apocalypse, so you got to get it while the getting is good.

3. Build an obstacle course between the television and their Snackadoos and Tootsie Shit-Pops.

4. Glue their cell phone to the ceiling. If they want to text their friends, they have to climb a ladder. Or, if you are really daring, take away their cell phone altogether. Seriously, does a five-year-old really need a cell phone? (Damn it, I can't wait for the apocalypse to restore some order to this planet.)

5. Make your child become an actor and steal all of his residuals. (It won't help them much, but it will make you wealthy without actually having to do anything yourself—just smart advice, really.)

THINGS TO SAVOR BEFORE THEY TURN TO ASH

The nice part about acquiring an apocalyptic mind-set is that it forces you to cherish the things most people take for granted. Below is a list of items that you should savor now, while you still have a chance.

Cleanliness

Personally, I shower approximately six times a day. I shower when I wake up, before each training session, after each training session, and before I go to bed. Obviously, I like the feeling of being clean. Each day I make the most of the fact that sparkling water flows freely from the faucets in our homes. Sometimes, I will let the water run just to hear its soothing melody.

When the apocalypse comes, clean water will be but a fond memory. Although I am sure it will prove very difficult to get used to my own filth, I think I will be able to deal with it. I mean, after a certain point, you stop smelling yourself, right? What will be harder to deal with is the filth of others. You see, in addition to losing clean water, we will also lose Bed Bath & Beyond, which currently does an excellent job at masking the fact that we are all little more than grimy animals. Without all the sweet-smelling perfumes and home wax kits, everyone's situation downstairs will get a lot more unruly. Instead of resembling a neatly manicured lawn, the post-apocalyptic bush will actually resemble a bush. The tidy landing strip all guys currently enjoy will transform into a damp woodland area. Personally, I have no desire to excavate such a landscape, for it is only a matter of time until you run into something horrible. What is the worst thing you can encounter? I have no idea because I wasn't an adult during the seventies, but I can certainly guess. Just think of what you would find beneath a mangrove forest—white aphids, small pieces of gristle, or perhaps something that smells like week-old crab Louis. If you do not take advantage of all the benefits a clean body supplies, you will regret it down the road.

Coffee

Coffee is a wonderful elixir that contains magical properties. And unlike most magical elixirs, it can be found on just about any street corner. While it has been proven that coffee in general reduces wrinkles, enlarges your genitalia, and grows hair in all the right places, certain coffees are superior to others. Who is king of this mountain? Starbucks, of course. Personally, I consume about eight Ventis a day. I know what you are thinking: "Forrest, don't you feel ashamed supporting that type of corporate monster?" No, I do not. Starbucks claims to help developing countries with free trade, and on each cup it has the word "recycled" printed on it. If the CEO of the company is off club-fucking baby harp seals on the weekends, I don't want to know about it. Of course, the downside to my current indulgence is that I will most likely go through serious withdrawals when the apocalypse comes. To make a full recovery, I will have to go through six excruciating stages:

STAGE ONE: Forrest is extremely tired. His basic motor skills are drastically reduced, and he has trouble speaking. He is forced to communicate with others through barbaric grunts. (Note from Erich: Forrest already speaks in barbaric grunts. Just listen to any one of his mush-mouth interviews.)

STAGE TWO: Forrest realizes that he is not going to get any more coffee, and extreme anger sets in. His rage overcomes the fatigue, and he attempts to cause extreme harm to a number of small animals. Luckily, without any caffeine in his system, he is unable to actually catch any animals.

STAGE THREE: Without caffeine keeping his digestive system running smoothly, Forrest loses the ability to defecate. He screams at random people. When no one is around, he acts out his rage toward trees, automobiles, and log cabins.

STAGE FOUR: Forrest blames his coauthor, Erich Krauss, for not somehow saving coffee. He searches for him far and wide in order to beat him senseless.

STAGE FIVE: Forrest attempts to find a coffee substitute. He chews bark from various trees and eats bugs that appear similar to coffee beans in shape and color. He gets diarrhea and is finally able to shit again.

STAGE SIX: Forrest adapts to having no coffee.

Drinking Water

Drink as much water as you can. When the apocalypse comes, the beverage of choice will be lukewarm urine.

Television

There will obviously be no television after the apocalypse, so it is very important that you watch all the really good shows now. This will prevent you from having to kill the people who are always talking about the shows you never saw. Here is my recommendation:

1. **LOST:** Everyone can agree on this one. It just has this way of pulling you in.

2. **DAMAGES:** I am getting into it. I never thought I could like a show where the leads were two chicks.

3. **SONS OF ANARCHY:** It is as cheese-dick as can be, but man, do I love it.

4. **TRUE BLOOD:** It is a ridiculous premise, it is a ridiculous show, and it is a glorified soap opera about vampires. I love it, and so will you.

5. **PSYCH:** James Roday is a god. I believe I said this in the first book.

6. **ARCHER:** Although this cartoon probably won't make it to the second season, the main character has become my new alter ego.

SHOWS THAT MIGHT CAUSE THE APOCALYPSE

All the British comedies that are supposedly better than the American versions. British people are just weird and I don't get their sense of humor. However, *Flight of the Conchords* is okay, but I think it comes out of New Zealand. Same difference, right?

Sense of Security

I secretly think that at any minute people are going to storm into my house and try to kill me and my wife. Maybe even harm my wife's poor cats. You're probably a lot less paranoid, so enjoy that sense of relaxation and freedom while you still can. Postapocalypse, someone will always be out to get ya, even when you are trying to take a dump!

A Comfortable Bed

Enjoy a comfortable bed, because postapocalypse, you will be sleeping on a rucksack on rocks—and that is if you are lucky! Don't complain how your mattress is lumpy, too soft, or too firm. Remember, a rucksack on rocks!

THINK YOU'RE READY?

So you think you're ready now? Wow, you're pretty confident. That's good: the apocalypse is going to need people like you. How else am I going to find people dumb enough to walk headfirst into my bear traps so that I can steal their food?

If you want to have even a remote chance of surviving, you better keep reading because you haven't seen shit yet. You might be ready for the inevitable, but you still don't have any idea what that will be (or even what "inevitable" means).

HOW SHIT WILL
GO DOWN

So here we are again, at the crossroads of a looming end-of-the-world scenario. Remember Y2K and that whole deal? The world's computer systems were going to crash, the power grids were going to shut off, planes were going to drop from the sky . . . Instead, everyone just got drunk, screwed their brains out, and then went on with life. Then, according alien-communicator Nancy Lieder, the end of the world was going to come in 2003 as a massive interstellar object known as Nibiru or Planet X collided with earth. The attacks of 9/11 were taken as an omen, and the end of times was nigh. We were all bracing (well, at least those of us that were so utterly pathetic we actually listened to a fat, old, insane woman). Again, the predictions led to absolutely nothing.

Now the next apocalyptic hurdle is looming on fate's horizon—

December 21, 2012. This date is derived from the double-wheeled cycles of the Mayan calendar, which complete their rotations every twenty-five thousand years. Strangely enough, another rotation begins right after this one ends, so I'm not quite sure how that translates into "the end of time." But then again, I just punch people in the face for a living . . . and sometimes in the gut, or the ribs, or balls, or wherever really.

In my opinion, trying to pinpoint the day the world will end is just plain stupid. There have been dozens of predictions over the years, and none of them have held up. Instead of focusing on calendars and wheels and such, we should take a hard look inward. There are nearly 7 billion people currently running around this rock like ants on a rotting pumpkin, and we're not exactly a gentle life-form. Instead of focusing on taking care of our home, we're constantly thinking up new ways to waste our limited resources and create bigger bombs to blow shit up. I don't know about you, but I don't need an ancient calendar to tell me that there is a good chance we will kick our own asses in the near future. There is a high probability that we will do ourselves in. It's not like we lack options. Crashing the global economy because we are too lazy to keep up with the math is a likely scenario, as is developing and spreading a viral pandemic. Can you predict when these events will occur? Most certainly not. But that doesn't make them any less real.

I don't have much hope that humans will get their shit together in time to avoid one of these scenarios, but even if we were to fix our greed and our population problems, we could still get our asses kicked back to the Stone Age by Mother Nature. Earthquakes, tsunamis, tornadoes, volcanic eruptions, asteroids, wildfires, and a stampeding pachyderm of Oprah Winfrey's studio audience are all occurrences that can wipe out hundreds of thousands of people in an extraordinarily brief amount of time. Matters get even worse when you imagine all of these events coinciding in one perfect storm of destruction.

There are also more fantastic possibilities. Throughout the history of man, every notable culture has had its own end-of-the-world prophecy. The Vikings had Ragnarök, the Christians have Armageddon, and even the Hopi Indians of the Southwest had an end-of-time prophecy. In recent years, everyone seems to be all stressed out over the Mayans' prediction, which states that the world will come to an end in 2012. But the very fact that people are stressed out over that one almost certainly means it's not going to happen, so I'm not sweating it.

Regardless of how it happens, there is hope. Unless the earth is smashed into pieces, certain species will always survive. And now that humans have evolved to a semi-intelligent state and can problem-solve, it is likely that come the end of the world, pockets of human civilization will continue to exist. Maybe not always in the manner we are accustomed to, but in some capacity. If you are among the lucky few to survive the Great Purge, the big question is, Do you want to survive? To give you an idea of what type of horrible shit you will have to endure when all hell breaks loose, here are several end-of-the-world scenarios ranging from the plausible to the "you're on crack if you honestly think this is how shit will go down."

WHEN $12 TRILLION JUST ISN'T ENOUGH:
THE ECONOMIC APOCALYPSE

I suspect that this book will shortly end up in the dollar bin at your local discount bookstore, but if you're one of the few who purchased it for the full retail price (idiot), chances are you have some money in your pocket to buy frivolous shit you don't really need. You have a nice place to live, a fun little backyard, a deck with a barbecue, and classy furniture. Your cupboards are all well stocked, allowing you to regularly stuff your face to the point where you find it difficult to rise off your designer leather couch. You spend most of your time playing video games and jerking off to Internet porn. You're happier than a pig rolling around in its own feces.

Now I want you to imagine all of it gone. Imagine that you awoke one morning to discover that all the money you have in the bank is worth less than toilet paper and all of your investments are down by a hundred percent? Although it might sound like a paranoid delusion, an economic collapse of this nature could very well happen in our lifetime.

I don't claim to be an economist. In fact, I don't claim to know much about nothin', no how, but the United States has multiple ways to screw

FORTUNE COOKIE WISDOM

I always thought that if enough people thought shit was gold, you could start crapping in a bag and spending it at the grocery store. That's why I bought my house when it cost a bazillion dollars. I knew that it wasn't worth that much, but since enough people believed in that value, I thought I would be fine. What the crash of the housing market taught me is that the only things of true value are those that will help you survive, which translates to food, water, and fertile land. So all those shiny things that we tend to place a shit-ton of value on, such as gold and diamonds, are pretty much worthless because they don't serve a purpose. Take my advice: buy a shit-ton of cows instead of a house. Gold sucks. I can only assume we have attached value to it because we like shiny things, like magpies do. All gold is good for is filling your teeth, and that's just because it is a malleable metal (yes, I've been looking for the opportunity to use the world "malleable").

the economic pooch. I mean, have you ever thought about what a dollar is *really* worth? You know you can get something for it. For instance, a dollar will buy you a bag of chips, a soda, or get you a closer gander at a stripper's meat curtains. We are told that it has value, and everyone in society has agreed to assign it value. But it's just a piece of paper. What is backing up its value?

Well, it used to be the gold, but in 1973 the United States completely separated the value of the dollar from any form of the gold standard. Separating currency from an actual physical asset allows governments to print as much money as they need to fund their pet projects, like running the country. Although this is pretty normal, and in moderation can be healthy for economic growth, flooding printed money into the economy in times of economic stress artificially solves problems without curing the underlying conditions that created the economic stress.

With a sudden overabundance of paper, the value of the dollar drops, while the prices of goods and services go up. This is called inflation, and although most of us are accustomed to this seemingly natural occurrence,

THINGS THAT WILL LOSE THEIR VALUE AFTER THE APOCALYPSE

The majority of things that hold value in our society now will be absolutely worthless come the apocalypse. For example, that shiny iPod you possess, your smartphone, and your day planner will be fucking worthless. Another thing that will lose value are your stuffed animals. I know they are really sentimental, but they will be fucking worthless. Except, of course, for my stuffed animal Mr. Tibbs. He will still be very valuable . . . Won't you, Mr. Tibbs . . . yes you will. Look at you, with your little button nose.

under the right conditions, it could royally fuck us. If we were to take on a large amount of national debt (which we already have), and belief in our government to pay back this debt suddenly became substantially weakened (which it has), inflation could lead to a little situation called "hyperinflation." (I always thought that when you place "hyper" in front of a word, it made that word better. I guess I was wrong.) It is pretty much the same thing as regular inflation, just severely magnified. At that point, money basically becomes paper with photos of really old white guys printed on the front. The worst part? Being so rough, it doesn't even make good toilet paper.

If in a very short period of time money lost its value, prices for living essentials like food and shelter became more than what people could pay, and jobs dried up left and right, our buying power would evaporate. This means that the goods and services currently provided to us by countries around the world would get a whole lot more expensive. Ever been to a third-world country where the exchange rate is like two hundred to one, and you end up paying a couple of hundred pesos or baht for a beer? If the value of the dollar dropped far enough, the same thing could happen here in the United States. Imagine a world where a lap dance or pregnancy test cost $6,000. Terrible . . . simply terrible.

This would inevitably lead to some pretty pissed-off folks walking around. There would also be some pretty pissed-off nations. Such a situation could go beyond a serious economic depression—it could lead to civil unrest and possibly even war. Unlike the collision of the earth with a "backdoor" asteroid, which you will learn about later, there are ways to spot this type of apocalypse. Below I have included some of the things to look out for (I'm telling you, the house of cards is falling, and I can smell the shit hitting the fan . . .).

1. **HIGH UNEMPLOYMENT:** This is pretty obvious. If people don't have jobs, they can't go snorkeling in the Bahamas, pimp out their ride, or buy their stripper girlfriends the breast implants they really, really need. Everyone stops paying their debts, and suddenly banks and other lenders don't have cash coming back in, which prevents them from lending to anyone else. But it is not like the banks are overly eager to lend money because no one has a fucking job. When unemployment gets super high, say 25 percent, start really worrying.

2. **RISING INTEREST RATES IN THE TEN-YEAR TREASURY BILL:** The ten-year Treasury bill is one of the ways the government raises money. It issues these bonds as a kind of IOU to the person or country buying them. In addition to paying back the loan, the bonds also pay interest. Usually the interest rate is quite low because the U.S. government's credit rating has always been strong, which means people believe they will cough up the cash when the time comes. If you see interest rates on the ten-year start to rise, it means that the government is having trouble selling the bonds and is trying to entice buyers. If the rate goes over 5 percent, it's time to start worrying. Because of the high interest rates, the U.S. government will have a very difficult time paying up on the loans. The rest of the world will no longer see the U.S. credit rating as strong, and suddenly finding buyers for U.S. bonds will become a lot harder. If this happens on a global scale, where many countries' debt is sold at exceedingly high interest rates, it could result in a global economic meltdown.

    P.S. It's all happening right now . . . Scared? Not scared enough.

3. **A SHARP RISE IN JOCK ITCH:** Although this may not seem like an economic indicator, it is. The less people have to spend on goods and services, the less they tend to spend on nonessentials.

FORTUNE COOKIE WISDOM

Sorry, but we traded our country for shitty plastic toys. We bought worthless items from China which they made through slave labor, and in turn they used the money to buy U.S. Treasury bonds. So, China has bought our debt, and now they own us. I learned the other day that we are in danger of losing our credit score, and I've been torn up about it ever since because I'm not sure what's brought me more happiness: a stable, democratic government or those really cheap, lead-painted Tonka trucks I buy every time I go to the toy store.

Without a job to go to or cash to spend out on the town, people will spend a lot more time at home. What will be the first thing they cross off their shopping list? That's right: soap. With laundry and personal hygiene becoming secondary to food and shelter, our unclean nut sacks will be spending a lot more time inside equally soiled underwear. The filthier your crotch gets, the more worried you should become. For all practical purposes, you should look at your junk like a Richter scale, but instead of measuring the magnitude of an earthquake, you will use it to monitor your level of filth. If it registers an 8.0 on the Cheese-Sack scale, it won't be long before the shit goes down.

4. **HIGH OIL PRICES:** If gas prices get too high, people can't afford to drive as much, which means they go out less and stop spending money. As a result, fewer things get sold and businesses stop being able to pay their rents or mortgages. People start to get laid off. In addition to this, transporting food and harvesting crops gets more expensive as a result of the rise in the oil prices, causing food to get more expensive. Those who are still employed need to pay more for commuting to and from work, which makes it harder for them to buy food. A vicious cycle, really. Although high gas prices should not cause you to go out and buy a bunch of guns (you should already have done that), when this is coupled with an already crippled economy, it is important to keep your eyes peeled and plan your escape routes.

ECONOMICS 101

For those of you who were completely lost on the last section, I am going to give you a quick lesson on economics. Basically, it all started with the barter system. In the old days, people would trade animal pelts for prostitutes (kill a beaver, get a beaver—that was the motto). Then we came to the New World and traded smallpox blankets to the Indians for their land and pretty much everything else they had. (What a fucking deal that was.) Eventually people stopped accepting smallpox blankets, and with just cause, so we agreed there should be a common united currency. For a while that was gold, but with gold being a pain in the ass to carry around, someone had the bright idea to use paper. They printed the portraits of a bunch of really old dead guys on the cover and called it money (yes, this didn't happen until the late nineteenth century). As this money thing caught on, you could use it to get really cool shit, like Happy Meals and all that great stuff for our bodies and environment. But getting increasingly lazy, we grew frustrated with all the counting, and decided to replace money with magical cards. These cards worked for a short while, but then a group of rebels blew up the buildings that stored all the records of how much everyone owed, leading to anarchy and eventually the apocalypse. The End.

5. **A DRASTIC DIP IN THE AMOUNT OF BLOW JOBS DISPENSED**: This indicator is in direct economic correlation to the increase in unclean genitalia described previously. With human funk being the new perfume and cologne, random afternoon blow jobs or "the shining of the bean" will all but vanish. Think you could endure the sour taste and terrible odor? Imagine going down on a homeless person (I tried to convince Erich that he needed to do this for research purposes, but he wouldn't go for it) . . . Think about it for a while, and then get back to me. If matters get so bad that crackheads stop giving so much as hand jobs because you are too stinky, it is only a matter of time until the world as we know it ends.

Although each of these factors sucks big-time, if they were to all occur simultaneously we would very well be looking at an economic apocalypse. Remember, just because the stock market may be going up, it doesn't mean that the economy is healthy and things are going good. A market propped up by artificial cash injections in the form of bailouts or drastic increases in the money supply is merely an illusion. Many times in history a country has had a strong stock market while the real foundations of its economy were rotting.

NOT JUST A TERRIBLE MOVIE PLOT: THE ASTEROID APOCALYPSE

Asteroids are the shit left over from the creation of the universe—the afterbirth, if you will. But instead of being a nice, runny, warm flow of human mucus and soupy-goodness, these fuckers are made of solid rock. Some are even composed of pure, dense iron. If an asteroid measuring more than two kilometers in diameter is spotted heading toward Earth, it is fancily nicknamed a "Planet Killer." I'm going to repeat that for clarity—PLANET KILLER, meaning no more planet. End of world.

Having trouble wrapping your head around this? Grab your bongs and I'll break it down for you. A collision would be nothing like the ones in the old Asteroid arcade game. Real asteroids are not a bunch of Lucky Charm–colored digital blobs, and when one hits you, most likely you will be dead, soon to be dead, or, if you are lucky, living in a world that makes Dante's third ring of hell look like a slip-'n'-slide party with the UFC Ring Girls. *Who the fuck is Dante, how many rings of hell are there, and who is the third ring reserved for?* Don't worry about any of that. Just trust me when I say that none of it is good news for you.

Now you're probably saying, "Forrest, won't we see an asteroid coming?" First of all, fuck off, it's "Mr. Griffin" to you. But yes, in many cases, we will. Scientists have built really big telescopes, but with most scientists being slightly perverted, there is a good chance the scopes will be pointed at some chick undressing in Iceland rather than at the night sky. Knowing this is a very real probability, they have come up with the term "backdoor asteroid" (see what I mean about scientists being perverted). A backdoor asteroid is one that sneaks past our radar, and if it should be larger than a kilometer in diameter, things will get way out of hand. Here is what you have to look forward to upon impact.

First off, this thing will hit our stratosphere at a shit-ton of degrees, which scientists say is hot enough to burn the pubes off a groundhog six feet below the crust of the earth. (There's another fantastic turn of phrase: "crust of the earth." Sounds like what was in the jockstrap I put in Bigger John's pillow case right after the first Tito fight!) With 70 percent of the earth's surface being covered by water, this flaming ball of molten death will most likely land in the ocean somewhere. It won't hit the surface and cool off—like a fat-fingered proctologist, that thing is going to hit the bottom of the ocean and keep on going, burrowing its way deep down into the earth. In addition to displacing all that water, it will also displace rock, gravel, and Davy Jones's locker itself. All this matter and water will shoot up into the atmosphere, where it will be scorched by the now-incendiary skies. Eventually, though, it has to come down, and when it does, it won't do any good. The shit will "literally" be going down.

Let me illustrate this for you using a more practical, real-world scenario. Let's say you have to squeeze out one of those double-fist-size, rock-hard balls of Indian clay from your nervous butt hole. You know what I mean, the kind of turd that actually makes you hesitate for a moment when you realize what is coming. The one where you have to mentally prep for the inevitable pain and perhaps even the humiliating Groan-Out-Loud. Well, imagine letting one of those go in a public restroom equipped with those taller toilets. You know the kind, where your butt is like two feet from the surface of the water. When that petrified shit ball hits the surface, it will displace the water below with such force that you will receive a dose of toilet water straight up your chocolate starfish.

In the case of a real asteroid, the toilet is earth, the toilet water is the ocean, the compressed mass of fecal ore is the asteroid, and your colon is so far in outer space it might as well be Uranus (drumroll, please). How-ever, instead of cool, soothing shit water (which can actually feel quite good if your sphincter is burning from last night's chimichanga), a hail-storm of molten earth and boiling water will fall back to the earth's surface in a radius of a fuck-ton of miles (yes, a fuck-ton is bigger than a shit-ton). Quite literally, a rain of fire.

If you think that being up in the mountains, far away from the point of impact, will help keep you safe, think again. Next comes a scorching, five-hundred-mile-per-hour wind, burning everything in its path. These winds, created by the overheated atmosphere, would carry the falling debris and spread this fiery cheer over hundreds of miles, instantly ignit-ing trees and man-made structures. Then tsunamis created by the impact would rise up to a hundred and fifty feet and sweep outward from ground zero and extinguish some of the flames once they reach land. Yes, I know you are thinking the same thing as me—good ol' Mother Nature has the same sense of humor as a small boy watching a snail drag its bubbling, dying corpse of slime across a pile of rock salt.

The impact will also give us fantastic earthquakes. These things will shake the earth much like a frustrated babysitter shakes a crying baby.[7] Millions of people living in densely populated urban centers such as New York City, Beijing, Mexico City, and São Paulo will be crushed under moun-tains of cement-and-steel infrastructure. But none of that really matters because the world will already have caught on fire, and not in the way Lance Bass hoped. No *Project Runway* here, buddy! Just a massive wildfire that will make Smokey the Bear put a bullet in his furry head.

Am I just telling you horror stories to keep you up at night? Am I blow-ing this whole asteroid thing out of proportion? Let me give you this bit of news. It is estimated that the likelihood of an asteroid hitting Earth is six thousand to one. And that number is not in our favor—I'm talking six thousand to one that such an event *will* occur. It's simply a matter of when and how big it will be. But don't give up all hope. After all, the odds were much worse when Han Solo went into that asteroid field, and he somehow

---

[7] Yes, I too was once a babysitter. Think that's funny? Fuck you. I babysat my brother Lief when I was fourteen, and he would often cry for hours upon hours. Of course I didn't shake him, as that would be a horrible thing to do. But I did scream at him for a while to make him stop. Probably not the best tactic now that I look back on it, but, man, it sure did work.

pulled out alive. However, I strongly suggest taking my advice below, as it will dramatically increase your odds of surviving an asteroid attack.

Hints for surviving an asteroid attack:

1. Stay away from asteroids.

2. Dig a hole deep into the bowels of the earth and then never come out.

3. Build a spaceship and then fly away just prior to impact.

4. Develop a machine that can turn you into a cockroach. Those nasty little fuckers can live through anything, including the heel of my boot.

5. Sorry, just kidding. There ain't shit you can do about this one. It's a fucking asteroid.

THE REASON EVERYONE IN THE 1950s WAS SCARED SHITLESS: THE NUCLEAR APOCALYPSE

This is not nuclear proliferation.

Have you ever seen a country really, really, insanely pissed off? France totally doesn't count, by the way. I'm talking about a country that's actually a threat. If a country got totally fucked over, say, as a result of an economic collapse, there is no telling how far they would go. Don't believe me? Just look at that crackhead prostitute who hangs out on the corner of Las Vegas Boulevard and Flamingo. She will do some pretty crazy shit for five bucks, or so I've heard, and she can get all the clean water and food she wants down at the shelter. (Note: Do not look at her too hard or you won't be able to eat your lunch. However, it is great if you are trying to cut weight. As a matter of fact, if you are way overweight, you might want to consider bedding her, as it will permanently reduce your appetite.)

People will do just about anything when desperate, and that includes scorching the tits off Mother Earth. But how will these types of countries get their dirty hands on an atom bomb? It's called "Nuclear Proliferation," son. Now I am sure you've heard that term bandied back and forth during your lifetime, but it isn't what happens when a fart follows you back to the dinner table while on a date, and it's not what happens when a stripper's HHH breast implant explodes during an oil wrestling match at a dingy, riverside bar on the outskirts of Meth Town USA.

Nuclear proliferation is a term used to describe the spread of nuclear weapons or nuclear technology to countries that are not on the "cool" list. For example, if the USA and Russia, both of which are recognized nuclear states, were playing a game of football, and a little Guatemalan kid suddenly ran out on the field, snatched up the ball, and then went skittering into the locker room, nuclear proliferation would have occurred. Of course, the football would have to be a nuclear weapon and the Russians would actually have to learn how to play football, but you catch my drift.[8]

This is a very real scenario. When the Soviet Union fell in 1991, not only did the world lose the sense of fear that came from watching *Red Dawn*, but many of the Soviets' weapons that had been stockpiled over the course of the cold war simply disappeared, as did some of their key scientists and the materials necessary to develop a nuclear weapon system. Much of this junk has never been accounted for, and it could have found its way anywhere. If one of these nukes ended up in the hands of a pissed-off dictator whose country has been leveled by a global economic collapse, what would stop him from kicking off a massive fireworks display that will end civilization as we know it?

In addition to a nuke possibly sitting in the basement of a dilapidated shack in some third-world country that hates the Western world, cyber-

---

[8] If you are one of those nerds who read this sentence and thought, "Well, in Europe, 'football' means soccer, and the Russians aren't half bad at that," if you are thinking anything along these lines, do the world a favor and run your head into a brick wall. This book is distributed in America, and that's my freakin' target market, so "football" means fucking football. Get it! Oh, and fuck you. I seriously doubt you could come up with a better analogy.

terrorism is another threat we face. Cyber-terrorism could arise when a fanatical group wishing to cause harm to a specific nation (America, it always has to be America—I guess it's because we're the poster child for Fat and Happy) ends up procuring a really smart computer nerd, convinces him to hack into a country's nuclear weapons launching system, and then drops a payload on an unsuspecting nation. This is a very real scenario, which is why security is so tight at Comic-Con. Think about it: it wouldn't be that hard for a terrorist cell to stake out a *Star Trek* convention or sign up for *Avatar* language lessons. After the meeting in the parking lot, they jack the smartest geek in the group. The terrorists know he won't put up much of a fight, as years of playing Halo in a windowless room and emerging once a year for his annual nerd fest have made him exceedingly doughy.

While nerd-kind is highly intelligent and keen with problem solving, they have a nagging inferiority complex. By repeatedly telling the geek how smart he is, combined with the conversion speech the Emperor used on Luke Skywalker and providing him with seventy-two virgins while he is actually alive, the terrorists could win the geek's loyalty and have him hack into any computer system on the planet.

Apocalyptic Movies You Must See

1. *The Stand*: Best apocalyptic movie of all time. And I don't want to get a bunch of letters telling me that I am wrong because it was a miniseries. A miniseries is a movie, shithead, it's just a really long one broken up into parts.

2. *Carriers*: This movie was recommended to me by Stephen King in *Entertainment Weekly*. My big problem with this flick is that the main characters wear these flimsy surgical masks in an attempt to avoid a virus that has wiped out a large majority of the population. Obviously, such masks would do absolutely nothing to save them. The reason I recommend this movie is that (spoiler alert, asshole) nearly all the characters die before the end. Other than their deaths, everything in the movie is totally unrealistic.

3. *28 Days Later*: As I mentioned in my last book, this movie reinvented the zombie genre simply by making the walking dead capable of running super fast. Although much of this movie was unrealistic, it accurately portrayed how quickly viruses can spread and how dangerous they can

be. I know this because of all the advanced medical training I've received during my frequent trips to the ER.

4. *28 Weeks Later*: Same as the first movie, only bloodier and starring the guy who picks fights with everyone in *Trainspotting*.

5. *Escape from New York*: This movie gives us very little information about the apocalypse itself, but New York does become a prison, which I am pretty sure is what it is presently becoming. Other than perhaps a little foreshadowing, the best part of this movie is Kurt Russell's mullet.

6. *Mad Max*: I think this movie is very realistic about how homoeroticism will manifest when the shit hits the fan. Seemingly overnight, people will transform from businessmen into gay, leather-clad barbarians. Personally, I know for a fact that I will be wearing a leather leotard and tights minutes after the first bomb lands.

7. *The Road*: Not sure if this movie was very realistic, but it was depressing as shit. It made me question whether or not I even want to survive the apocalypse.

8. *Planet of the Apes*: I don't know if it is actually an apocalyptic movie because we haven't outlined the parameters of what can be classified as apocalyptic, but monkeys overtaking everything sounds pretty fucking apocalyptic to me. In any case, while the original is good, the remake is fucking unwatchable, except for that female ape/Mark Wahlberg love-story side plot . . . Did I say that out loud? I meant the movie is just terrible; forget I ever said anything about that side plot. Would you excuse me? I'm just gonna go throw on that DVD for a few minutes . . .

9. *Star Wars*: Not actually an apocalyptic movie, but it is awesome.

Back when I was a kid, they used to show a movie called *The Day After*, and it scared the living shit out of everyone. It wasn't filled with the special effects they have now, but you got the point. A nuclear blast would seriously fuck some shit up. However, today, people seem to be so blasé about the possibility of a nuclear war. To snap you back to reality, here is a likely scenario of what you can expect:

One afternoon, you are sitting on your front stoop, sipping on your gin 'n' juice, trying to recall where you stashed your blunt. Your hoes are upstairs in your tiny studio apartment, drinking cheap champagne and gettin' it on, and you're contemplating going up there and joining them in the mix . . . If only you could find your damn blunt! (Sound familiar? Yes, I stole it from a Snoop Dogg horror movie.) Suddenly a really old, creepy man who happens to work at the cemetery wanders by, looks at you, and says in his grave, old-man voice, "A storm is a-brewin'." Then he hobbles off.

As you watch the geezer zigzag down the street, you hear what sounds like a siren wailing in the distance. Seconds later, there comes a terrible roar from above, and you look up to see what appears to be a trail of fire streaking across the darkening sky. Your eyes track it until it disappears over the horizon, and just as you are lulling yourself back into relaxed contemplation, a deafening *BOOM* rocks your eardrums and a bright white flash blinds you. As you regain your vision, you see a ball of flame gather up into a familiar amalgam of orange and black. Within seconds it is there, the classic calling card of the end of the world—the Mushroom Cloud.

You immediately forget about your blunt and go sprinting upstairs hoping to get one last romp with Laticia and Uganda, but it is too late. Immediately after the nuke hit, the air around the detonation rose to twenty thousand degrees Fahrenheit. The blast proceeded to suck up all the air underneath and around the detonation, and then a split second later it pushed it all back out in a shock wave. You see, a nuclear explosion contains so much energy that it actually creates an electromagnetic pulse that radiates in all directions, flattening everything in its path.

Just as you are removing your pants, you see your blunt lying on the floor and pick it up. You take a hit, but it is not the type of hit you were hoping for. That's right, you take a nuclear blast straight to your face. I would go into gory detail about what the shock wave does to your body, but there might be kids reading this book, simply because I have warned them not to (which was my ploy all along), so I will skip right to the end, which is where you, your house, your bitches, and of course your blunt all get vaporized. That's absolutely correct, vaporized. Remember that episode of the original *Star Trek* where they turned people into little cubes of dust. That's you.

Nuclear bombs are fucking terrifying. And it's not just the big fancy explosion and the super-awesome shock wave. When the atomic bomb exploded over Nagasaki in 1945, it shot radioactive fallout sixty thousand feet into the atmosphere. That shit didn't just come straight back down—

it got sucked up in prevailing wind currents and traveled long distances before eventually finding its way back to earth. That's why if you are anywhere near a blast zone and survive, they tell you to "shelter in." In idiot terms, that means stay the fuck inside. Do not go outside to look at the pretty sky. Get into your fallout shelter as quickly as possible and then wait for the radiation to subside. If you ignored my advice and did not build a fallout shelter, you're most likely screwed. But you should at least give survival a shot by sealing up all the door frames and window ledges with duct tape, shutting off any outside source of ventilation, and then going down into the basement. If you do not have a basement or fallout shelter, crawl under your desk like they used to tell kids to do during the Cuban missile crisis in the early sixties. This will in no way save you—I just think it is an amazing way for you to die. On the upside, the desk will most likely fall on you and serve as your coffin.

What happens next is wholly dependent upon your location in relation to the blast. If you are living in the target city, the one that has been struck, you are smack-dab in the thick of some mayhem. Since you had the foresight to purchase this book, I'm going to give you a tip: save some of the money you would normally spend on booze and your Internet porn subscriptions and go buy yourself a radiation dosimeter that tracks the level of radiation, which is measured in rads.

At the very least, you want to get a radiation badge, which looks much like a credit card. Anything measuring more than one hundred rads is considered "hot" (saw it on *Fringe*, so it has got to be legit). If the area in which you are residing is registering hot, no one is coming for you. The First Responder teams, such as the Chemical Biologic Incident Response Force (CBIRF), label zones that measure a hundred rads or greater as No Go Zones, and they ignore that part of town altogether. Chances are you will be stuck there for several days. In cities that have a population greater than 7 million, such as Los Angeles and New York City, the No Go Zone will produce anywhere from one hundred to two hundred thousand fatalities within the first twelve hours. Those who do survive but did not construct a fallout shelter will most likely be soaked with a heavy dose of radiation, which is evidenced by severe burns and sickness.

ANIMALS KNOW WHEN IT'S BETTER JUST TO DIE

If you do not have the money to purchase a radiation detector, just go down to your local pet shop and pick up a shit-ton of canaries. Apparently, they die super quick from radiation and will let you know when to get the hell out of Dodge (yes, I stole this from *Close Encounters of the Third Kind*).

Outside of the No Go Zone, you have the Fallout Zone. If you managed to seal up your doors and windows or get into your fallout shelter quickly enough, you might have a glimpse of hope at truly surviving. Some degree of radiation sickness should be expected. If you purchased a radiation dosimeter like I suggested, you can always test yourself to see how fucked you are. If you don't have one, you can gauge your level of sickness by your symptoms. Minor radiation poisoning can lead to throbbing headaches or light skin burns. Significant doses are said to be able to cause genetic mutations. I don't think this means that overnight you will grow a dick out of your forehead, but it does mean that you'll have a stronger likelihood of having deformed babies should you decide to procreate and bring a child into a jacked-up, godforsaken, post-nuclear-war world. If you ever wondered where all the deformed creatures come from in movies such as *Total Recall*, you got your answer. It's sick fucks like you who want to get your groove on after sucking down large amounts of radiation. You've probably spent many a dark and lonely night thinking about that three-titted girl.

To avoid having to name your child "Thing" or "It," I would highly recommend remaining indoors for at least four days. But be warned, once you do venture outside, you will have to work your way through a gauntlet of dead bodies, rubble, and all sorts of shell-shocked and desperate people who may be completely fucked in the head. As I mentioned in the escape route section, stay off the main roadways and keep to lesser-traveled paths. However, be on the lookout for any Red Cross or other medical units.

If you manage to link up with a unit trained specifically to handle major crisis, you will be sorted out in what is called the DIME system—Delay Treatment, Immediate, Minimal, and Expected (yes, the government loves acronyms). If you see yourself being marked with a green tag, you are basically fine and won't receive much attention, but you can breathe a sigh of relief because you've just advanced to the next round: post-nuclear-war survivor. If you get marked with a yellow tag, you have minimal injuries and will most likely survive. In my personal opinion, the yellow tag is the worst because you will be waiting around for hours and hours, bored out of your mind. If you get a red tag, you are in the immediate category and will receive priority treatment because they think they can save you. If you get a black tag, you have been labeled as "expected"—as in "expected to die" (there simply is no nice way to say that). You won't receive shit, except maybe some morphine for the pain, which at this point may not be such a bad thing.

Going out in a nuclear blast during the end of the world isn't a shameful death, unless of course you were doing something unmentionable during the actual impact. For example, if you were trying to figure out if the chick you were jerking to online was actually a dude, and then you noticed the Adam's apple at the precise moment the bomb hit, I'm afraid your death isn't as heroic as you may have hoped. In fact, once in the afterlife, expect to be the laughingstock of the next world.

If you get released from a medical unit with a clean bill of health or you do not link up with such a unit, it is important to remember that a shit load of people will be fleeing the city. They will attempt to find refuge in towns and states that cannot support an instantaneous mass immigration of this kind. Survivors will be competing for resources, and this will undoubtedly piss off the locals. In a short period of time, refugee camps will be established. Personally, I advise avoiding them at all cost. You want to go solo instead. Just strike it out on your own and live like the wolf—El Lobo. Howling at the moon in your anguish. Always hunting. Always yearning.

However, if this does not work out for you or you get corralled by law enforcement officers, you're going to have to learn how to survive in a refugee camp. It will become a dog-eat-dog world very quickly, and I feel it is my duty to give you some much-needed pointers. How do I know so much about refugee camps? Well, I used to watch that HBO prison show *Oz* all the time, until it got super-duper gay. And there is a strong chance that I watched too much of it, as I am now using words like "super-duper."

FORTUNE COOKIE WISDOM

The apocalypse isn't all doom and gloom. Sure, everyone is dead, the world is in chaos, and all those near-extinct species are now extinct . . . well, most every species is extinct. But you must think of the many benefits. There will be no more reality TV, which is the lowest form of entertainment. Even lower than curling (a pathetic sport that is somehow still in the Olympics). The obvious exception is *TUF* because it is a show where people with actual skill compete against one another for an actual goal. (It did wonders for me. Without *TUF*, you would not be reading this book and, consequently, dying a horrible death in the apocalypse . . . Oh, and that show where they compete to make the best cake is pretty legit too.)

In addition to no more reality TV, the roads will be far less crowded, which means fewer instances of road rage. In fact, most cases of road rage will be me kicking unoccupied vehicles. There will also be no lines anywhere—try to wrap your head around that. Of course, there will be nothing left to actually do, but at least you won't have to wait in line to do it. So your family and friends may have died, but there will be no traffic. Come on, that's a fair trade.

LIKE SUMMER CAMP, ONLY DIFFERENT: HOW TO TOUGH IT OUT AS A REFUGEE

Refugee camps are designed for the unwanted, and so the majority of the time they are constructed on very inhospitable terrain. If you are in Louisiana, expect to be placed in the swamps. If you are in Nevada, expect to be placed in the middle of the fucking desert. If you are in Arkansas—well, anywhere in Arkansas is pretty fucking shitty.

Since they placed you in the crappiest part of the state, there will be no permanent structures. Although tents will be erected overnight, most of them will fall over in the first storm. You will most likely have to sleep outside, but instead of being out in nature with a good deal of breathing room, you will be packed into these camps tighter than a pedophile's shit in San Quentin. Basically you're going to be like the aliens in *District 9*, except without the cat food. (Though come to think if it, you'll probably be pretty hungry, so it won't take long for cat food to become a desired luxury . . . and yeah, I mean you will be selling your body for a can of cat food.) All night there will be the obligatory sobs and anguished wails (kind of like what I hear from my wife during and after sex). To avoid going mad, you are going to have to train yourself to stay hard. I don't mean walking around 24/7 exclaiming, "I am the owner of a boner!" I mean you want to have to stay emotionally tough. You can't let things faze you, no matter how terrifying they may be.

Food will be scarce, and so you must get used to taking things from people who are less aggressive and dominant than yourself. Just like in fighting, survival is based on who really wants it. There are many ways to

develop this mental toughness prior to an actual scenario. For instance, I find it helpful to take things from small children and babies with little or no remorse. It's just a good way to get started. Next time you see a child relishing an ice-cream cone, walk by and simply snatch the dessert from the child's clutches. It also helps to scream as loudly as possible to scare the living shit out of him. This adds to the power of your action. Even if you are in training and trying to eat healthy, snatching ice-cream cones, cotton candy, Popsicles, etc., is great practice. You don't even have to eat

it: just drop the tasty treat on the ground in front of the child. This not only helps you forge your emotional toughness, but it does the same for the child. Children need to experience more of these types of life lessons if they're going to make it. Trust me, you're doing that kid and yourself a favor. It's a win-win . . . Although, it can be kind of difficult explaining that to the parents and the judge.

The next step to becoming refugee-camp tough is to start punching people. I obviously have a bit of a head start in this department, but you too can cultivate your ability to strike another for personal gain so long as you start now. For example, it is okay to take practice swings at those who are weaker than yourself, so long as it is done in the name of your post-apocalyptic training.

Even with this toughness, though, refugee camps are just going to suck, so again, my advice is to stay on your own and avoid refugee camps. In a postapocalyptic world, trust no one. When things begin to settle down and you have the urge to rejoin society, the dosimeter in your Go Bag will come in handy for determining whether or not you will be accepted back into life with others. Measure yourself before you try to reintegrate with any kind of organized group or law enforcement types, as they will most certainly measure you before allowing you to mingle with their constituency. If you are registering above a hundred rads, you will be treated like the redheaded stepchild of mankind. Even if you are below the necessary amount of radiation, your new friends might attempt to give you a "cleansing," which is a whole new joy of this modern world to look forward to.

Hints on Surviving a Nuclear War

1. Avoid living near major metropolitan cities, military bases, or the White House.

2. The Emergency Alert System, which replaced the Emergency Broadcast System in 1997, broadcasts emergencies over the radio, television, and even satellite radio. Keep one of these channels open at all times.

3. Purchase a battery-powered radio for those times when the power goes out.

4. Have at least fourteen days of emergency supplies in your fallout shelter.

5. Build an underground home. In addition to help protect you from fallout, it will dramatically cut down on your electric bill.

6. In case you are not at home when a nuclear attack occurs, purchase a radiation suit and store it in the back of your car.

7. If you are exposed to fallout or radioactive dust, remove all of your clothes before entering your fallout shelter.

8. Avoid vacationing in North Korea or the Middle East.

GIANT SPIDERS ARE SCARY AS SHIT

If you think the notion of giant spiders is crazy, you haven't watched enough post-nuclear-war movies. These documentaries have taught me one thing—be very wary of giant insects that have grown to prehistoric stature after ingesting large amounts of radiation. Personally, I cannot think of anything more terrifying. Spiders are all over the place, and in the animal kingdom they are ruthless. While radiation has a tendency to deform and kill humans, it seems to make spiders and other insects larger and more powerful. When all jacked up on green nuclear waste, the little fuckers that you've been smashing for years are going to be the size of minivans, and they will come looking for revenge.

Next time you capture a spider in a jar, grab a magnifying glass and take a good look at it. They are hairier than a female Armenian power lifter, and they have eight eyes that surround their body, allowing them to see in all directions. They are perfect killing machines. If you desire to see their ruthlessness firsthand, throw a more docile insect into that jar. When viewing the spectacle through a magnifying glass, you will most likely shit your pants at the savagery. Instead of tearing its food to pieces, the spider drives its fangs into the flesh of its victim and injects a poison. This poison doesn't kill the poor little buggy, oh no, it liquefies its innards while it is still alive. I recommend watching this horror show very closely, and then I want to hear you tell me you are not afraid of giant fucking spiders.

P.S. Once you're finished studying your future foe, use your magnifying glass to burn that little bastard-fuck to a crisp. At the very least, fill the jar with water or gasoline. Just murder the fucking thing 'cause that's one less spider we will have to deal with postapocalypse.

Apocalyptic Movies You Should Never See

1. *Armageddon*: I really wanted to like the movie because an asteroid impacting Earth is such a feasible scenario for the apocalypse. If scientists spot an asteroid heading toward Earth, our only chance of survival could very well be to send out a mining crew to blow the thing up. If such a thing actually occurred, I am sure the sales of Aerosmith CDs would shoot through the roof. However, I find the movie so ridiculously stupid, it actually makes me angry.

2. *Deep Impact*: Sounds like it should be porn, but unfortunately it's not. This came out around the same time as *Armageddon*. Why do theme movies always seem to come in pairs? In any case, the movie was actually worse than *Armageddon*. Morgan Freeman is president and that's about the only thing I remember beyond the fact that it's about an asteroid. Hopefully, the real apocalypse doesn't have this much drama or bad acting. I'm banking on a whole lot more action and explosions.

3. *Waterworld*: I don't know if there is enough water to cover the whole world, but if there is, I hope I am the first one to develop gills. But even with gills, this movie will still suck.

IT AIN'T BEDROCK, IT DAMN SURE AIN'T FRAGGLE ROCK—IT'S RAGNARÖK, MOTHERFUCKERS

Before I go into the story of Ragnarök, I just want to clarify something. Things will get real nerdy-sounding real fast. Just so you are aware, the story of Ragnarök is where all the Hobbit shit, Dungeons & Dragons, and some of the canned metal tunes came from. I am going to use names like Midgrade the Realm of Men, and Asgard (not Assguard—ASGARD, but don't worry, ass guards will be covered later in the book, as you will probably need one in the apocalypse). If you think I've been listening to techno all day while playing PC games in my basement, you're wrong. That's what you've been doing. I've been in the library, reading up on all this shit . . . well, at least my coauthor has. So if anyone is a nerd, it's him . . . and you . . . especially you.

This is the real story of how the Vikings viewed the end of time. And when I say "Vikings," I am not referring to the ones with "lifebars" or "Hit-

Points" or "damage points" or who-the-fuck-cares points. The kind of Vikings I'm talking about are the raping, pillaging, looting, and killing kind. So put aside your initial reaction to flush my head in a toilet or Saran Wrap me to a flagpole and listen, because even though the nerds of the world jacked up this story to make themselves feel like they could slay anything from the safety of their computer keyboards, the truth is that this story is all about cutting people and hacking them to death with hatchets and axes and tearing things in half and stuff. It is a story from the manliest men to ever exist. Anyway, check it out.

So Ragnarök is going to come after mankind has been fighting for three solid years in winter conditions. I'm talking hard-core war for three years straight in the freezing cold. By this time, a lot of us will be dead or starving or really fucking beat down. During this massive battle, mankind kinda loses its mind. People get sicko-pervo on each other. The prediction says that fathers will start trying to kill their own sons, while mothers will try to hook up with their sons. And sisters and brothers will start getting it on as well. Sounds like some pretty isolated people wrote it, right? Apparently, the Vikings had some deep Freudian issues (maybe this is where the realm of Nerdgard started to relate to them, I don't know).

At any rate, there will be no rules whatsoever, so if Ragnarök really does come to fruition, just go crazy and do whatever the hell you want. But whatever you decide to do, just make sure you dress warm. According to the ancient texts, three straight years of winter wasn't enough. With the onset of Ragnarök, another winter will set in, except this one will be so freakin' cold that they actually give it a name—Fimbulverr. Sounds like what you did with your stinky pinkie the other night, if you know what I mean.

Once this winter comes, we start to meet the bad guys in all of this. Two brother wolves, Skoll and Hati, turn up after chasing shit around the universe for an eternity. Their main target had been the sun and the moon, and about the time of Ragnarök, they finally catch up to them. Being stupid dogs, instead of turning them into their chew toys, they decide to eat the sun and the moon outright. If they were my mutts, I would either give them a swift kick to the ribs for their insolence or send them to Michael Vick for a little obedience training. But that's just me.

While the two stupid dogs are feasting, a huge earthquake shakes the shit out of the entire earth, causing trees and mountains to fall. Unfortunately, the quake breaks the chain that had been holding back another wolf named Loki, who carries the nickname "the Trickster." What a douche. Sounds like a freakin' DJ at some lame-ass techno club. "Hi. I'm Loki, but you can just call me DJ Trickster."

So now there are three wolves on the loose. Either the Vikings liked wolves a great deal more than they should have, or they just couldn't think up any more characters for the stories.

As all this is happening, an insanely giant sea serpent slithers onto dry land. As a matter of fact, this thing isn't just insanely giant—it is super-insanely giant. So giant that it causes a tsunami to sweep across the globe. This serpent has another one of those jacked-up names—Jormungand. I know, a little much, right? But what do you expect—they were fucking Vikings. (Man, there seems to be a kraken or a krakenlike monster in everything these days.)

Now, this is where things start to get weird. The giants are another race of creatures in this whole sordid affair, and they have a creepy ship called Naglfar, which is apparently made from the fingernails of dead men. That's got to be a shit load of fingernails. I mean, can you imagine how gross that fucking ship would smell? Anyway, as these giants come sailing into the picture, the Serpent Jormungand and a great wolf named Fenrir decide they are buddies and join together to form one rank of evil and strife. They march side by side.

If you look to the north, you can see that Fenrir's mouth is so gaped that his top jaw scrapes the heavens of our earth while his lower jaw, wrought with jagged teeth, drags across the trembling ground. To the east, DJ Trickster is streaking toward you in a flaming rocket ship made from every condom ever used throughout the history of fucking. (Okay, I made the used-condom-rocket-ship part up, but after the warship made from fingernails, I didn't feel I was reaching.) Everywhere you look there are monsters and death, but suddenly from the west appears one shining ray of hope, one dream of salvation—the gods. Badass gods. Not only are they super pissed off, but they get their rocks off on beating the asses of supernatural beings. It's fun for them, and they don't mind dying in battle. For them, dying

FORTUNE COOKIE WISDOM

Valhalla is the coolest place ever. The realm where dead Vikings battle all day and feast and fuck all night.

in battle is fucking awesome! One god, Heimdall, sounds one of those classic horns to alert the other gods to what is transpiring on earth. And they spring to action.

Unfortunately they don't actually "spring" into action. There ends up being a lull because the gods have to have a meeting to talk about shit. Personally, I hope it is one of those Council of War meetings where everyone sits around a big table and feasts on hunks of bloody meat and drinks from barrels of ale, just like in medieval times. Hopefully it's not like the usual shit when government officials get together and take forever to make an important decision, and then don't commit to that decision when it is finally made. I say this because during the meeting, Odin, who's the head of all gods, gets on his horse, which happens to have eight legs (could be from nuclear radiation, so watch out for the giant spiders), and rides to a magical spring to get advice from Mimnir, which might be a mermaid or some shit (this wasn't made all that clear in the Cliff's Notes). She isn't pleased with his presence. "Get the fuck out of here and go to the battlefield," she says. "What are you, a little kid? I thought you were king of the damn Aesir gods!"

Ashamed, he goes and assembles all the other gods (finally), as well as all the dead Vikings that live in Valhalla—the place where good Vikings who die in battle end up so they can die in battle later on with Odin at Ragnarök.

While all these gods and dead men are waking up and having their coffee, all the bad guys join up. Jormungand, the scaly, poison-spitting schlong; Fenrir, the big bad wolf; a fellow named Surt, who is the sentinel for the Realm of Fire—(when he's not fighting at Ragnarök, Surt is a part-time bouncer at Club Savage; he enjoys sushi, long walks on the beach, and good conversation)—as well as the Fire Giants and Ice Giants. They all merge into one battalion and start marching to the battlefield, which is called Vigrid. During the hike, they cross Bifröst Bridge. Now, this is a rainbow bridge, which I find a little weird. I mean, either they took a break to star in a Skittles commercial or they were heading to a Nordic Gay Pride parade. Either way, a little out of character for the manliest monsters around.

Then the action starts. Approximately 432,000 dead Vikings, all wearing golden helmets, along with the gods, meet the Legions of Evil in mortal combat at Vigrid. Although this apocalypse has yet to happen, the ancient texts give us a play-by-play for all the primary characters. Odin, the All-Father and King of the Aesir gods, engages the wolf Fenrir in battle first. Basically, the wolf wins by swallowing him from the get-go. Who the fuck made this pussy king? He's supposed to kick some major ass, but instead he gets eaten alive by a giant dog. But then again, I guess being a god and all, he is probably as old as dirt, and so it would be like an eighty-five-year-old man dragging his old bones across the junkyard in an attempt to fight a pit bull. Pretty disappointing.

The next fight on the Ragnarök card is in the bantamweight division—Loki vs. Heimdall. The bout is billed as DJ Trickster versus the Blower of the Magic Horn. For a while it looks like "good" will get the upper hand on "evil" as Heimdall employs his magic horn in sinister ways, but after the two roll around for a while, they end up slapping each other to death. Neither one wins.

Then Thor, who has my vote for the most badass Viking god, takes on the serpent Jormungand. Thor uses his strength and his giant hammer, and Jormungand uses his serpent fangs. Thor beats the crap out of Jormungand, but our hero ends up dying a few minutes later from the venom he ingests. Come to think of it, this bout sounds a little fishy as well. Thor is said to have a "Great Hammer," and he fights an extremely large and thick snake who "he has met before." Then he ends up dying by getting injected with secretions from that snake. And here I was thinking Thor was such a macho guy.

Just when things begin to look bleak for the forces of good, a true badass emerges—Vidar, Odin's son. Pissed off that Fenrir ate his father, he steps on the mutt's lower jaw, grabs his upper jaw, and tears the fucking thing in half. Now that's what I'm talking 'bout.

Unfortunately, this victory means very little. In the final throes of battle, the giant flamer Surt rains fire on all nine of the Vikings' worlds. Pretty much everyone dies—all of mankind, the gods, the giants, and animals. Even the Elves and Dwarves die, meaning there is no hope for Mini-Me, the Keeblers, Time Bandits, or Urijah Faber. This is it. All worlds burn and sink into the seas.

This kind of begs the question How do I survive when everyone is wiped out? Sorry for the obvious, but you just don't. If the Viking story of Ragnarök, the great battle between the Aesir gods and the legions of the underworld, does in fact come to pass, we are all pretty much fucked. But if you have any gumption whatsoever, any balls at all, you will fight to the death, because that's pretty much all you'll be able to do. After all, it could mean the difference between dying by a blade or being porked to death by a depraved Fire Giant. You get to pick. If you choose the former, I have included some tips below on how to take on one of the more common foes of Ragnarök.

HOW TO KILL A SUPERNATURAL WOLF

(Editor's Note: Delete following section—offensive and homoerotic potty talk. Childish—reader will hate.)

When Ragnarök comes, you're gonna want to know how to fight and kill a supernatural wolf. Luckily, the super-badass wolves will already be fighting some of the gods, so you will most likely be pitted against one of the lesser wolves, such as Papsmear and Queernir. Despite being enormous and, for all intents and purposes, mythical, they will act the same as all dumb dogs and charge you. If you follow my step-by-step instructions below, there is a good chance that you will step off the battlefield victorious. You will die a horrible, fiery death a short while later, but that is inevitable.

Step 1: As the wolf charges you, dive off to the side to avoid its gaping jaws and stank breath, and then quickly roll underneath it so that you are gazing up at its underbelly. Unless the mutt has been fixed, you should see an engorged set of red balls swinging above your head like bells in a tower.

Step 2: Remove your rope from your homemade utility belt, lasso that set of nuts, and then climb up the rope. Once you reach the top, cling to the punching-bag-size scrotum and shimmy around to the backside. Do not cling to the front of the scrotum, as the animal will have a tree-trunk-like torpedo whipping around. Ever been hit upside the head with a rubber dildo? No? Yeah . . . uh, me neither. But anyway, supposing you had been hit upside the head with a rubber dildo, this is a thousand times worse.

Step 3a (option one): Remove a pipe bomb from your homemade utility belt and cram it up the wolf's anus like a suppository.

Step 3b (option two): This option comes into play when you are not armed with a pipe bomb. Lacking the option of turning the wolf inside out, you are going to have to kill it using your blade. Luckily, all supernatural wolves have the same weak spot, which is located between the dick and the balls—not the "taint," which is between the balls and ass. I don't have a word for the spot you are looking for, and I certainly hope you don't either, as it would mean you spend far too much time talking about dicks and balls. Unless, of course, you are a woman, and then it's totally cool.

Anywho, the wolf's massive schlong will most likely be guarding this spot, and the only way to gain access to it will be to arouse the wolf to erection. I have no information as to how to do this either. My only advice is to be creative. Once the animal is showing lipstick, the artery will be exposed and ready to slice. Cut deeply and strongly, and you will be victorious.

Note to Reader: If you actually wasted your time reading multiple paragraphs on how to kill a supernatural wolf, which, I remind you, is a creature that will never exist, I would like to give you a call sometime. Not to be your buddy or pal: I simply want to know if people like you truly exist.

P.S. Is there even a word for a person who has a wolf genital fetish?

AIN'T NO CONDOM TO PROTECT YOU FROM THIS: THE VIRAL APOCALYPSE

It starts off as a slight tickle in the throat, a little lump when you swallow, maybe a little soreness. You get congested and your nose begins to run. Sneezing follows shortly thereafter. Within a day, you develop a dry, hacking cough and your breath shortens. The moment you realize you're in trouble is when playing video games becomes impossible because of the energy required. By the end of the second day, you have severe nausea and are puking and pissing out of your backside, which is blistering sore from the continuous wiping. Your headache turns to fever and you lose all body strength.

Day three brings the lesions. They start off small, but they get bigger and deeper as you scratch them. Soon they cover your entire body—they're in your mouth and all over your genitals. You cover yourself in toilet paper and pretend to be one of those lepers from the movies about the Middle Ages or a mummy from ancient Egypt. Either way your prognosis is not good. You lie immobilized in a pool of sweat, blood, and various excretions. Your cough settles deeply in your lungs, and bright green mucus oozes from your encrusted nostrils and stinging eyes. It dries in the back of your cottony throat. Your fever rises and, as you lie there, you swear you can smell your brain cooking in your skull.

The coughing continues, but it is no longer an upper-respiratory hack. It is deep, and every hack is painful. Golf-ball-size globs of phlegm force themselves out of your lungs, Day-Glo and streaked with red. Sometimes you are unable to spit them up, and so you end up swallowing them. You feel like you could drown in your own fluids at any moment. Just as you think that matters couldn't get any worse, your skin deteriorates and begins to fall away. Your veins and arteries can be seen through thinning, waxy layers of epidermis, which cling like rice paper to your body.

There is no remedy. No cure. There is nothing for the pain. In fact no one is coming to help you at all, for you are in quarantine, and there are millions like you—this is more than an epidemic. This is a Viral Apocalypse!

ONLY YOU CAN PREVENT THE VIRAL APOCALYPSE

You probably can't do shit to prevent the viral apocalypse unless you're a scientist working in an underground bunker doing viral research on monkeys, but you can at least have some common courtesy, which is something most people know absolutely nothing about. You see, microscopic viruses would have a much harder time turning into a global killer if people covered their mouths when they coughed and sneezed. And I'm not talking about covering your mouth with your hand: What good does that do? Sure, you might have not blown your nastiness directly into my face, but you proceeded to touch and infect everything within a ten-meter radius.

The worst is when people don't wash their hands thoroughly after taking a dump. When I have friends over at my house, I find myself listening intently after the flush to hear how long the sink runs, just to make sure things are straight. Many of my sick-fuck friends need monitoring, believe me. So, in conclusion, I never want to hear these words come out of your mouth: *Oh yeah, I feel like shit. I have a terrible fever, but I'm a real trouper and came to work anyway.* Fuck you! If you are sick with the plague, lock yourself in your basement and stay there until you rot.

Did my description terrify you? Well, unless you actually shit yourself, you are not nearly scared enough. If you actually did shit yourself, then hopefully it's because you were reading this book in the bathroom, where it's supposed to be read. If you weren't reading it in the bathroom and you shit yourself, don't even think about using the pages to wipe with. This is your mess and I'll be damned if I'm gonna help clean it up.

One of the most plausible end-of-the-world scenarios is an incurable viral pandemic. The virus could come about naturally through mutations in the animal world and then get passed to humans, or it could be created accidently by scientists or on purpose by domestic or foreign bioterrorists. Thankfully most of the stuff we catch these days is either curable bacterial strains or viruses that our bodies can fight off and develop immunities to. Currently, just the pathetically weak die from flu viruses. No one gives this much thought because it is usually just the elderly and children, both of whom are pretty much useless in society. But this won't always be the case.

Now, we've all seen the zombie movies where a virus spreads rapidly through humanity, causing horrible death and then reanimation. Although these movies are ridiculous because the zombies somehow survive with missing limbs, which could never actually happen (I hope), these cinematic masterpieces are very realistic in that it is quite feasible that a man-made, incurable kind of virulence will be released into the general public. What sinister minds could do such a thing? Who are these mad scientists who are laboring to kill us all with the next crushing bug?

The principal cause of a man-made viral threat lies in the genetic alteration of existing viruses for use in biowarfare. Now, of course I would never suggest that our illustrious government would be involved in something that was declared a violation of international law, but there are plenty of

FORREST FACTOID

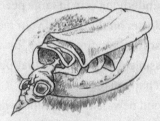 Chicken eggs are one of the main incubators for viral research. Who knew? I thought they were just for slinging at passing cars or pasting houses with! But it makes sense when you think about it. Eggs are really just abortions in a candy shell, right? Ever open an egg and find that little black dot floating inside? That means it's actually been fertilized! Once I cracked open an egg and found blood. Yep, that cured me of eggs for a while. I've heard that if you go organic with eggs, you also run the risk of discovering a partially developed chicken fetus. If you ever encounter something as tremendous as this, I suggest you invite some buddies over one night, buy a bunch of beer, make sure everyone gets tore the fuck back, then go out to pick up some burritos for the crew. While driving home, slip that slimy little fetus into one of the burritos, mix them up, and then distribute them to your friends once you get home. As everyone digs in, break out the video camera and pan around slowly for the lucky winner. It's kind of like Russian roulette, except no one knows they are playing except for you.

groups and governments that don't adhere to these agreements—or didn't, as in the case of the Soviet Union. Remember how I told you that when the USSR fell, a shit-ton of nukes kinda disappeared. Well, so did a crap load of weaponized biowarfare agents. One of these agents was a genetically engineered strain of smallpox, which has been one of the deadliest diseases in the history of man.

This nasty little viral infection was responsible for killing an estimated 500 million people in the twentieth century, and some experts believe it has been around since approximately 10,000 BC. So this stone-cold killer has been wreaking havoc on humans for thousands of years. How does it do its dirty work? Well, it is caused by a virus called "variola" that is transmitted through inhalation or direct exposure to infected bodily fluids. The virus gets into the nose, throat, and respiratory system, and then heads for the lymph nodes, where it sticks and festers. Open sores pop up on your skin and in your mouth and throat, making drinking orange or grapefruit juice extraordinarily uncomfortable. In some cases, the lesions can combine into large patches that slip off the underlying skin in large peels, much like slippery fruit roll-ups. They can cluster on the soles of your feet and on your palms, making hopscotch, masturbation, fire walking, bitch slapping, and giving foot jobs all but impossible. Did I mention that pus can dribble out of your penis? Yeah, that can happen too.

Sounds pretty terrible, doesn't it? The good news is that smallpox was declared "eradicated" in 1979. The bad news is that the virus had become so rare, we widely discontinued the vaccine around 1970, making all the people born after that date extremely susceptible to the infection. This wasn't considered a big deal because the nasty little fucker had been exterminated. I guess at the time no one thought that there could be a group so hateful they would pour resources into bringing it back from the dead. If the USSR's former stash found its way into the hands of a group that hated Americans, and this group somehow found a way to release it into the population, it could wipe out a large portion of our country. Smallpox only kills around 30 percent of the people who get infected with it, but when you are talking about nearly 300 million people scampering around the land of the free, that is a lot of graves you will have to dig.

What is disturbing is that there have been other strains of the "pox" virus discovered in the wild, as well as strains developed in the laboratory, that can infect both animals and humans (great thinking!). This includes cowpox, monkey pox, and . . . man, I feel ashamed to even say it . . . mouse pox. I mean, really? Mouse pox. I wouldn't be surprised if in the near future some scientist will have to write an apology letter to the world explaining how sorry he is for introducing squirrel pox. This is how I imagine the letter would go:

Dear World,

I am very sorry for inventing squirrel pox. I was working on a project to enlarge male genitalia, got sidetracked, and ended up fucking around with the smallpox virus. One thing led to another; I ended up developing this terrible virus that could wipe out a large portion of the world's population, and then decided to inject it into various squirrels to see what happened. But the last thing we want in this time of crisis is to be pointing fingers, am I right?

If you for some reason come into contact with a squirrel and get the disease, it follows the usual progression of smallpox: fever, nausea, and the pustulelike bumps that turn to lesions. But after the lesions explode, you go through what I like to call a "turning" process. You get big puffy cheeks, grow a bushy tail, and patches of fur pop up in random places. For all intents and purposes, you turn into a giant squirrel. If you have a family member who happens to get infected with this virus, I strongly recommend strapping them down to a bed or tree to prevent them from sprinting across the road at the precise moment a car is coming. Anyway, sorry for this mishap. And good luck!

Yours truly,

Richard

Personally, I feel this is the worst type of apocalypse. I would much rather get vaporized by a mushroom cloud or eat the hot dust of a super-volcano than slowly rot in my bed. To avoid dying a horrible death, take my advice below.

1. Stay away from people. They are disgusting creatures. (I know what you are thinking: "So Forrest, you are telling us to avoid human contact with anyone but our most significant loved ones, but you roll around with sweaty men for a living?" Well, that's only because I haven't yet found a way to make a living without rolling around with sweaty men . . . Do as I say, not as I do.)

2. Wear a body condom wherever you go. If you don't have a body condom, just slip into one of those large plastic bags that dry cleaning comes in and fit a rubber 1970s swim cap on your head. Personally, I tried to go with the full-on contamination suit. Unfortunately, this was short-lived. In addition to my sponsors telling me I couldn't do appearances in a plastic jumpsuit, Dana White informed me that the Nevada State Athletic Commission turned down my request to wear one in the cage. Despite these minor setbacks, I am hoping to get contamination suits into the new fall fashion line. Will you help me on this crusade?

3. Become a homeless person and live in a trash can. Apparently, homeless people can survive pretty much anything.

4. Kill every single person on the planet . . . and pigs. Those little fuckers are nasty germ carriers.

THE HOT NEW THING TO BE AFRAID OF: SUPER-VOLCANO APOCALYPSE

Seventy-five thousand years ago on the island of Sumatra, the human race was brought to the very edge of extinction by one of nature's most powerful and devastating forces. I'm not talking about Cain Velasquez's right cross, though that tends to be pretty powerful and devastating as well. I'm talking about the eruption of a super-volcano. It's exactly what it sounds like—a really big volcano. Although these things are very rare, they fuck shit up beyond all recognition when they blow.

Regular volcanoes like Mount St. Helens and Mount Vesuvius are usually shaped like nipples or penises (whichever you prefer), and as magma boils inside, pressure builds, until one day they erupt and spew molten rock out of their blowhole. Super-volcanoes, despite being exponentially larger, do not have the traditional cones. Instead, they are largely hidden beneath the surface of the earth. If the shape of regular volcanoes can be described as a nipple or penis, super-volcanoes should be described as a giant, yawning butt hole. The magma of super-volcanoes bubbles underneath the ground in gargantuan reservoirs, held at bay by a massive blockade of rock known as a caldera. Over hundreds of thousands of years, pressure builds in the depths. When the pressure reaches a critical threshold, the magma blows through the caldera, spewing shit into the atmosphere.

To help you better understand this phenomenon, let me use another third-grade fecal analogy. Say there is a morbidly obese man who gets a bad case of diarrhea, but that diarrhea can't squeeze itself out of his swelling anus because he lost an anal bead in his rectum. As the obese man continues to gorge himself, the diarrhea burbles in his great bowels, creating an insane amount of pressure. Then one fateful afternoon while he is loading up his shopping carts at Food 4 Less, the pressure becomes too great, the anal bead becomes dislodged, and gallons upon gallons of explosive shit hurtle into the atmosphere of his tremendous trousers. This is exactly what happens with a super-volcano. The only difference is that there are no feces of any kind involved—but there is a ton of hot magma and ash.

When the butt hole in Sumatra blew seventy-five thousand years ago, it shot so much ash into the atmosphere that the sun was actually blotted out. The ash came down like snow, covering the ground a foot deep more than twenty-five hundred miles from the eruption. The catastrophic event wiped out the majority of the human race living at the time, leaving only a few thousand survivors to struggle through a seemingly never-ending winter. Although there is no evidence of any kind to support this theory, I believe the survivors were forced to turn to incest and cannibalism.

The next blast will most likely come from Yellowstone National Park, which is home to a caldera more than eighty-five kilometers wide and forty-five kilometers tall. Scientists have discovered that this super-volcano erupts every six hundred thousand years, and with the last blast having

THINGS FORREST HATES

- People who smoke.

- People who drive.

- People who breathe.

- People who have been brainwashed by a certain diet and talk badly about the things you eat.

- People who used to be addicted to alcohol and now think that everyone who occasionally uses alcohol is somehow an addict who needs their help.

- People who bash everything that is fun, such as eating bad food or drinking alcohol.

- Fat people who order a cheeseburger and a Diet Coke. (In fact, so many fat people drink Diet Coke, Forrest used to think that diet soda made you fat. Turns out it is just a strange coincidence.)

- Close talkers. Even worse still, close talkers who follow you around as you try to walk away from them.

- Anyone who talks about themselves in the third person. Forrest Griffin hates that.

- Salespeople who refuse to give you refunds.

- People who wear spandex shirts out to the bar.

- People who use too much gel. Unless, of course, the gel is Rogaine.

- People who are balding. Completely bald is totally cool, just not those who are currently going through the balding process.

occurred 640,000 years ago, we are overdue. This baby has got to come out, and Mother Earth is pushing like a son of a bitch. Since 1923, the earth over the caldera itself has swollen and risen more than two feet. It is not a matter of *if* this thing will blow, but rather a matter of *when*. If it should erupt in our lifetime, let me give you a little preview of what could happen.

First, a series of earthquakes will rock the area around Yellowstone, shattering the seal on the caldera and allowing all that magma to eject. It is estimated that falling ash and lava will extinguish all life within a six-hundred-mile radius, and do so with approximately one thousand cubic kilometers of lava. Ash will get ejected into the atmosphere, and when it comes down it will cover lands as far away as the Gulf of Mexico. In a very short period of time, all the farmlands of the Midwest will be covered in ash and destroyed, which will be a major blow to the national and global food supply.

Tens of thousands of people will die pretty much within the first few minutes from hot ash and molten rock. How terrible would this type of death be? Think back to those occasions when you nuked a microwavable burrito too long, and when you went to pick it up, you got that napalm-like cheese-and-bean goo all over your fingers. Now imagine the cheese and beans from a really big burrito dripping on your entire body. Now times that pain by fifty thousandish, let's say. That is pretty much what you are looking at. Luckily, you will be seared into oblivion almost instantaneously, so pain really won't be a factor.

If you manage to avoid hot shit falling on your body and killing you, all is still not a bushel of canned peaches. The ash and debris flung into the atmosphere will very likely block out all the sunlight and drive the world into a state of nuclear winter. When the super-volcano in Sumatra blew its load into the sky, the overall temperature of the earth dropped by just over twenty degrees. Just as with all the ash covering the ground, this will dramatically reduce the world's food supply, which in turn could lead to starvation, extreme bitchiness, and eventually nuclear war.

Hints for surviving the hot blast of a super-volcano:

1. Build an island in the middle of the ocean, kinda like they did in *Waterworld*. Do not leave your island or let Kevin Costner star in any movie made on your island.

2. Get on the boat with Bilbo and Frodo and sail to Valinor.

3. Volunteer on a Russian space station.

4. Kill yourself.

THE END OF THE WORLD ISN'T JUST FOR PAGANS: A SINNER'S GUIDE TO REVELATION

The Christian Bible has its own version of the apocalypse. A lot of people refer to this as "Armageddon," but this is the incorrect word. In fact, Armageddon is the name of the actual place in Israel where the final conflict between Good and Evil will supposedly take place. The end-of-the-world prophecy in the Bible is referred to as Revelation or, according to Apostle John, the Book of Revelation. How did Apostle John know what he was talking about? Well, he saw a bunch of crazy shit go down in these two "visions" he had. Anyone who is named John and has regular visions is undoubtedly Irish, so I have a tendency to believe him. After all, we all know that God favors the Irish and gives them holy visions regularly. I could get deeper into it, but I would be saying too much.

When John goes into one of his more intense visionary states, he hears voices beckoning him up to heaven to meet God. During one such vision, John finds twenty-four old dudes kicking it with some animals, one of which happens to be a lamb. John of course attempts to kick the lamb because he never managed to catch the one that ate his rose bushes down on earth, but the old men quickly stop him. They tell John that the lamb symbolizes Jesus. Now, I don't know if John thought this was a little weird, but I certainly do. If you are the Son of God, you can choose whatever form you want. I would have picked something cooler, like a lion, a giant eagle, a marmoset, or a Tyrannosaurus. Obviously, Jesus never won the "If you were an animal, what would you be?" game.

Anyway, this all-powerful lamb is the one picked by God to learn and divulge the true sequence of the end of the world. The lamb does this through the cracking of the Seven Seals; potentially more evidence of John's heritage, as Seals could be interpreted as those on bottles of whiskey, tapped kegs, or ancient clay jugs of wine. With the cracking of

FORREST FACTOIDS

Forrest Griffin is only to be referred to in the third person omniscient . . . he will also accept Grand Master G.

Forrest has an elevator in his single-story trailer for obvious reasons.

Forrest Griffin only drives barefoot.

Attaining a bachelor's degree takes seven years in Forrest Griffin time.

Forrest Griffin doesn't get knocked out—he just chooses to take naps at odd times.

Forrest Griffin reuses condoms.

Forrest Griffin wears a parachute at all times, just in case.

Forrest Griffin doesn't know his pets' names—he simply refers to them as pets 1 through 4.

Forrest does calisthenics before sex.

Forrest uses car keys instead of Q-Tips. In an unrelated matter, Forrest gets a lot of ear infections.

Forrest Griffin can communicate with trees simply because of his first name. (However, trees have nothing to say. They just bitch a lot about not being able to walk.)

Babies hate Forrest because they know . . . cats love Forrest because they know . . .

each Seal came a vision of how the world will end. How did John see these visions? Apparently, he saw them through the lamb's eyes. I know, sounds a little Ragnarökish, but I am not going to be the one to talk smack. I mean, what if, right?

The vision for the First Seal is that of a king riding a white horse. I thought it was odd that this dude would ride on a white horse and not a white pony. Does this mean that he will prefer heroin to cocaine? I don't know, but this king is also quite the conqueror, so probably not. If he were truly riding the white horse, he'd just doze off in the middle of his sentences and most likely wouldn't do much tooling around. But his drug of choice means little because it is believed that he represents the Antichrist or false prophet. The one who says he is God. Few people will believe him at first, but he will actually be able to work miracles, like making Eddie Murphy funny again. I don't know about you, but if someone pulled that out of their hat of tricks, I would be a believer. This guy ends up fooling a ton of people into following him, and for a moment he becomes more popular than Oprah.

The cracking of the next Seal leads to the vision of a rider on a red horse. This too is quite strange because I have never actually seen a "red" horse. I have seen brownish-red horses, but not actually one that is fire-engine red. I suppose in a supernatural dream it is important to suspend disbelief at some points. Well, this rider is almost as bad as the first one because he brings massive wars and conflict. A lot of people who are really into this story feel that the rider on the red horse is currently among us. If you think about it, it makes sense. In the past hundred years, we've seen World War I, World War II, the Korean War, the Vietnam War, the cold war, Desert Storm, the wars in Afghanistan and Iraq, *Dancing with the Stars*, Halo, *Are You Smarter Than a 5th Grader?*, and countless other raging battles. The signs are all there, so what comes next in Apostle John's visions should interest us all.

When the Third Seal is broken, John sees a rider on a black horse. This horseman brings with him Famine—which reminds me, I'm starving right now! I'll be right back . . .

. . . Okay, back. When I wrote the word "famine" I knew I needed to go out and get some Quiznos. That shit rules when you are hungry. I don't think they'll have Quiznos around when all this biblical shit goes down, so I recommend getting the good grinds while you can. Anyway, the world experiences a bunch of famine, which is a pretty realistic scenario. Other than the "seeing through the lamb's eyes" part, I'm still on board.

With the breaking of the Fourth Seal, the rider on the pale horse emerges. For some reason, the pale horse is different from the white horse. I don't know about you, but I have always considered white a pretty pale color. Perhaps the pale horse is translucent like one of those weird shrimp that Japanese people eat while the little fellas are still alive (when I said "little fellas," I was referring to the shrimp, not the Japanese). Perhaps this means that the fourth and final horseman is actually riding an invisible, giant shrimp or sea horse. Now that I think about it, all this horseman stuff is kinda strange. If John is actually seeing into the future, why is he still seeing people riding horses? Shouldn't he be seeing people driving cars or hovercrafts or light cycles or something? Anyway, the rider of the pale horse brings Pestilence. After looking up that word, I discovered that it means plaguelike sickness or infectious diseases. We've covered how this concept could be a real-deal apocalyptic scenario, so things are starting to look rather grave.

The cracking of the Fifth Seal shows that all the people who had died in God's name will be really pissed off, and they'll begin bitching and moaning to be avenged. Not very "godly," if you ask me. I mean, isn't a part of martyrdom being satisfied with the fact that you gave your life for God? Vengeance just seems a little out of place here. But looking back in history at how some of these folks were killed—being skinned alive, boiled in water and oil, burned at the stake, and one unlucky sap getting his guts ripped out and wrapped around a drum while a bunch of people beat on the thing—I guess you can't really blame them. Under the conditions, a little payback seems to be in order.

When the Sixth Seal is cracked, John sees earthquakes and all sorts of other natural disasters causing havoc on the earth. Basically, shit starts getting really bad. The lamb quickly cracks the Seventh Seal, hoping things will get better, but that's when angels come in and start blowing on their trumpets, which happens to be the most annoying instrument ever created. (That's why they use them in the military to get your ass out of bed at 0500 hours . . . Or is that a bugle?) Instead of things getting better, they get a whole lot worse. Over the course of seven trumpets being blown, all hell breaks loose.

To start with, one-third of all forests and plant life is wiped off the face of the earth, one-third of all the oceans and rivers and well water becomes poisonous, and one-third of the sky goes dark. Pretty bad, I know, but things only get worse. An army consisting of 200 million people starts killing everyone they can find. John must have been a really fast counter to know it was 200 million. I would never have been able to figure that out. I would have said something more like, "A huge fucking army kills a shit load of people." Instead, John seemed to know exactly how many, and that they kill one-third of all human beings (again with the thirds!).

Somewhere in the middle of all these crazy visions, John seems to get hungry and, finding nothing to eat around him, ends up scarfing down a small book. It is described as being sweet when he first starts munching on it, but then it gives him a stomachache. Even if I was really hungry, I don't think I would eat a book, though this book is pretty fucking amazing, so I'm sure it tastes good too. Speaking of which, did I already go over Quiznos and how good it is? I'm sure those twenty-four old dudes watching him trip out were getting pretty hungry as well. With that many people, they could have ordered a six-foot sub. There are usually never enough people to get a six-foot sub. Obviously a missed opportunity there.

So he eats the book. Apparently this leads to another vision because he sees 144,000 people on top of the holy Mount Zion, and they are all hanging out with that lamb. In addition to this, they all have God's name written on their foreheads. Note to Self: If shit goes down, grab a Sharpie and make sure to write God's name on your forehead. Hanging out with a lamb on top of a mountain will be a lot better than what is going on down on the earth. Don't believe me? Let me keep going.

The Ark of the Covenant suddenly shows up in heaven—that's right, the funny box that Indiana Jones discovered, the one that melted all those Nazi guys' faces off. Seriously, I always wondered what happened to that thing after the last scene in the movie when it ends up in the gigantic warehouse. Clearly what happened was that Indiana Jones later broke into that huge U.S. government warehouse, stole the Ark, and brought it up to heaven. Indiana Jones certainly had his thinking cap on. After seeing the damage it could do, hiding it in heaven was a really smart move. I am not sure how having it turn up in heaven helps or hurts the situation, but that is what the Bible says. From what comes next, it leads me to believe it is a bad omen.

Satan is cast down to earth, which I think is a pretty dick move. I mean, if you've already got the guy, why not kill him! There's no point in unleashing him back into the world just to meet up with him in a later battle. I guess it's like fighting a guy you know you can beat down at will. Every time you knock him down, you let him back up just so you can beat him again and really show your dominance. In any case, that is what will happen. Satan immediately starts killing everyone, and then a monster comes out of the ocean and starts doing the same. Eventually Satan, who is on land, makes mankind worship the sea monster, kind of like two guys in prison ping-ponging some unfortunate jailhouse bitch. To make matters worse, the angels are given Seven Bowls, and each bowl is filled with God's wrath. That's right, God's wrath, which apparently has not yet started.

Sores start to pop up on the bodies of everyone who worships the devil and the sea monster, even if they were forced into doing so, and every drop of water on earth turns to blood. Yeah, that blows. The sun burns the living hell out of the earth, everything is blacked out, and another earthquake hits and levels all the mountains and sinks all the islands (that means no more Pure Cane sugar. Fucking hell! I despise the taste of sucrose in my coffee). But instead of simply calling it quits there, both Good and Evil begin to prepare for the final battle at Armageddon.

Then God gets bored again and decides to let Satan out . . . again. Maybe he's been real good and he can come out of his room now. Of course a tiger can't change its spots, and Satan goes back to waging war and torturing folks. So God has to round him back up again and put him in the lake of fire. It is about this time that God has had enough of the bullshit and decides to have Judgment Day, where he condemns Satan, all of his followers, and every evil fuck in the world to eternal damnation. He just picks them all up and dumps them in the lake of fire for good. Once accomplished, he remakes the earth to be a nice, chill place to hang out. The end.

With all that said, I am sure you are wondering how you can survive such an apocalypse.

Hints for Surviving Armageddon

1. Be kind to other people.

2. When in a public restroom, do not urinate all over the seat. That is a ticket straight to hell.

3. Do not cut people off on the freeway, and if you are in the fast lane, go fast.

4. Do not pick on people who are smaller than you. Unless, of course, they deserve it.

5. Give to people less fortunate than you.

4

SURVIVING THE
INITIAL SHIT STORM

I f the shit went down and you followed my instructions, you survived the initial death toll by taking refuge in your fallout shelter, boogied out of town using your escape route, and now you're chilling out in your safe zone, swinging in a hammock and sipping a warm beer. Assuming you didn't get caught by a demon wolf named Loki while you tried to escape, you fucking made it, buddy! Now, if you didn't take my advice, you are probably lost in the forest and scared as hell because you can hear the "bad men" off in the distance, shouting about how they want to have another go at ya (ah, yes, the characters from *Deliverance* are gonna make you squeal like a pig).

This scenario is much more likely than you actually having followed my step-by-step instructions, so you are definitely going to need some additional skills to survive (and perhaps some anal lube). I strongly recommend that you find a cave or something, break out your flashlight, and keep reading. These coming pages may very well save your life, or give you something to read while you're taking shit. Either way, a job well done on my part.

MARTIAL LAW

With an estimated global population of nearly a shit-ton of people, it is safe to say that unless Ragnarök turns out to be more than just my favorite fairy tale or an asteroid obliterates our planet into pieces, mankind will not get totally wiped out during the apocalypse. There will be small pockets of people who survive. They might be forced to live in some pretty inhospitable conditions, but they will still survive. The United States government realizes this, and because the physical and mental state of these people will be in question, they developed something called Continuity of Government, or the COG Plan.

There exists a specific directive to this plan called NSPD-51, which states that in case of a "disaster," the U.S federal government has the authority to seize all the functions of both state and local governments (don't worry, I played no part in researching any of this). All that power is transferred to the Executive Branch of the government (the Office of the President and his cabinet of advisers . . . and no, the President doesn't keep his advisers in an actual cabinet, except for maybe Bush, because those guys were undoubtedly never around). In addition to this, members of the Legislative Branch (House of Representatives and Senate) and the Judicial Branch are demoted to advisers (serving wenches). In other words, they lose all real power and are subjected to the will of the Executive Branch. (Note: We gathered this information from a separatist camp in Montana. They also told Bigger John he needed more guns.)

It is important to remember that these actions can only be undertaken in case of a "disaster" or "Catastrophic Emergency," which is defined as "any incident, regardless of location, that results in extraordinary levels of mass casualties, damage, or disruption severely affecting the U.S. population, infrastructure, environment, economy, or government functions . . ."

(Note from Forrest: Blah, blah, blah) So, if any of the disasters we have covered actually transpire, you can pretty much expect the Executive Branch of the government to claim all power, eliminating all the checks and balances currently in place. For all practical purposes, our country would become a dictatorship.

Before I go any further, I want to be clear that I am not passing judgment on this concept. I understand why it is an essential contingency. If one of the scenarios I described earlier were in fact to occur, it would be pandemonium. While nobody wants to see the Executive Branch with any more power, this would actually be necessary in case of an emergency. The President would need the ability to make decisions in a streamlined and succinct manner, without all those checks and balances that we call democracy. Just think of what things would look like if Thor was battling it out with a giant snake in the middle of your neighborhood. The madness would be multiplied by a thousand because of comic book fans alone. Some type of plan must exist to bring those nerds back under control. However, it is more than a little scary to think that that the amount of power we are talking about here has already been quantified and assigned to a specific entity. It is even scarier to think of how that power might be used. And, if you give it some thought, it is even more scarier (yeah you heard what I said) to think that there is someone out there whose only job is to think about how to keep the government running if shit like this goes down—and that we're paying him a full-time salary.[9]

Immediately after the disaster, martial law would almost certainly be declared. Martial law is simply a nice way to say that you are now living in a society completely controlled and regulated by the government. If you're wondering what this world would be like, just think of the book *1984*, only with less stuff. (What? You didn't read *1984*. You're an idiot.) Your value in the society is suddenly based upon what you can do to further this government's efforts or goals. For example, if it were my dictatorship, your worth will be based upon how good of a training partner you are for me, and if you bring me delicious treats and coffee. Basically, if you treat me like Sean Connery in the 1975 movie *The Man Who Would Be King*, and give me gold

---

[9] And it is super-duper scary when you learn that you had a one-night stand with a chick that used to be a man. Trust me, that shit is fucking terrifying.

and jewels like one of those natives, you'll be OK, so long as you don't get all uppity when you realize I am not actually a god, chop off my head, and throw it off a cliff (that part of the movie fucking sucked). Personally, I am not too worried about my place in the new system, as I possess some skills. However, I'd be a little concerned if I were you. I mean, I imagine your most valuable skill is being able to jerk it while simultaneously playing an online game of Call of Duty.

Disagreeing with the government's overall game plan is no longer an option—if you do not follow their orders, you risk imprisonment or execution (arguing with them is much like arguing with Greg Jackson between rounds—it just ain't gonna happen). And if you are deemed undesirable due to your health, age, intelligence, etc., you may end up being expendable. Of course, all of this only applies to extreme cases, such as if 90 percent of the human race was suddenly wiped out in the blink of an eye or if we had a major collapse of the U.S. economy. Either way, this is all important stuff to consider.

Life under martial law would be a life of regimentation. You would work the job you were told to work, and for as long as you were told to do it. You would be compensated however the government saw fit. The government would institute curfews and regulate the information that reaches the general public. Food and medical supplies would be rationed according to your value and status in the new social structure. I know, this system failed in both North Korea and Russia, but the government would still try it thinking they could succeed. After all, we're talking about the government.[10]

Again, I am not saying this would necessarily be a bad thing for a society in the midst of a major disaster situation. It may actually help maintain order and keep us all from raping and killing each other.[11] Maybe even allow us to regroup and start rebuilding in a practical and efficient way. Deciding whether or not to adhere to the new structure of power boils down to one question: Do you trust the government to use that kind of

---

[10] Again, I am personally going to be just fine, as I am a naturally born hoarder. Back when I was a kid, I used to steal ketchup packets everywhere I went, and then suck them down in the privacy (pronounced with an English accent—*priv-a-see*) of my room. If you are smart, you instinctively know hoarders are survivors. Just look at squirrels—they hoard everything, and they've been around longer than sharks (not sure if that is true—might want to look that shit up).

[11] Seriously, if we didn't have a government right now, I would have killed half a dozen people because of road rage.

power honestly and in your best interest? If the answer is yes, you trust the government will do what is best, then you should fall into line and do as you are told (and you can sleep tight tonight, Santa is going to bring you lots of presents this year for being such a good boy). But if you answer is no, you don't trust the government, then you'd better prepare yourself for life on the lam.

Personally, I will want to go it on my own. It's not that I distrust the government—I simply don't want to be milling around among the masses when shit goes down. It's going to be hard to bring my perfect utopia to fruition, and having a bunch of other assholes around is only going to make things more difficult. I don't want to be told what to do or how to live. I would rather forge a new life on my own. If you are like me[12] or if you distrust the government, there are a few things that you must prepare for.

First things first, you must view law enforcement officers and military personnel working to implement this master plan as threats. Their job is to ensure that everyone alive is accounted for under their new system, and it is your job to elude that system and find an isolated spot in which to build your new utopia. They're not going to want a bunch of freethinkers lurking around because it may cause harm to their design, and this is understandable. But it won't be good if they manage to capture you. I'm not advocating going up against them or even trying to dismantle their operations, but if you want to live your own way, you will need to avoid them at all costs. For all intents and purposes, the government will have the mind-set of Spock, and we all know his beliefs—The Few Must Be Sacrificed For The Many.[13] It is the same as the phrase "For the Greater Good." If you're one of the Many, all is well, but if you have some sort of affliction[14] or can't pull your weight, sorry buddy, you are one of the "Few" and the "Greater Good" will sacrifice your ass. If you fall into this category[15], you will become one of the hunted. Most of those hunting you will be organized, armed, well nourished, and trained for this type of situation. To elude them, you must be trained even

---

[12] A Real Man.

[13] I actually did not know this because I am not a nerd. I figured you were most likely a nerd, and I wanted to make you feel at home.

[14] We already established the fact that you are a nerd, so you obviously have a laundry list of afflictions.

[15] Seriously, we're still on this. You are a nerd, which means you are one of The Few. Deal with it! Step away from World of Warcraft for a moment and open your fucking ears.

better, which is where the techniques offered later in this book will come in handy (also, watch *Rambo*. That is where I got 90 percent of the information in this book. The other 10 percent I got from my mother).

As I mentioned earlier, the best way to avoid the ensuing madness and the rigid social structure that will be hammered out of the rubble and mayhem is to get on the move before the "organizers" step in and start running the show. Of course, you want to remain sheltered until the event causing all the death subsides, but get on the move shortly thereafter. If you wait too long, there is a good chance that the government will limit the mobility of the general populace by setting up checkpoints and possibly even camps to facilitate their containment efforts. The trick is to get the hell out of Dodge and then find a location that has clean water, vegetation, and possibly even a healthy amount of wild game. In other words, head to Montana. Just make sure your plot of land is not desired by the government, as that will undoubtedly lead to a confrontation which you are not going to win.

MANLINESS AND THE APOCALYPSE

I know this book is about the apocalypse, but I felt compelled to address manliness in today's society, or the lack thereof. After the apocalypse, this lack of manliness is going to be a real problem, so it's important that we start addressing this issue now. If you take a hard look around, you'll notice that men's hairy nutsacks have gone the way of the appendix. That's right, the vast majority of men have essentially become eunuchs. What are the signs? Well, the fact that tattoos and tanning beds have replaced the good old-fashioned workbooks and callused hands as indicators of manliness is a good start. Even professional fighters, who are supposed to be ultra-manly, have gone soft. After all, it's kind of hard to be a real man when you play more video games than twelve-year-old boys in China. I am not saying that fighters are not tough, because many of them are very tough. But there is a difference between being tough and being manly. You can be tough as hell, own a pit bull, and even ride a motorcycle, and still not be manly.

If you want to be a real man, at the very least you must learn how to

APOCALYPSE MANLINESS TIPS

1. Refer to groceries as supplies. Example: I am going out for supplies.

2. Start every sentence with: "There are times in a man's life where he's got to stand for something . . ."

3. When in doubt, do what Ted Nugent would do. You can start this pre-apocalypse.

fix shit—and I am not talking about your cable. Every guy, both manly and unmanly, knows how to rig his cable box. I'm talking about big shit. Today, most fighters don't have a clue how to fix their plumbing or heat and air—they don't have the slightest clue what Freon is or what it does.

How did this happen? Well, a lot of it had to do with the digital age. Due to all the technological advances, men have forgotten how to hunt women. Instead of chasing women in bars, they pick them up on the Internet, send text messages, and, when all their electronic attempts to get laid fail, they look at Internet porn. The day the great chase became skewed, the lion inside of men died. I know what you are thinking, "Forrest, I still hunt women, it is just a different kind of hunt." No, you are wrong. Typing into a search engine is not hunting, and I don't care if you spend two hours a day on the MILF Hunter website. We have been coddled by technology, and as a result, we have lost the manliness that our fathers earned at a young age.

Men have gotten lazy—plain and simple. Blue-collar workers have always been a little lackadaisical, but now even construction workers have gone soft. Sure, they might be able to lay tile, but they don't know how to lay brick. Sure, they might be able to construct a wall, but they don't know how to fix a water heater. Back in the day, the men who worked with their hands knew how to do everything.

If you fall into this sackless category, don't beat yourself up too bad—you're not alone. I do not work on my car or fix shit after I break it. I am not out there doing ultra-manly things, like vandalism. Just like you, I seek out help when something goes wrong. Most guys call their fathers when shit suddenly stops working, but not having one of them, I call my mother. Yes, my mother is manlier than me. Back when I was a kid, she did all the traditional guy stuff. She went out and worked all day, and then came home and repaired anything that had broken around the house during her absence.

With that shit all taken care of, I assumed the traditional woman's role. In other words, I cooked and cleaned. I probably would have learned how to do all the hard stuff when I struck out on my own, but there was no need to tinker in front of the water heater for nineteen hours, trying to figure out the gizmos inside. If my mom couldn't give me step-by-step instructions over the phone, I could find the answers on the Internet. And if those answers were too complicated, I could use the Internet to find someone to interpret those instructions or simply come out and do the repairs himself.

However, technology is not entirely to blame. There are two other factors contributing to our lack of manliness—the hormones in our meats and women. Yes, I said it, women are to blame for the downward spiral of man, but not for the reasons you might think. Becoming more independent, women have stopped wanting as many kids, and so a large percentage of our female population takes birth control pills, which are chock-full of estrogen. Well, that estrogen doesn't just disappear. With every flush, it gets put back into our water supply, which in turn finds its way into every man on the planet. Did you know that when it rains, you are actually being doused with estrogen? I know this might seem like a cheap way out, but all that womanly DNA (I know estrogen is probably not DNA, but not having the slightest clue what estrogen actually is, that is what I have decided to call it) has got to be having some negative side effects, am I right?

I know the lack of manliness in our society might not seem like that much of a problem now, but it is getting worse every year. We have to think about future generations. When all fathers are just as dumb as their kids, nothing will ever get accomplished. I mean, when fathers come home from an eight-hour workday and start playing video games and surfing on the computer instead of fixing the washing machine, the entire foundation our society is built upon will begin to crumble.

If you are as worried as I am and want to attempt to fix the problem, do not run out and try to sleep with fifty women. Again, manliness is not about the number of women you can bed. If you truly want to become manly for the sake of the next generation, you should start by going out and getting a manly job. What is a manly job? Well, any type of work that endangers your health is a good place to start.

The manliest job I ever had was working on a road crew. We would uncover these massive septic tanks, and being the new guy, I would have to go down in there to remove any of the debris that had fallen into it. So I would head down into the shit pit in a pair of boots and waders, shovel rocks and raw sewage into a metal bucket, and then someone up top would pull the bucket up. Of course, rocks and human feces would fall out of the bucket and rain on my head, which was the part that made the job manly. The first time I crawled out of the pit, a fellow worker named off thirty diseases I could contract from this type of work, the most permanent one being hepatitis. So, yeah, I kinda of have a hint of what it is like to be a real man.

If you get a dangerous job and still feel somewhat unmanly, I have included a list of things you can do to make your balls drop further.

1. Marry a destitute woman that has a lot of children you have to take care of.

2. Do anything wilderness oriented—hunting, fishing, wildernessing. But I don't want to see you out there looking at your phone or GPS system. Get a compass, camp, and learn how to navigate by the stars.

3. Learn how to fix your vehicle. This is perhaps the most frustrating thing on earth, which in turn will add large amounts of manliness points. Personally, I learned how to fix a car in the most manly situation possible—on the side of an active freeway, with semis damn near killing me.

4. Grow a beard. If you are like me and your Irish curse prevents you from growing a beard, get some wicked back hair.

5. Wear boots . . . for a purpose. If you wear steel-toed boots, you better get a job where heavy shit frequently falls on your feet.

6. Eat meat you cooked and caught yourself. Don't be a pussy by shooting a deer and bringing it to a processing plant. Clean that shit yourself.

7. Get a gun. However, if you get a gun and don't learn how to use it, you lose manliness points.

8. Wear slippers around the house and possibly even a smoking jacket. I know, doesn't seem too manly, but it is.

9. Wake up early. I'm talking before 5 A.M.

10. Milk things. If that "thing" is your girlfriend or wife, you get extra points.

11. Sports are relatively manly. I mean, the little bit of manliness I have, I learned from football coaches.

Now, I know a lot of you are probably pretty disturbed right now and want to correct your lack of manliness. Some of you will take my advice above, but others will undoubtedly think that taking directions is the unmanliest thing of all, and attempt to strike out on this mission alone. To prevent you from steering in the completely wrong direction, I have included a list of things that you might feel are manly but are actually very unmanly. I only do this because I care.

1. Beating your woman is not manly. When angry with your old lady, the manliest thing you can do is step out for a pack of smokes and then never show back up. That is what my dad did.

2. As I already stated, getting tattoos is not manly. Unless, of course, you are a sailor or legit biker.

3. Muscles are not manly. Don't be a pony show, as my old boss used to say.

4. Do not wear jewelry. I know pirates used to wear earrings, but they did that for a reason. They had no home, no family, and lived on a ship with a bunch of thieves. Their two gold earrings were to pay for their burial when they died in battle. Whoever stumbled upon their battle-torn corpse would use one gold earring to pay for their burial, and then keep the other for themselves. Unless you plan on dying in battle, do not wear earrings.

FORTUNE COOKIE WISDOM

Manliness isn't like on the show *Mad Men*—that is a re-creation of what we think it would have been like. The manliest thing we have going today are Old Spice commercials, which I actually think might hold the key to regaining our manliness. That's right, commercials are the best shot we have at regaining our manliness. Yeah, we're fucked.

I know all of this might seem like a lot of work, but for the sake of those who will follow us, please make your best effort to become a real man. And don't set aside time for it like you do for the gym—you have to make manly things a way of life. Start a local petition in your area to outlaw estrogen pills. Of course, a large part of the estrogen we ingest could be eliminated by eating organic, but altering yourself in such a manner isn't very manly, so stick with the petition and contacting your congressman. I feel if all of us men band together, we might have a chance of getting estrogen eradicated from our water supply. Unfortunately, that will probably mean a lot more kids running around, but taking care of kids is pretty fucking manly . . . So long as you actually take care of them.

BOB'S USED CAR LOT OF THE APOCALYPSE

You don't need to read this section if you followed my instructions and built a Vehicle of Death, but I realize that shit happens. If you're a woman, you most likely stood in front of the car that you planned to convert for a long time, confused by all the parts under the hood. Eventually you started crying, kicked the bumper in anger, and then cried even harder because you hurt your foot. A few minutes later, you went inside and ate a box of bon bons[16], never again to visit your little pet project. If you are a man, you most likely used the project as an excuse to get away from the missus. Although you spent approximately nineteen hours a day in the garage, you never actually worked on the damn thing because you were too busy drinking beer, looking at porn, and telling your buddies who came over how cool your Vehicle of Death would be when it was finished.

---

[16] Bon bons are delicious.

In either case, you don't have a monster of a ride to plow through all the mayhem that's choking the streets. All you have is your family sedan, and under the current conditions, that won't get you out of your neighborhood. Of course, I told you to have a backup escape route, one you could negotiate on foot, but if you were too lazy or teary-eyed to work on the Vehicle of Death, you probably never got around to doing this either. So you are in a bit of a pickle, but luckily Uncle Forrest is here to bail you out . . . Again.

Below, I offer instructions on how to hot-wire a car, but since we're not at the apocalypse yet, keep in mind that hotwiring cars is still illegal. I'm not suggesting that you go out and do this now. But once the shit hits, all bets are off and you'll do what you need to. Before I get into the actual act of hot-wiring, though, I feel it is important to talk a little bit about the type of vehicle you want to commandeer. The most important thing to remember is that shortly after the apocalypse happens, survivors are going to go gas crazy. Gun battles will break out at every gas station in America, and the winners will most likely suck the pumps dry. So whatever car you commandeer, it is important that it has enough gas in the tank to get you where you are going. If you chose a safe zone several hundred miles away, you will want to stick with vehicles that run off diesel. With the majority of cars running off regular gasoline, diesel will be a lot more available, especially when all the truckers fall asleep due to the lack of meth. And if you can't find any diesel at gas stations or the pumps have stopped working, you can always siphon from the generators in machine shops.

VEHICLES YOU SHOULD COMMANDEER

1. **SEMIS:** Whether or not to commandeer (notice how we said "commandeer" and not "steal") a semi requires careful consideration. If you know exactly where you are going and want to haul a ton of shit needed to survive for the long term, it's obviously a good choice. Once you have the semi, all you have to do is back up to the loading ramp at Costco and begin stocking up on the Cheetos and diapers. Just make sure that you steal

a cool big rig, like the one with the clown face from *Maximum Overdrive*. (Seriously, I better not see you driving around a basic, piece of shit International.)

However, a semi is not something you want to be cruising around in, looking for a place to set up shop. They are not very fast, so outrunning marauders is usually out of the question unless the truck that you pick happens to be Optimus Prime, in which case you have to worry about having Shia LaBeouf around and that will pretty much suck.

Despite what they show in the movies, semis really aren't that great at smashing through blockades, either. Big rigs have their cooling systems in the front of the truck, so if you ram something with it, don't be surprised to break down on the side of the road a few minutes later. I know what you are thinking, "But what about Mad Max, he rammed all sorts of shit." Yes he did, but if it were real life instead of fiction, a few minutes later, the pursuing gang of gay motorcyclists would pull him from his ride and ram *him* in a ditch in the desert.

Another weakness of big rigs is their tires. Although they have a lot of them, they are large and easy to shoot by people in pursuing vehicles. If you've ever watched an episode of *COPS*, you know that most vehicles can drive just fine with one of their tires blown out. Not the same can be said for semis, due to their length. Lose a couple of back tires and you'll go careening all over the road, lose control, crash into a ditch, and then . . . well, you know what happens then. To top all of this off, semis are a fucking bitch to drive because they have 20,000 gears.

2. **SCHOOL BUSES:** School buses are better than either semis or RVs if you are traveling with a group of people because they have a ton of windows to shoot out of. If you don't have guns or are running low on ammunition, you can simply throw things out the window, including the more annoying members of your crew. I mean, that would get pretty much anyone to stop chasing you, am I right? Just picture it. You are chasing a yellow school bus packed with helpless survivors, eager to claim your spoils.

Suddenly they begin chucking old people and whiny teenagers out of the bus windows. Would you still chase them? I sure as hell wouldn't. (I bet you're starting to see why I landed this book deal. I have all sorts of useful wisdom to impart.) In addition to having more windows, school buses are also a lot easier to modify than either a semi or an RV. You can deck it out with barbed wire, skulls, and all sorts of other menacing-looking ornaments. And with a bright orange bus, you will never have any difficulty spotting your ride in a crowded parking lot. The downside is that school buses suck gas big-time and tend to have governors installed to prevent angry bus drivers from doing a hundred and ten on the freeway and producing one of those gruesome scenes from the driver's ed video, *Red Asphalt*. If you chose to commandeer one, I suggest loading the back with multiple barrels of petrol and removing the governor from the engine.

3. **TRUCKS:** If you do not have people or a ton of shit to haul, a truck is an excellent choice. They get decent gas mileage, do well off-road, and if you install a snowplow or steel grille on the front, they are decent for ramming shit. However, there are a couple of things you must do to make a pickup a safe traveling vehicle. First, store several guns and some ammunition in the cab. Second, knock out the back window and store backup ammunition at the front of the bed. Remember, if you have ammunition, you never want it to be too far away from it. Third, properly tie shit down in the back. Although it is the apocalypse, you're still in America. If you want to pack a mountain of shit in the back of your truck and then tie it down with dental floss, move to a third-world country. Lastly, always bring a pet monkey so that he can drive the car while you shoot out the window at pursuers. It is also possible for you to drive and the monkey to shoot, but I have discovered that monkeys have lousy aim. Quite possibly the monkey will shoot you.

4. **HUMMERS:** Despite all the negative shit I said about these gaudy, overpriced vehicles and their owners in my last book, a Hummer is actually a good vehicle to commandeer during the apocalypse

for obvious reasons. They are roomy, rugged, have massive gas tanks, and do exceptionally well off-road. However, if you steal a Hummer with the three-piece rims that Snoop Dog talks about when he raps, you have made a huge mistake.

VEHICLES NOT TO COMMANDEER

1. **TRACTORS:** Although tractors are super cool because they allow you to destroy all kinds of things such as scoreboards, barns, and other vehicles, they are not very practical. They burn a shit load of gas and top out at just a few miles an hour. Unless you are looking to dig a pit of death for people to fall into, avoid hot-wiring heavy machinery.

2. **SPORTS CARS:** While it might seem like a good idea to commandeer a sports car because they can go super fast, you don't have to be Einstein to figure out why they are a terrible postapocalyptic vehicle. First off, it is difficult to fit two big bodies into one of these sleek pieces of machinery, let alone all the extra shit you would want if you go through the effort of obtaining a vehicle. There is no room for an extra gas tank, your various weapons, or a stockpile of ammunition. In addition to this, having the ability to maneuver through various types of rugged terrain will be much more important than speed. With abandoned vehicles and bodies littering the streets, as well as all the damage to the pavement caused by the thousands of accidents that occurred as people attempted to flee, having a low-clearance vehicle is just about the stupidest thing you could choose. I know why a sports car jumped into your mind in the first place: you want to look cool. Well, a sports car will not make you look cool.[17] If you were a douche bag before you climbed into a sports car, you will still be a douche bag once you're behind the wheel. However, if you absolutely insist on commandeering a sports car, stick with American-made vehicles. They have more

---

[17] It will make you look dead.

clearance, more torque, larger tanks, bigger trunks, and handle much better off-road. (Just remember, you're still a douche bag.)

3. **ELECTRIC CARS:** Do I really need to explain this one?

BE FAST, BE FURIOUS

This is obviously something I had to research, and I really wish I had done it sooner. If I had known how easy it was to hot-wire a car, I never would have fought my ass off with Stephan Bonnar to win that crappy Scion. If you are working at Taco Bell or cleaning the diapers of the elderly in order to purchase the vehicle of your dreams, quit your job right now. To have the vehicle of your dreams, all you need is a flat-head screwdriver, a pair of pliers that can strip electrical wires, and a box of Kleenex. The first two tools are to steal the car itself, and the Kleenex is to wipe the jizz off the dashboard when you realize how much easier your life just got.

Before you pre-cum in your shorts thinking about your neighbor's Mercedes and how good you will look sitting behind its wheel, it is important to mention that not all cars can be hot-wired. Many of the cars that came off the conveyer belt in the past half a decade are armed with kill switches. You poke, prod, or talk dirty to them, and they shut down completely, much like most of the women I have met. Unless you are a professional car thief, stick with older models. This shouldn't be a problem because the only time you should consider stealing a car is when you need transportation in a postapocalyptic world. (Please ignore what I said above about quitting your job and stealing a car . . . That was bad advice, and I really don't want to get sued over this book as I did with the last one. Remember stealing = bad until martial law is declared.)

1. **STEP 1:** Check all doors to see if the car is locked. If the doors are locked, smash one of the back windows. Despite what you see in the movies, do not smash one of the front windows. This will deposit shards of broken glass all over the front seats that will surely end up in your ass cheeks. Unless, of course, you like the thought of shards of glass slowly embedding themselves in your colon.

2. **STEP 1A:** Check driver's-side visor to see if the owner of the car
   has left their keys there. I've never quite figured out who is a big
   enough moron to actually do this, but it seems to happen with such
   frequency in the movies that it must be true, though the people who
   do it are probably the people whose e-mail passwords are 12345.
   (Fuck, now I have to change my email password . . . and my PIN.)

3. **STEP 2:** Locate the hole where you stick in the keys. This device
   is referred to as the ignition tumbler, but with these words being
   too intricate for either you or me, I will just call it the vagina
   of the steering wheel. Once located, pry off the plastic covers
   surrounding the vagina.

4. **STEP 3:** Remove the flat-head screwdriver from your utility belt
   and jam it into the vagina. If your screwdriver is short, you will
   most likely need to slide it in all the way up to the hilt. Personally,
   I do not have this problem because I carry a large screwdriver.

   Once you have penetrated the vagina, grip the screwdriver's
   handle with both hands and twist like a mother. (In case some of
   you forgot we were talking about hot-wiring a car, do not attempt to
   perform this procedure on your girlfriend; it will not win you any
   brownie points . . . but who am I kidding, we all know you do not
   have a girlfriend! . . . Oh, yeah, that's right, that Australian girl you
   are seeing, the one you met while on vacation with your parents
   last May. The one none of your friends will ever get to meet because
   she lives so far away. I read ya.) Anyway, if you have a strong grip
   and are lucky, the ignition switch will turn and the car will start.
   This is the best-case scenario because you won't need to fuck
   around with wires and risk getting electrocuted. From that point
   on, starting the car will be as simple as turning the screwdriver.

5. **STEP 4:** If you are attempting to hot-wire a car at this moment
   and are currently reading step four, you are a loser. You rolled
   the dice and shit the bed. Although God has completely given up
   on you, do not give up on yourself.

   Release your grip on the screwdriver, reach underneath the
   ignition tumbler, and locate the panel that has five to eight wires

attached to it. This is where things get a little tricky—you want to locate the positive and negative wires that go up into the steering column. Different cars use different colored wires, but most of the time they are both red. Once located, pull them from the steering column, strip about an inch of the plastic coating off the ends, and then twist them together. It is important to mention that these wires are hot, which might lead to a small shock. (Translation: Ignore the fact that all your muscles have tightened up, urine is dripping down your leg, and spit is flying from between your clenched teeth.) Completing this step supplies electricity for your ignition components so the engine is able to start.

6. **STEP 5:** Return to the assortment of wires and locate the ignition wire, which in many cars is brown. Again, strip approximately an inch of the plastic coating off the tip.

7. **STEP 6:** Lightly touch the ignition wire to the two red wires you already twisted together. In most cases, the car should start. Note: This is the part of the process where it is quite possible to receive a rather strong electrical shock. To avoid this, do not hold the metal tip of the brown wire. Hold farther up, where the plastic is still intact. After you have gotten the car started, separate the brown wires from the red wires so they are no longer touching.

8. **STEP 7:** If you still can't get the car running, throw a tantrum and vent your frustration about your incompetence.

9. **STEP 8:** Your tantrum alerted a motorcycle gang to your presence. Run!

(INSERT MILDLY AMUSING BLOWJOB JOKE) OR HOW TO SIPHON GAS

Unlike the Vehicle of Death I told you to build, most cars you find on the street will not have an extra gas tank built into the back. As a result, you won't get very far unless you learn how to siphon gas. Luckily, I offer step-by-step instructions below. When I am finished, you will be able to siphon better than an underage runaway on Hollywood Boulevard pulling for his next fix of China White. While this knowledge might be able to save you from getting stranded in the middle of a desert, it can also get you in trouble. There are several objects on which you do NOT want to practice your siphoning techniques. Below is a brief list of do's and don'ts.

Okay to Siphon

- Cars
- Boats
- Lawn mowers
- Generators

Not Okay to Siphon

- Curdled milk
- Kerosene lamps
- Drano
- Toilets
- Spittoons
- Animals (especially not raccoons and cheetahs)
- Bottles of glue
- The curious penis dangling through the hole in your bathroom stall at the freeway rest stop.

Step-by-Step for Siphoning Gas

STEP 1: Obtain some type of rubber hose that is smaller in diameter than a garden hose and larger than a catheter. DO NOT use a catheter.

STEP 2: Slide the hose deep into the gas tank's shaft.

STEP 3: Position a receptacle below the car's gas tank.

STEP 4: Stroke the rubber tube with one hand, place your opposite hand on the base of the tube, wrap your lips around the tip, and begin sucking. The goal is to feel the fluid rising in the tube, and then quickly remove your lips before it blows. (If you get a mouthful, do not swallow. You're not trying to impress anyone here.)

STEP 5: Move out of the way and allow the tube to spit its precious fluid into the opening of the receptacle you placed on the ground.

STEP 6: Allow gravity to pull gas from the tank into the receptacle.

STEP 7: Clean yourself up with Kleenex.

STEP 8: Never tell anyone what you have done. Not ever.

BRONCO BUSTIN' FOR DUMMIES

Horses will be an excellent source of postapocalypse transportation because they can go where vehicles cannot. They can climb mountains, move gracefully through dense forests, traverse deserts, and swim across rivers. They also run off grass rather than gasoline, which, unless there is a nuclear winter, will be much more readily available. The most difficult part will be finding a horse. All the domesticated horses will probably get eaten pretty quickly, so you will have to locate and catch a wild horse. Before I give you step-by-step instructions on how to accomplish this, I must mention that breaking a horse is actually quite cruel. Although old westerns make it seem like a very natural process, anytime you steal an animal from its natural habitat, shatter its will, and then make it serve you, it's a pretty dick move. But hey, if you need to get around, you need to get around.

Step-by-Step for Breaking a Horse

STEP 1: Find a wild horse: Thanks to the white man, wild horses are pretty scarce. The best place to find one is at wild-horse refuges, which are scattered around the United States. The problem is that these refuges are the same places where we have corralled all the Injuns, so you must be careful not to get scalped!

STEP 2: Move toward the horse: When you spot a wild horse, you do not want to spook it. Running toward it waving your arms and shouting is a bad idea. You want to move toward the animal slowly and speak softly to it. It doesn't matter what you say, so long as you speak softly. For example, you can say, "Nice girl. You're a nice girl, aren't you? I am your friend, that's right. I want to be your friend and take care of you." Or you can say, "Hey shit stick, I am going to steal your freedom and make you my slave. If you disobey me, I will stab you with my spurs. Don't worry, I will still let you eat grass—not the fresh grass you have now, but rather shitty, dried cubes of hay that taste more like cubes of shit. But be grateful that I will feed you at all. You are a dumb animal and I can kill and eat you anytime." Both are just as effective so long as you talk softly.

STEP 3: Obtain control of the horse: Pull up beside the horse and begin rubbing its neck. Do not pat the horse as you would a dumb child—stroke it nicely, as you would a cat or some other creature you care about. While stroking, slowly place a rope around its neck. If the horse finds this arousing, like David Carradine, quickly move on to another horse.

STEP 4: Shatter the horse's horseliness by treating it like a pimply-faced junior high school student; this can be achieved by sliding headgear onto its face. Such gear is often referred to as a halter, but it looks nothing like the sexy little tops women wear. Next, grip the bottom portion of this headgear and begin to walk. The goal here is to teach the animal to move when and where you want. To break its will, feel free to write insulting things about it on the stalls of the boys' locker room; however, do not attempt to stuff the horse in a trash can or flush its head in a toilet as you would a junior high weakling that you are tormenting for sport. You want to be demeaning, but not totally abusive.

STEP 5: Continue to be mean and annoying: Jab your finger in the horse's side until it moves away from your prodding. Repeat on all sides of the horse until it submits to your every command.

STEP 6: Continue to dress the horse as if it were a child you hated: But instead of forcing it to wear a pair of footed pajamas, put a saddle onto its back. Remember, horses are against God, which is why they are always naked. You must help them find the Lord.

STEP 7: The Bridle: The bridle is much like a ball gag, but instead of putting it on your spouse, you use it on a horse. It consists of a headset, a bit that goes into the horse's food hole, and reins that you can use to steer the animal into places it does not wish to go. Just like getting the ball gag into your partner's (or sometimes repulsive prostitute's) mouth, it can be difficult to place the bit into a horse's mouth. If it refuses to open its chops, slide your finger into the various corners of the animal's hay cave. The horse will find this very annoying and eventually open wide. Once you've accomplished this, slide in the bit and strap it in place.

STEP 8: Mount the horse: Mounting a horse is nothing like mounting a woman. Although both are oftentimes unenthusiastic about being mounted, horses are much larger animals than women. They also have hooves that can annihilate a healthy pair of testicles. With only one remaining testicle, I am very careful to avoid hooves and high heels. As a result, I attempt to mount both of these magnificent creatures very rarely.

To reduce your risk of injury, mount the horse very slowly and then just sit there. Do not stand up on the horse or lie back to get a suntan. Once it is comfortable with your presence, force it to move forward by pressing your legs into its sides. For some reason, horses understand this as the "move forward" command.

STEP 9: Turning. Moving in only straight lines sucks because eventually you will run into something. As a result, the next step is to teach your slave horse to turn. If you want to turn left, press your left leg into his side and pull on the left rein. To get it to move to the right, press your right leg into its side and pull on the right rein. To get it to stop, pull back on the reins. In addition to this, you must learn all the proper terminology, such as "whoa" and "Easy, boy" and " 'smatterchew." This will make you sound like a real cowboy.

STEP 10: Throw a tantrum because you can't get the horse to do what you want.

STEP 11: Your tantrum alerted Injuns to your presence. Run!

THE FLAT ORIGAMI: HOW TO READ A MAP, AND MAYBE EVEN FOLD THEM

First off, let me start by telling you that the wilderness sucks. There are no showers, stores, washing machines, or shitters. All the wilderness offers is dirt, trees, animals, and insects.

In order to spend as little time as is humanly possible under these terrible conditions, it is important to know where you are going. This can be tough because there are also no street signs in the wilderness. Occasionally there is a ribbon tied around a tree or an *X* etched into a rock, but following these will either confuse you more or lead you into the mouth of a grizzly bear den. Unlike when you were a child and hid under the kitchen sink, no one will come looking for you if you get lost.[18] You are totally and completely alone, and to avoid certain death, you must learn how to read a map. And I am not talking about Hollywood Star maps that show you how to get to the houses of various celebrities, though those are super cool, especially if you are a stalker. I'm talking about topographic maps, like the one shown above. Trust me, there is no need to go all Christopher Columbus and attempt to discover Australia for a second time.

How to Do Lines

Topographic maps are filled with a bunch of wavy lines. While at first glance it might appear as though the mapmaker left the map in the backseat of his car where his idiot son had at it with a Magic Marker, these lines are actually there for a reason. The most important lines to familiarize yourself with are the brown ones, as they represent contours, which is a fancy way of saying "points with the same elevation." What is nice about these lines is that they allow you to visualize a three-dimensional image from a two-dimensional drawing. On the next page, there are blank boxes where you can test your hand at conjuring up these three-dimensional images as well as actual topographic maps for you to study. Obviously, this is an important

---

[18] Personally, I was not able to hide under the sink as a child because my mom got those damn cabinet locks. Probably had something to do with the fact that I constantly tried to drink the Windex. It's not that I liked the taste, I just thought it was a pretty color.

skill to have because it tells you what stands in front of you and the easiest way to get around obstacles. If *Butch Cassidy and the Sundance Kid* had been in the possession of a topographic map, they never would have had to jump off that cliff.

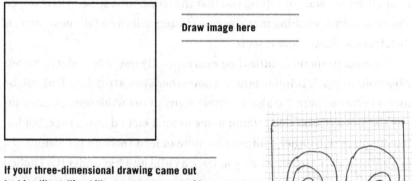

Draw image here

If your three-dimensional drawing came out looking like rolling hills, you can now consider yourself an adequate map reader. If it ended up looking like a pair of breasts, you are more of a pervert than a mapster.

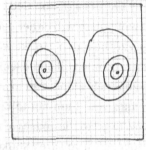

Draw image here

If your three-dimensional image looks like an outcropping of granite coming off two small hills, congratulations! You can now consider yourself an expert map reader. If it came out looking like morning wood, you have dicks-on-the-brain, and that is totally your business, my friend; I don't judge.

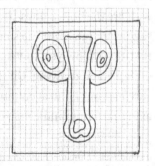

Legend (Not Just a Great Movie)

Marsh ˅⁄ ˅⁄ ˅⁄ ˅⁄ ˅⁄	Unimproved Road - - - - -	
Scrub		
Campsite △	Hard or improved surface	
Loose Rock	Open pit/ Mine quarry ✕	
Trail - - - - -		
Managed Woodland ˅⁄ ˅⁄ ˅⁄		
Spot elevation ✕726		

In addition to learning how to read contour lines, you must also familiarize yourself with the legend at the bottom of the map. In this area, the map will show the symbols used to describe certain information on the map. At left, I list some of the more common ones.

Sample Map

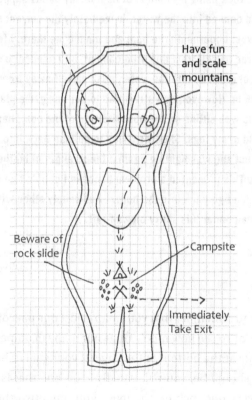

Have fun and scale mountains

Beware of rock slide

Campsite

Immediately Take Exit

HOW MUCH I HATE THE OUTDOORS

As you are probably guessing by now, I don't much like the outdoors. Well, when I was thirteen, my mother decided we were going to have a bonding experience. Instead of taking me to Disneyland or somewhere cool, she decided to take me white-water rafting. There were seven or eight of us on the oversized inner tube, and being a large kid, I was put in charge of the left side of the boat by the guide. He told me my job was to make sure we didn't get stuck on any rocks, and I was more than excited to take on this task, as it made me feel like I was wearing my big boy pants.

About ten minutes into our adventure, sure enough, we get stuck on a rock. I had wedged my paddle down between the side of the raft, so I tried to push us off the rock using my hands. Of course, my hands slipped off, and my entire torso dunked into the water. Immediately the current swept my head and life vest underneath the boat and pinned me there. I felt no need to panic—to free myself from this predicament, all I needed to do was slide the lower half of my body into the water, push myself away from the boat, and climb back in. However, as I attempted to put this game plan into effect, my mother, who was sitting on the opposite side of the boat, began to panic and grab a hold of my legs. She was trying to pull me back into the boat with all her might, but she was fighting against the strength of Mother Nature and losing terribly. This presented a problem because I couldn't go out of the boat and I couldn't go back into the boat. I was simply stuck with my head and chest pinned under this shitty blowup raft.

Grids

It is important to remember that your map is just one part of a much larger map—the world! To see how much area your map encompasses, you want to visit the scale at the bottom of the page. If your goal in having a map is survival, as it should be, you will usually want one that is 1:24,000. This means that every one inch on the map represents two thousand feet of actual land. Knowing this, you can measure how many inches you have to

After about twenty seconds fighting to free my legs from my mother's death grip, I realized that I would soon pass out. Not knowing what to do, I kicked my mother as hard as I could in her chest and face. As you would expect, this caused her to release her hold, allowing me to follow through with my initial game plan. I slide out of the boat, pulled myself out from under the raft, and then hopped back into the boat. At the time, I did not even care that I had come close to death. The only thing that I cared about was the fact that everyone on the boat was now staring at me with open mouths.

I was exhausted and totally out of breath, but since I had daddy issues, I didn't want to look like a jackass in front of the guy who had given me some authority (yeah, I could have been a stripper), so I breathed slowly out of my nose and pretended that I was looking around at the scenery. A few seconds later, I grabbed my paddle and focused my gaze downstream. I should have probably checked on my mother, who had just received a mule kick to the chest and face, but I figured she was probably okay because she had a life vest on. To this day, neither one of us have every brought the subject up. It was akin to farting during sex in that you and your partner just move on and pretend that it never happened. In any case, the moral of the story is that the wild will try to fucking kill you any chance it gets, and I fucking hate it.

go on your map, and know how many feet you have left to reach your target area on land. For a carry-along measuring tool, you should now measure your penis and convert it to feet using the scale above. Once this is accomplished, all you will need to do is place your johnson on the map to know exactly how far you have to travel to reach your destination. Even if your pecker can only be used to measure six-thousand-foot increments, it may not be as useless as your past girlfriends have told you.

POSTAPOCALYPTIC
DIET-AND-EXERCISE PROGRAM

The human digestive system is not designed to handle processed foods and large amounts of sugar. It is not designed to handle foods that are vitamin fortified, a practice that only began about seventy years ago. If you want to be healthy during the apocalypse, you should eat the same foods our distant ancestors ate, such as nuts, twigs, and berries. It is also extremely important to eat for your body type . . . No, no, fucking no!

If you plan on trying to maintain your specialized, trendy diet in a postapocalyptic world, you are a filthy mouth-breather and will most likely die a horrible death, which is fine because you deserve it. Eat whatever you can find that isn't rotten or spoiled. Eat untreated shoe leather if that is what you have on hand. The human body will adapt. Don't baby your body; it wants to live. It will take whatever calories you give it and turn them into energy. Remember, no one cares if you are ripped when you are fucking dead. If you are thinking, "How will I maintain my daily workout regimen without proper meals?" then you are an even greater idiot. The postapocalyptic exercise program will consist of RUNNING FOR YOUR FUCKING LIFE from syphilis zombies, as well as building shelters and hunting. Basically, staying alive will be all the workout you need. I swear, every time I talk to you it is like I am dealing with my brother's kids!

The Apocalyptic Standard Body Mass Index Chart

Frail: You are weak and fragile. Although you are considered attractive in our current society, after the apocalypse, a large bird or gust of wind will most likely carry you away. Note: Postapocalypse, vomiting up food will be punishable by decapitation and being cooked on a spit.

Skinny: You are thin and quick. Although you will probably have no trouble running from lunatics, you most likely have a fast metabolism. Your survival will depend on your ability to eat every few hours. May I recommend shoe leather?

Athletic: You are strong and fit. As you can tell, this drawing was made in my current likeness. If you resemble me, you have an excellent chance of surviving any type of natural disaster. Trust me, we'll be just fine.

Fat: You are one of the jolly folk. If you somehow survive the initial shit storm, your long-term survival will depend upon your body type. As we have all learned from the UFC, there are certain fat guys who are extremely athletic and agile. If you are this type of fat, you might actually have a leg up on those who are athletic because you can survive on your man tits and the medicine ball you call a stomach for a good deal of time. However, if you are the type of fat guy who has trouble getting out of his chair, you most likely won't last a week. But seriously, if you're that kind of fat, do you really want to survive in a world without Cheetos?

Morbidly Obese: You are morbidly obese. You have to pay for sex and most likely cannot see your genitals, so what is the point in surviving the apocalypse? Might as well end things now before getting licked to death by your fifteen cats.

HUNTING

Hunting will be a pretty big deal after the apocalypse, but despite how manly I come across, I am not an avid or expert hunter. I've only been hunting three times, and on two of those occasions absolutely nothing happened. I just sat around in the woods, bored as shit. The only time something eventful happened was when I was twelve. My stepfather Abe took me out into the woods to train me to be a man, and I pretended the best I could that I really wanted to shoot me a deer. When a deer did in fact cross our path, my hand remained frozen and my stepfather put that beautiful creature down.

Once the life had drained out of this magnificent creature, we dragged it back to the car. Yes, that's right, I said car. My stepfather did not own a truck—he owned a Lincoln Continental. The two of us spent the next half an hour stuffing a giant, bloody deer corpse into the trunk. When we were finished, did I look like a shell-shocked kid who had watched his parents be murdered while he hid under the bed? Yes, I most certainly did. To make matters worse, we took the deer home and my stepfather proceeded to skin and gut it. My job was to clean up afterward. So, as you would guess, the only knowledge I took away from the whole situation was how to fit a very large body into the trunk of a car and clean up a bunch of blood and guts. This would have been very useful if I had turned out to be a mafia hitman (which might actually have happened when looking at the trauma I went through that day).

The only living thing that I ever shot was a duck, and even that disturbed me greatly. We were out in the marshlands, and I shot one out of the sky. Immediately the dog took off after it, and I was paranoid as hell that it would bring the duck back half alive and I would have to break its neck or something. I mean, imagine how terrible that would be. You get shot, a dog picks you up in its filthy mouth, you get dragged around through the mud, and then dropped at someone's feet, only to get your fucking neck broken. Horrible. Simply fucking horrible.

So, as much as I would like to give you advice in the hunting department, you are going to have to get this knowledge elsewhere. I am going to retreat the darkness of the closet and weep to myself for the next half an hour or so . . . Thanks so much for making me bring these painful memories back to the surface.

THE SCENT OF A WOMAN (HOW TO CATCH A FISH)

As I mentioned, you don't want to get picky with your diet. While making the trek to your safe zone, it is important to constantly be on the lookout for anything edible. If you are in the desert and happen to wander by a small creek, hunting for fish is an excellent way to get a decent meal.

The easiest way to catch a fish is with a fishing pole (you've probably noticed by now that I have a tendency to state the obvious). However, the chance that you managed to escape the city with a fishing pole is probably pretty slim. Your first instinct will most likely be to sharpen a stick or try to construct a homemade hook, but if you're like me, both will lead to some type of horrible accident where the testicles are torn or stabbed.

Your safest and most surefire approach is to catch fish with your hands. I know what you're thinking—"that's complete bullshit"—but it is completely true. Here is how you do it:

1. Locate a small creek no more than seven feet in width, and walk its length until you find an area that is stagnant. As a rule of thumb, you want the water to be three or four feet deep.

2. Remove all your clothes. This might seem silly, but remember, at night all you have keeping you warm is a small fire or a crappy lean-to shelter packed with leaves. If you get your clothes wet, you will most likely freeze. According to my coauthor, Erich, who taught survival school for years, if your clothes do get wet, the best way to stay warm is to perform a specialized method of naked spooning, which he attempted to show me despite our clothes being perfectly dry.

3. Wade over to the bank of the creek. Due to the eroding forces of water, there will usually be a cavernous region directly

underneath the bank. When an invading force is in the water, fish will often retreat to this area and burrow their heads into the walls. Once in their hiding places, instead of bolting when a threat approaches as they do when in open waters, they will generally remain motionless.

4. Dip a hand into the water and move it very slowly across the wall of the creek underneath the bank. Believe it or not, this can be very nerve-racking, and your first reaction when coming into contact with slimy flesh is to jolt your hand away. Of course, this will cause the fish to quickly vacate, so you must maintain your cool.

5. There are two methods of capture once you have found a fish. The advanced method is to slide your hand slowly up its body until your fingers are in its gills, apply pressure to trap the fish, and then calmly pull it out of the water. While this is the most surefire method, it requires a very light touch and steady hand. If you're an amateur, the best approach is to use speed. The instant you touch the fish, jam your hand into its body and pin it up against the wall of the creek. Next, dip your opposite hand in and use both hands to pull it out. However, fish are very, very slimy, and without a firm pinch on their gills, you will most likely lose about 50 percent of your catches.

6. Once you have a fish, throw it at least ten feet away from the bank to ensure that it won't flip-flop back into the water.

7. After catching all you can eat, hold each fish down and kill it by bashing its head with a rock. For the morons out there, I must once again state the obvious: Do not obliterate the fish with a large boulder.

8. With fish, you can consume everything but the guts. This means the head and the bones. As a matter of fact, the bones are the best part. After slowly roasting them over the fire for half an hour, they taste just like crackers. Shitty-tasting crackers that

have the consistency of porcupine, mind you, but still better than bulrushes or cattails, both of which taste like piss.

9. Throw a tantrum because you can't catch a fish.

10. Your tantrum has alerted a starving bear to your presence. Run!

8 EASY STEPS TO MILKING A COW

If you don't come across a creek while fleeing to your safety zone, you are going to have to find an alternate source of food. Raiding convenience stores and supermarkets is a bad plan because all of the other survivors will have the same idea. If someone made it there before you, there is a good chance he or she will be ready to defend their food supply with either weapons or booby traps. A much safer option is to eat off the fat of the land. This is where cows come in.

Currently, there are more than 1.3 billion cows in the world, and a large percentage of those are in the United States. They are perhaps the stupidest animal in creation and have absolutely no defense mechanisms to speak of (bulls are different, obviously). Basically, a mentally challenged person could go around killing one cow after another with a wooden club—that is how easy they are to hunt. Although cows will be the primary food source for apocalyptic survivors, without our beef being slaughtered and shipped all over the world, the remaining cows will last a long fucking time. Good news for us!

While it is possible to skin and eat a cow, if your goal is to make it to your safe zone alive, this will most likely take too much time. Milking a cow is a much better option. It is extremely quick and can provide that extra energy you need to make it those last few miles to safety. Below I offer step-by-step instructions on how to steal this precious life-juice from these dumb animals:

STEP 1: Locate a somewhat attractive cow.

STEP 2: Sit next to the cow and wash its udders with a warm cloth, much like they do in massage parlors.

STEP 3: Place a bucket underneath the udders to catch the milk. If you do not have a bucket, simply open your mouth and place your face underneath the udders. This is known as "udder-to-mouth."

STEP 4: Begin the milking process by squeezing one of the cow's teats between your forefinger and thumb. Next, squeeze your other fingers around the teat, forcing the milky goodness to flow. Note: It is okay to whisper sweet nothings into the cow's ear, as it often gets them in the moooooooood. However, never look up into the cow's eyes because chances are it will be looking down at you. If your eyes meet, it gets a little awkward. Instead of getting all personal, you want to keep the whole experience very distant, like you would when visiting your friendly neighborhood glory hole.

STEP 5: Let go of the teat.

STEP 6: Again squeeze the teat. When it feels soft and flabby, the cow has given you all she's got to give.

STEP 7: Throw a tantrum because the cow is not cooperating.

STEP 8: Your tantrum alerted a bull to your presence. Run!

MILKING ALTERNATIVES

Although cows are by far the easiest animals to milk, if you like to live on the wild side or have no other choice, there is a broad assortment of other animals that also produce drinkable milk. Luckily, you can find many of these animals in your local zoo. But before you go charging down there with a bucket and eager lips, it is very important that you realize milking these wild creatures can not only be extremely time-consuming, but also extremely dangerous.

Great Ape

Jane Goodall taught us two things about great apes: they can be very violent, but they can also be very nurturing. If you walk up to one in your everyday street clothes and attempt to suckle from its teat, chances are it will tear off your arms, rip your body in half, and then use your torso as a toilet. I mean, if there were such

a thing as rape in the animal world, uninvited suckling at the teat would probably be it.

If you value your life, you must get the ape to offer you her teat. This can be accomplished by dressing up in a monkey outfit and hanging out with the other great ape toddlers. The goal is to make the mother feel utterly sorry for you, so you are going to want to fail at everything monkeylike. For example, keep falling out of the trees, show yourself to be incompetent at peeling bananas properly, hit yourself in the face when you attempt to pound on your chest, and miss every target you aim at with your feces.

Once you are recognized as the complete loser of the group, the mother will eventually come to you, cradle you in her arms, and put her hairy teat directly into your mouth. The problem is getting away from the mother once she has adopted you. As we have all learned from nature documentaries and the end of *Trading Places*, ape males are real pricks. They are always huffing, sprinting at trees, and bitch-slapping bushes. They are constantly showing off, and the chicks hate them for it. After she's fed you, there is a good chance that the female ape will want to mate with you, simply because you are smaller and less violent than a real male ape. Do not try to fight this. Instead, just grin and bear it. The good news is that a man cannot impregnate a female ape because they have incompatible chromosomes. I actually looked that shit up. (I'm sorry about this—I don't know why they let me write a book, let alone *books*. Will I ever run out of material? Not if they let me talk about milking apes.)

Kangaroo

Kangaroos kick really fucking hard, they have a long, whiplike tail, super-sharp claws, gnarly teeth, and they can run up to forty miles per hour. Needless to say, these attributes make milking one extremely difficult, but not impossible. Every animal has a weakness, and with the kangaroo it is her pouch. Whenever I feel like hanging out in a kangaroo's pouch, or a Roo-Hammock as I like to call it, I just gather up all the needed items, which include four feet of nylon rope, a Snickers bar, a kerosene lantern, and a roll of duct tape (duct tape works for everything, don't it?). I would tell you how to use these items to make your entry into the pouch, but that is self-explanatory. Once you are all wrapped up in the warm flesh-blanket, you have direct access to the teat and can suckle away for hours.

Giraffe

You would think that a giraffe would be an easy animal to milk because of its height. I mean, it seems like you should just be able to walk underneath one, turn your head up, and begin sucking out milk as if it were coming from a beer bong. As it turns out, giraffes do not like other animals to be directly underneath them, suckling on their teats. Instead of standing there and letting you get your fill, they have a tendency to bolt. I thought it might be possible to kind of run underneath them as they scurried about, breathing out of my nose as I suckled with my mouth, but they are a good deal faster than I imagined. A healthy giraffe can run up to thirty-seven miles per hour!

I almost wrote this animal off as a practical source for milk, but a lightbulb went off in my head and I decided to use a motorcycle. This actually works really well. The goal is to drive directly underneath the giraffe, stand up on your seat, suckle for a brief moment, sit back down, steer, and then stand back up for another quick hit at the teat. It takes a little while to get full, but giraffe milk fucking rules. (For fuck sakes, why aren't people stopping me? I really didn't think I could get away with this much simply for being semi-famous. In addition to being allowed to put complete nonsense into this book, *Revolver* magazine, which is a pretty big magazine, allowed me to write an article on the sexist animal. Just how far do I have to go before someone stops me? I am crying for help here, people. Why can't anyone hear my screams?)

Animals That You Should Not Attempt to Milk

- **LIZARDS:** If they have nipples at all, they are too small to find.

- **PENGUINS:** They keep slipping from your hands as you try to suckle.

- **SLEEPING BEARS:** Not down with being milked in any way, shape, or form.

- **HUMANS:** I am still researching this one.

- **WOLVES:** Very, very dirty animals. The milk from their one protruding red udder strangely tastes like piss. Other times, it is just waaaaay too salty.

- **RED ANTS:** A really bad experiment on my part

- **LOCUSTS:** Do not, under any circumstances, attempt to milk a swarm of locust.

THE FORREST GRIFFIN SURVIVAL EXPERIENCE

I know I'm sending you mixed messages. I tell you I hate the wild, and then I go on and on about all these survival tactics. You are probably starting to wonder if you can trust this hot knowledge I am giving you. Well, although I personally don't like spending time in the outdoors, I have been cast ruthlessly into the wild on several occasions and survived.

The most traumatic of these experiences was just before my twenty-first birthday when I was in the police academy. In the evening after class, I went back to the dorms and discovered the doors were locked. I tried my key card several times, and each time it did absolutely nothing. A few seconds later, I read a sign on the door that said CLOSED FOR SPRING BREAK. Somehow, I missed the fact that they were shutting the dorms down for the entire week. I was homeless, and to make matters worse, all of the friends I felt comfortable calling were out of town. Not knowing what to do, I returned to my Mazda 626 and just kind of sat there, and not comfortably I might add. I got the car because I'd seen it sitting on some guy's front lawn. When I knocked on his door to inquire about it, his exact words were, "If you can get that blankety-blank-blank off my fucking lawn, you can do whatever the fuck you want with it." I had it towed away, and then my stepfather fixed it up. He took the choke off our lawnmower, drilled a hole into my dashboard, and slapped that sucker in. So, I basically had a 1920s automobile. When I started it, I would have to throttle it up for several minutes using the choke, which proved to be a real panty dropper while on dates.

Anyway, I was fucking homeless, sitting in my piece-of-shit ride. With nowhere to go, I drove to the grocery store, purchased a box of Little Debbie treats and a cheap bottle of wine, and then sat on the curb out in front of the dormitory for the next eight hours. When it started getting cold, I purchased a ticket to an all-night movie theater so I would have somewhere warm to sleep for a few hours. I spent that entire week in that Mazda 626, subsisting on cheap wine and Little Debbies, so don't you tell me I don't know how to fucking survive.

HOW TO FIGHT A WILD ANIMAL

I included this section because it seems like every time I do an interview, a reporter asks me how I would fight a certain type of animal. Sure, they open with the canned "Who is your next opponent?" and "How is your training going?" questions, but it always comes back to me fighting animals. Unfortunately, I know very little about engaging animals in hand-to-paw combat. I do, however, know quite a bit about being viciously attacked by animals.

The most violent animal beat-down I have received came from a giraffe. This happened as a teenager, when a buddy and I decided to pay a visit to the zoo (I know, sounds super gay, but I swear we weren't holding hands or any bullshit like that). As we were cruising around, checking shit out, I saw a giraffe with his head reaching over the chain-link fence separating him from the outside world. He was chewing on some cud, just kind of staring blankly out at freedom. Without thinking, I ran toward the fence, climbed up it, and threw my arm around his big-ass neck. The goal was to have my buddy snap a picture of the two of us, but before he could even pull out his camera, the ferocious giraffe attacked. In one swift movement, it placed a fairly large chunk of my head into its rancorous oversize mouth, which prevented me from leaping off the fence. I, of course, screamed bloody murder, but my friend was absolutely no help. He instantly fell on the ground in a fit of laughter.

I'm quite sure the evil giraffe could have crushed my head like a grape, but realized that it would be put down if he did. Fighting the overwhelming urge to end my life, he released my head from his death grip after a few moments, and my hat fell on the opposite side of the fence. After being viciously attacked by the brutal giraffe, I wasn't going to attempt to retrieve my favorite hat. I walked away with a bruised face and feeling very insignificant.[19]

Since that day, I've had numerous other very close calls with some of

---

[19] Giraffes are evil, evil animals that should be avoided at all costs. Unless, of course, you are trying to milk them from a motorcycle like Evil Knievel would.

the more ferocious members of the animal kingdom. When I was fifteen, I spent a summer in North Carolina, and in order to get from my house over to a friend's house, I had to cross a river. This gave me two choices—I could walk two miles to a bridge or I could ignore a series of "No Trespassing" signs, hop a chain-link fence, and swim across the body of water. Inherently lazy, every day I chose the swim.

Then one afternoon, right before I was about to enter the water to make my way across, a group of people sitting on a deck on my side of the river began screaming and shouting at me. Ignoring them, I began walking toward the bank, but now they were not only screaming and shouting, but also waving their arms madly in the air. After taking two steps into the water, I got really pissed off and began walking down the muddy bank toward them.

"What the fuck is your problem?" I shouted at the group of middle-aged men and women. "I had to hop a fence, big fucking deal. Give me a fine, I don't care. I was just trying to cross the river, man!"

As with most people in North Carolina on a summer afternoon, they were all drinking beer. "Sorry about all the yelling," one man said as he pointed in the direction I had come from. "Just look over there at your footprints."

I did as the man said and followed my footprints, and about two hundred yards back, drifting in the water where I had been preparing to enter the river, was an eight-foot alligator. Although it might not have been as big as the alligators you see on the Discovery Channel, an eight-foot alligator is pretty fucking huge when you see it in the wild. I almost shit my pants. The people informed me that they had posted the NO TRESPASSING signs and put up the chain-link fence for a reason—this little area was a wildlife refuge and was filled with alligator nests (not sure if alligators have nests or not, but that is what I was told).

The next close call I had occurred in South Africa. I went there with my friends Rory and Numo, and wanting to see what the real Africa was all about, we decided to visit a lion refuge. Unlike zoos where all the animals are confined to cramped cages, this place let all the animals run free. (What's up with that? Freedom is for people.) This obviously ruled walking around the park out of the question, but supposedly it was safe to drive.

Both Forrest and his cat are easily amused by paper bags.

Forrest's thoughts: "I bet these birds taste delicious." Jaime's thoughts: "I hope Forrest isn't thinking about eating these birds."

Forrest and Bigger John at Forrest's wedding. Moments after this photo was taken, Bigger John attempted to propose to Forrest.

Proper postapocalyptic attire.

You have absolutely no proof that they're gay.

If you see a strong resemblance, that's because they are related— and I'm talking about the two guys *and* the monkeys on the shirts.

I really had no idea that coming down would be the hard part.

After Forrest's third arrest for road rage, this is the only vehicle he can legally drive.

Me, postapocalypse.

Bonding with my brother.

Alternate cover shot #1. You talkin' to me?

Alternate cover shot #2

Forrest's thoughts: "This is the happiest day of my life."

Luke's thoughts: "I can't believe he is doing this."

John's thoughts: "I give it a year, tops."

Leaf's thoughts: "When did he even start *liking* girls?"

Bigger John: "Does this mean Forrest really isn't going to take me to Vermont and marry me like he promised?"

Please, no one tell him Santa doesn't exist.

Postcoital

Walking cats is harder than you think.

Someone let the monkeys out of the cage.
Randy Couture, Some Guy, Stephan Bonner, Ron Frazier, Mike Pyle, Tim Credeur, Jay Hieron

Forrest trying to get the deer drunk so he can have his way with them . . . His most lascivious fantasy come true.

Don't worry mom. I can't get any uglier.

Forre
you c
Forre
loves
read
guys
out f
went
dese
If you
the s
I war
confi

FORTUNE COOKIE WISDOM

Beware of anyone who drinks excessive amounts of Mountain Dew. Back when I was a police office, anytime I broke into a meth laboratory or pulled someone over who was trafficking drugs, I found a shit-ton of empty Mountain Dew containers on the floor of their trailer or backseat of their car.

I figured we would be in an armor-plated Range Rover or something, but they packed all three of us into a shitty little Yugo. I was fighting heavyweight at the time, and Rory is a pretty big dude as well, so we were quite literally sitting on top of one another.

The driver cranked up the engine and drove over to the front entrance gate, and that's when I realized that visiting a lion refuge in South Africa might not have been the best move. The guy who opened the gate had one eye, one arm, and his face had deep scars from where a lion had mauled him. Immediately I thought, "This guy's only job is to let you in and out of the park. What the fuck happens to the people who actually go inside?"

I bit my tongue and didn't say anything, and at first everything was cool—I could see a shit load of lions off in the distance, but none of them charged the vehicle or anything like that. It was actually an enjoyable experience.

Then the Yugo started to overheat. Outside it was 112 degrees, and once the driver shut off the air conditioner, the confines of the car quickly became an oven. I asked if we could roll down a window, and the driver immediately began shaking his head.

"You don't want them to smell you," he said.

Great.

When the car didn't cool, the driver turned on the heater. Other than cooking our nut sacks in our underwear, it did nothing to solve the overheating problem. After another few hundred yards, steam began pouring from the hood and the driver pulled over. "I can not drive anymore," he said.

I figured that they had some sort of system worked out for when one of the cars broke down, but apparently that wasn't the case because no one came by to lend a hand. There was no roadside assistance of any kind. We just sat there in the car, waiting. And with each moment that passed, the lions became more and more curious and began inching their way toward us.

Figuring it was only a matter of time until the lions ripped off one of the flimsy doors to the Yugo and ate my ugly ass, I made my friend Numo get out and piss in the radiator. And yes, if the lions had attacked him, I would have locked all the doors and watched the feast transpire, but that's only because you're not supposed to disturb animals when they are eating. Park rules, you know.

Luckily, my quick thinking paid off, the engine cooled, and we were able to get the hell out of Dodge. As we were leaving the park, I noticed that the guy who let us out had all of his body parts intact. If they had a marketing guy, he needed to get fired. Yeah, let's have the guy who looks like he was mauled by fifty lions let everyone into the park. That will do wonders to soothe the nerves of our guests.

But the more I thought about it, the more it made sense. In South Africa they don't make you sign waivers before participating in dangerous shit, and sticking a guy who had obviously been attacked by lions at the front gate was their disclaimer—their way of letting you know that what you were about to do was pretty fucking stupid.

So as you can see, I am far from the Beast Master. Come to think of it, the only fight I ever won with an animal was against an ex-girlfriend's cockatoo, but all I had to do was open the door and chase it outside with my superior, broom-wielding prowess. With my current track record, the best advice I can give on fighting animals is to simply not do it. If you fight an animal and lose, there is a good chance that you will get eaten. This even applies to dogs. I still have a scar on my right arm that constantly reminds me that even these much smaller creatures are fierce opponents.

ANIMALISTIC ATTRACTION

 Seeing that we are already on the topic of animals, it is time to talk about a very hard truth: after the shit hits the fan, there probably won't be that many people left to mate with, so you are going to have to get creative. What do I mean by "get creative"? What else could I mean? Have sex with animals, of course.

Although it might seem simple to grab the nearest animal and give it a good shagging, most four-legged creatures will not willingly allow you to simply mount and penetrate them. They will undoubtedly put up a fight, and taking a hoof or paw to the face can suck big-time. It is also extremely important to ravish an animal that you personally find sexy. To avoid having to go through this type of decision making postapocalypse, I suggest that you put some thought into the animal you would most like to lay pipe to right now.

As far as women go, they all want to have sex with dolphins. Don't believe me? Just look at any woman's house. What do you see all over the place—that's right, dolphins. I think the reason for this . . . strike that . . . The reason for this is that women love a giant phallic symbol. Dolphins even feel like penises. They are basically a big blue penis, like the schlong of that dude in *Watchmen*.

In fact, a lot of women go so far as to tattoo dolphins on their lower back and ankles. If you see a chick with a dolphin tattoo, there is no doubt she is into cock, and will be willing to bone down. However, watch out for chicks with butterfly tattoos. The butterfly represents ~~lesbianism~~ feminism, and chicks who go so far as to get a butterfly tattoo are most likely into carpet munching and scissoring and all that. The same can be said for guys who get gorilla or ape tattoos—they like to have sex with other men. It is a fact.

Personally, the animal I find the sexiest is undoubtedly the deer. I love the way they move, with that little come-hither tail of theirs and those big glossy eyes. When you creep up on one in the forest and she pops her head up, all nervous like, and your eyes meet, you can tell she is flirting with you. If you are wondering when these amorous feelings first started, I can pinpoint it exactly. It all started the first time I saw *Bambi*—and I say first time because there were many. In fact, certain spots on my VHS copy of the movie are pretty much worn out. And yes, you guessed it: those spots are the scenes in which Bambi's mother makes an appearance.

If you go back and watch *Bambi* today, you will realize what I realized at the age of five: Bambi's mother is fucking hot. She is one hot piece of tail, literally. As a matter of fact, if you don't want to fuck Bambi's mom, you're gay.

If you find my attraction to deer a little disturbing, do not worry—I can't actually catch them. That is a part of what makes them so attractive. Now, they do have tame deer that you can visit in the petting zoo and feed, but those deer are all fat. What kind of sicko do you think I am? I am not into fat deer—I am not into any kind of fat animals. If I wanted to hump a hippo, I would hump a hippo. But I don't. And don't worry, sheep are not beautiful creatures. They are ugly. They are the ugly, fat, drunken sorority girls that won't leave you alone at a party, and who wants them? Certainly not me.

Now that I have shared with you some of my inner feelings about the animal world, I would like you to sit back in your chair and think about what animal you find the sexiest. Is it some kind of tropical bird? Do you find the lioness as she glides across the plains strangely alluring? Or do you find a creature of the sea the most tantalizing? I'm being serious: sit back and give it some deep thought. It is very important to think about this now so that when you spot that animal postapocalypse, you can immediately commence with the fulfillment of your needs . . . no . . . of your desires.

Serious Note to Reader: Unfortunately for you, I like tests, and this was one of them. If you actually made it through my bit on animal fucking, you failed. I mean, who would keep reading a book that talks about humping animals? I know after the apocalypse there will be no laws against that shit, but come on, where is your pride? You should be ashamed of yourself. Deeply, deeply ashamed. However, you have to admit that deer are kind of sexy. If someone held a gun to my head and insisted that I fuck some type of animal, it would most certainly be a deer. (Erich, I told you to hold that gun to my head . . . just do it and close your eyes; this will only take a second.) I mean, those eyes are so big and glassy. You can get lost in those eyes . . .

HOW TO PREVENT MUD BUTT (AKA SWAMP ASS)

Properly wiping your backside shouldn't be your primary concern when trying to escape town and make it to your safe zone, but if you let matters get too carried away back there, you will develop a condition often referred to as Mud Butt. Trust me, this is very uncomfortable.

Personally, I have never shit in the actual woods. I've shit my pants more than a few times, but according to Erich, this has no bearing on the apocalypse. When it comes to shitting in the woods, he is undoubtedly the expert. He insisted that we include a "shitting" section in the book, which I found a little odd. After listening to a few of his stories, you gotta wonder if his goal is to actually teach people how to shit or simply to make them feel better about themselves because they have not shit all over themselves in the wild. If you are like me[20], you will probably agree that Erich has some bizarre fascination with fecal matter. After all, he has German blood. If you were to hack into his computer, there is no doubt that you would find some *shizer* videos in a secret file. Anyway, here is the section on shit:

For the longest time, I thought the best way to wipe your ass in the woods was with whatever you could find—leaves, weeds, bark, small animals—but then Erich proceeded to tell me half a dozen of his wilderness shit stories, the worst one being the time he hiked the Machu Picchu trail in Peru. He was up at fourteen thousand feet and decided he had to take a dump. He found a nice field filled with grass, dropped his drawers, made his deposit, and then broke off a handful of grass to wipe his ass. Although the grass was green, it was not as fresh as he'd first thought. It basically turned to dust in his hand.

Being a dirty, filthy mongrel, he wiped with it anyway, and ended up with shit on his mitt. Not far from the field he heard a small babbling creek, but it was located down a steep embankment of shale. Being a genius, he attempted to scale down the slope and ended up slipping and sliding all the way down. By this point, shit had migrated from his hand to select parts of his torso. He attempted to get at the water, but the stream was completely encased in thornbushes. After a full five minutes tangling with the bush, he gave up. He climbed back up the slope of shale, again slipping and sliding, and by the time he reached the top, he had shit on his torso, legs, and face. With no other option, he was forced to hike another eight miles literally covered in shit and with an ass full of prickly grass particles.

---

[20] It is good to be like me.

Learning from his mistakes, I have devised the ultimate way to shit in the wild. All it requires is a single, somewhat healthy leaf:

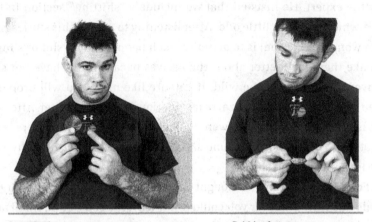

Get a leaf.　　　　　　　　　　Fold leaf once.

Fold leaf twice.　　　　Tear semi-circle off corner of leaf.

Unfold leaf and stick thumb through hole.

Stick thumb up ass.

Slide leaf up thumb to remove fecal matter.

Use severed piece of the leaf you tore off to dig shit out from under fingernail.

Display your somewhat clean thumb.

WHY YES, I DO SPEAK SIGN LANGUAGE

If you are traveling with a group of people, you want to develop hand signals. Although they make you look like a sock puppeteer when you do them alone, they make you look like some type of commando when other people are around, even if the people have no idea what the hand signals mean. But beware, sometimes hand signals have more than one meaning. To prevent you from getting confused, I have included some of the more popular hand signals below and the various meanings they have.

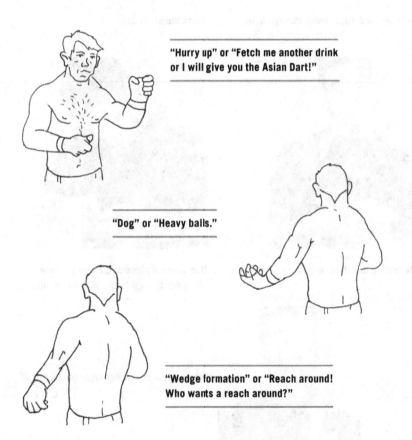

"Hurry up" or "Fetch me another drink or I will give you the Asian Dart!"

"Dog" or "Heavy balls."

"Wedge formation" or "Reach around! Who wants a reach around?"

"I understand" or "Look at my awesome hand puppet."

"Live long and prosper" or "Hope you die a horrible death."

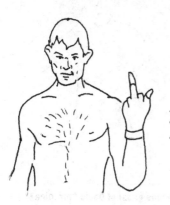

"Fuck you" or "Wanna spin on my finger?"

"Gas leak" or "Twist my nipples while I check your oil . . . ohhh, yeah, creamy cheese delight."

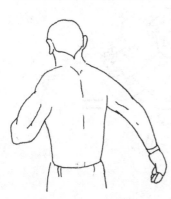

"Move up" or "Put it in here."

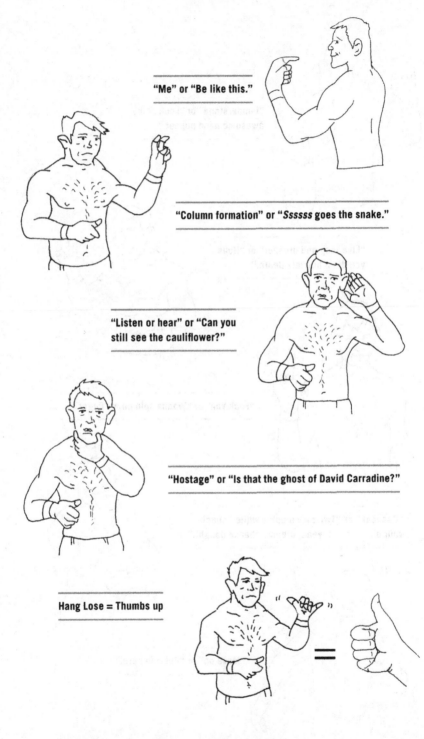

"Me" or "Be like this."

"Column formation" or "*Sssss* goes the snake."

"Listen or hear" or "Can you still see the cauliflower?"

"Hostage" or "Is that the ghost of David Carradine?"

Hang Lose = Thumbs up

THE MOST DANGEROUS PEOPLE OF THE APOCALYPSE

It is pretty obvious that while making the escape to your safe zone, you want to avoid well-armed, unsavory people. However, there are less obvious people who will pose an equal amount of danger. I have included the list below.

Note to Reader: Erich predominantly wrote this section. I tell you this not because I am a nice guy or because I don't want to take credit for the ideas of others—I obviously have no problem with that (see *Got Fight?*). The reason I tell you this is that I want to absolve myself of the forthcoming ill will directed at hippies. You see, Erich was kidnapped by a clan of nomadic hippies as a small child and was forced to live among them. This explains his lack of hygiene, as well as his passion for "roughing it." When I met Erich, he was sleeping on a pile of clothes and trash that looked like the pit of a hamster's nest, in the closet of a million-dollar house. Gallon jugs of urine and water, which he drank from regardless of what they actually contained, surrounded him. I asked him why he lived in such a manner, and he simply replied, "I am preparing." That is when I knew I had found a writer for my apocalypse book.

Why does Erich, who seems to despise hippies, choose to live like them? Well, I can only liken it to Hitler hating the Jews but being part Jewish. At heart, Erich wants to be a hippie, but he can't do it because it is frowned upon in our society. Erich yearns for the apocalypse so he can be freed from these shackles—free to live like a filthy hippie. And I am not talking about the hippies that secretly have money or families with money, and will reach a point where they will quit being hippies and convert to yuppyism. Erich hates those hippies even more than the others—he sees them as fakers hidden under dirty dreads. After the apocalypse, Erich will show the world what being a hippie is really about.

Hippies

Hippies themselves are not very dangerous. As a matter of fact, the majority of them
will not try to hurt you in any way, even if it
means their very survival. This should dis-
gust you, but it is not why you should fear
them. Hippies are primarily dangerous
because of their hugs. I am not sure why, but
hippies seem to love giving hugs. When they
approach you, hug ready, you are immediately thrown off by their odd smell, which is
a mixture of patchouli and garbage. My guess is they wear patchouli in an
attempt to cover up the smell of garbage emanating from their bodies, but
it doesn't work out like that. It simply produces two distinct smells that
shatter your senses and leave you terribly discombobulated. Like trying to
cover the smell of a meaty man-shit with some bathroom spray. While you
stand there stunned, they wrap their arms around your body, forcing you
to come into contact with their gross body hair.

Although it is possible to live through such an embrace, the majority of
the time one of their hippie buddies will begin playing their terrible music
on either an acoustic guitar or bongo drum. When subjected to their smell,
hugs, gross body hair, and terrible music all at the same time, a victim is
likely to suffer intense seizures. To avoid such an outcome, if you see a hippie approaching you postapocalypse with his arms outstretched, you want
to bolt. Luckily, hippies eat only seeds, nuts, and herbs, and this combined
with massive amounts of weed smoking makes them very slow runners.

The other dangerous aspect about hippies is their compassion. They
love to go against "the man" and save things. This will be even more common postapocalypse because there will be no one there to dissuade them
with billy clubs, tear gas, and, my favorite, rubber bullets. In a matter of
days after the shit goes down, the hippies that have survived will gather in
massive groups, and after several weeks of odiferous lovemaking, someone in the group will get the bright idea to save something, causing their
masses to begin to wander. Within a couple of days, there is a good chance

they will find their way into the city zoo. And guess what? They will release all the starving animals, thinking they are doing a good deed. Unlike normal people, the hippies will not just release the cute, cuddly animals. In their world, a pee-bug is just as important as a panda, and all the cages will be flung open with glee. Despite the angry and ravenous state of the wild animals, they will not feed on the hippies because they are too smelly. As the lions and tigers and packs of wolves go stalking down the street in search of less gamy game, the hippie mass will continue to wander.

Eventually they will find their way into the city prison. Again, they will do this "good deed" of theirs and release all the inmates. And of course the inmates will not kill the hippies because they are simply too smelly. The butt-hungry killers will head out into the streets to find something non-smelly to fuck and/or kill, and the hippie mass will continue its wandering.

After a few more days pass, they will stumble into a science laboratory where testing is done on animals. They will do yet another "good deed" and release the starving, genetically altered, Ebola-infected chimpanzees, all of which are crazed and enraged with syphilis and hungry for vengeance and human flesh (this might actually cause the apocalypse—see *28 Days Later*). Fortunately, these creatures will be so tortured that there is a good chance they will kill the hippie mass, but the damage will already have been done. If you happen to find yourself on the streets of a city where a hippie mass has been, you have zero chance of survival. As a result, avoid San Francisco and most towns in Oregon.

Fat People

Obviously, most fat people cannot move very quickly; thus, most of them will not survive the apocalypse. But there is currently a shit load of fat people, and some will manage to avoid the various pitfalls by blind luck. It will be like the ultimate fat camp—they will learn to survive on nuts, berries, fruits, and vegetables for the first time in their lives. After making this switch, they will feel extremely powerful and have amazing energy supplies. Will they realize the errors of their ways and be changed by their newfound diet? Most certainly not. They will be ready to consume anything in sight, including you.

The majority of overly fat survivors will not last long, but there will undoubtedly be at least a couple who make it past the first few weeks, and they will be very dangerous. Not so much out in the open—fat people are like slow-moving zombies in that they are easy to get away from. The places you must be careful of are confined spaces. Although fat people are extremely large, they are kind of gooey, and they can fit themselves into some pretty tight places, like closets and underneath beds. They are also extremely patient. After all, they are not concerned with what concerns normal-weight people. They care nothing about warmth because all their extra adipose keeps them toasty at night. They can't see their penises, so sex is out of the question. And all the entertainment they need is wrapped up in a Twinkie. Their sole focus will be to get more food, so they will cram their bodies into tight places and wait for weeks for someone to walk by. If you happen to wander past one of their hiding places, you are pretty much doomed. They will leap out at you, wrap their gelatinous arms around your body, and then drop on top of you and smother you with their colossal boob-belly mass. The worst part is they will not even wait until you are dead to begin feasting. For this reason, avoid all confined spaces. If you absolutely must enter a building, check all the cupboards, cabinets, and broom closets before settling in.

Children

Children of the apocalypse must be avoided at all costs. The more innocent a child looks, the more dangerous he or she will be. While adults are scrounging for flashlights, food, and batteries, children will scrounge for candy. After three weeks of eating nothing but Snickers, Kit Kats, and Ho Hos, they will be spun out big-time. They will hit the streets in their Big Wheels looking to dish out some pain, cackling the Mario Brothers' theme  song. Armed with toy military helmets, BB guns, wrist rockets, and pocket-knives, they will be like extremely smart and crafty gremlins.

How much harm could they do? A fucking lot. Remember, these little wrecking machines did not grow up playing with sticks in the backyard.

They have been playing Halo and Call of Duty since the day they were born, and they can shoot the ball sack off an eagle soaring two hundred yards overhead. These are not real kids you are dealing with—they are American kids, spoiled rotten and used to getting what they want. If the picture is still blurry, imagine the little tribe of parentless kids from *Thunderdome*. It will be exactly like that, except the postapocalyptic kids in the real world will not be singing songs and cheering. They will be beating your head in with Tonka toys and screaming at you to give them candy.

And if for some reason they do not choose to kill you, they will undoubtedly try to talk you into taking care of them. With their upturned eyes, they will play the guilt card and make you share your food, shelter, and clothing. Bear in mind, these are not actually your children. If they are your children, you should probably take care of them . . . probably.

Surviving on your own is hard enough, but when you add a bunch of hungry mouths into the picture, things get really difficult really quick. If you should encounter a rug rat in the wasteland, you only have one choice: Run! (Note: This form of orphan trickery can also happen pre-apocalypse. If some woman claims that you are the father of her child, she is lying. Screw genetic testing, it is all bullshit. Many of my friends have fallen for this very con.)

FILTHY FUCKING STREET URCHINS

The Homeless
Although you want nothing to do with hippies, fat people, or children, when the world as we know it ends, befriending a homeless person may very well save your life. Why? Because they are survivors, that's why. I know what you're thinking: "If 99.8 percent of the human population gets wiped off the face of the planet, there will only be

two homeless people left." Wrong. They will be everywhere. After a lifetime of subsisting on leftovers, they can eat a super-flu for lunch. After sleeping on the winter streets of New York and the summer streets of Vegas, they consider a huge natural disaster only a mild inconvenience. An economic collapse—get the fuck out of here. Looting and rioting is a carnival to homeless people. I'm telling you, every last homeless person will survive the end of the world, and if you manage to convince one to become your traveling mate, you will be as right as rain.

Your new homeless friend will teach you how to turn week-old cheese into a fantastic new cologne, divulge his secret recipes for cooking rat, and show you how to turn garbage into a fine sorbet. If the two of you get close, he may even demonstrate how to light a cigarette without igniting your breath, give you clues on how to break your phobia about masturbating in public, teach you how to filter coffee using your underwear, and show you how to build a fort under a bridge, in back alleys, or in the bushes. I'm telling you, homeless people are the ultimate urban warriors. But beware, gaining access to their secret society is not easy, so I recommend starting now. This can be achieved by volunteering down at your local shelter or just being kind and compassionate to those less fortunate. Just think of it as an investment. Personally, I have been volunteering at a shelter here in Las Vegas. Do I care about doing good deeds? Most certainly not. My only goal is to trick the homeless into allowing me into their inner circle when the shit hits the fan.

HOW TO FIGHT IN THE THUNDERDOME

Mad Max Beyond Thunderdome is obviously more than just a movie—it is a guide to know what shit will be like postapocalypse. Based upon this very real depiction of the near future, martial arts and the UFC will continue to grow in popularity. The only difference is that they will undoubtedly add some weapons in the mix and the rules will change. Instead of fighting in the Octagon, you will fight in a Thunderdome-type arena. And instead of striking your opponent with your fists, you will stab each other with swords and spears and shit. You might even have to fight a lion or two (if it was good enough for the Christians, it will be good enough for the apocalypse).

To prevent you from dying a quick death in this type of sporting event, I am going to give you a few tips. Most important, join one of those geeky medieval knight clubs to learn how to wield ancient weapons of death. The only downside is that any friends you currently have will disown you, and you may become brainwashed into thinking that covering your body in tinfoil will provide adequate protection in armed combat. While wrapping yourself in tinfoil does wonders to prevent the government from reading your mind, it provides absolutely no protection when being struck with heavy, sharp objects. Being involved in a medieval club might also lead you to believe that it is a good idea to wear a giant steel cup and leave your legs completely exposed. While this is a great fashion ensemble,[21] you might want to protect your femoral arteries. I know the Spartans like to keep their legs glistening in the sun for other men to gawk at, but you are not as fast and quick as a Spartan (and hopefully not as close to your comrades).

At the very least, you want to cover your legs in heavy leather. If you chose to go bare legged and someone stabs your femoral artery, you will bleed out very quickly. And dying from a leg wound is a pussy way to check out, especially when fighting in the Thunderdome.

WHEN YOU'RE ALL BUSTED UP

While making your way across the rubble to your safe zone, you want to do everything in your power to avoid injury. The best way to accomplish this is simply not to panic. Granted, there will be some pretty freaky shit going on, such as people with half-burned-off faces staggering toward you, animals that are all freaked out and confused, and perhaps even groups of half-crazed individuals on the hunt for human flesh. You might even see that giant spider with its eight legs, huge fangs, and million fucking eyes (woo, scared myself there). No matter what stands before you, do not panic.

---

[21] *Ensemble.* Definition: A slab of metal forged into a giant steal cup. Usage: You kicked me in the groin, but thank goodness I was wearing my ensemble.

MY WORST INJURIES

The worst injury I ever had was when I fought in South Africa. This was back in 2001 before MMA really took off, so the promoter offered me absolute shit. I basically fought for the trip. My opponent was a guy who had wrestled in the Olympics, and a few seconds into our fight, he picked me up and slammed me down on my shoulder. Being a Mickey Mouse event, we were in a boxing ring rather than a cage, and instead of a thick pad underneath the canvas, they had a tiny layer of foam on top of steel. The instant I landed, my shoulder popped out. I felt immediate pain, and when I glanced over at my shoulder, I saw what looked like the tit of a fourteen-year-old girl sitting on top of my deltoid. I would have quit right then, but my opponent began hitting me. I managed to get up, and we tussled for another few moments. As I was throwing punches and kicks, I kept looking over at my shoulder—as if staring at my injury would somehow make it go away.

Anyhow, my opponent got tired, I kneed him in the face, we went back to the ground, and I ended up on his back with one hook in. In some pretty serious pain at this point, I wanted to end the fight as quickly as possible. Genius me, I wrap my bad arm around his throat, grab my wrist with my other hand, and pulled my limp arm up into his throat until he tapped in submission. The second the referee separated us, I began rolling around on the canvas, screaming in pain. Although this was in no shape or way funny, the commentary of the South African announcer was. In his weird accent, he goes, "And the American with an interesting celebration . . . I think he is pretending he is on fire. Maybe it is a stop, drop, and roll type thing . . . Wow,

If you lose your head, there is a good chance that you will injure yourself by stepping in a hole, tripping over shit, or even running into stuff. Just keep your head and be cool. If you have to run, then run. But look where you are fucking going. If you have to jump over a fence, look on the other side first. This is all very common knowledge, but common sense seems to fly out the window when people get scared.

he is really getting into this . . . His face is all clinched up and everything."
Yeah, MMA has come a long way.

I received my second worst injury while working out with Bigger John in the gym. My shoulder was still fucked up from my fight in South Africa, and he had this notion that doing floor presses would somehow be better for me than doing bench presses. I hadn't done bench presses in years, and I had never done a floor press, but not thinking clearly, I decided to take John's advice. So, I laid on the floor, he hefted the bar up to me, and then spotted me on his knees (and yes, it was the gayest looking thing in the world). After about five repetitions, John leans forward to spot me, and I see a massive chunk of Copenhagen dip fly from his mouth in slow motion. I had two hundred pounds in my hands, and I did my best to squirm out of the way, but there was absolutely no avoiding it. That massive piece of saliva soaked dip landed right in my eye socket. Immediately my entire head started burning, and I begin shouting at John to take the weight. Instead of following my instructions, he began shouting back at me in his brutish voice.

"Fuck that, son, you got another rep or two in you! You got two more reps easy, son!"

I started screaming, trying to throw the weight off of me, but he held it in place. Without any options, I did my two reps, John took the weight, and I went running to the bathroom. After washing out my eyes, we finished our workout . . . And yes, I am still emotionally traumatized by that event.

However, even if you are calm and collected at all times, there is still a chance that you will injure yourself somewhere along the way, so I have included some basic medical skills in this section. It is important to note that I am not a practicing physician, and there is a good chance that by following the procedures listed below, you will die a horrible death. With that said, let's get started.

Mending a Broken Leg

If you injure your leg postapocalypse, chances are you will have to do your own diagnosis to discover if it is broken. To begin, examine your leg for any cuts, bruising, obvious deformities, or protruding bones. If all looks well, feel up and down your leg for any gaps or bumps in the bone; also move your leg as you normally would to check if it has full range of motion. If you discover that the bone is in fact broken, check the pulses around the bone to ensure that an artery hasn't been severed or compressed from the swollen tissues or broken bone. If the pulses feel fine, you have a chance of surviving.

Surgery is out of the question, so the only real option is to brace your leg. Although this will be tremendously painful, begin by aligning the broken bone to the best of your ability. This might require some elbow grease. Once you regain consciousness, place a rigid object underneath the leg, such as a rolled-up newspaper or a flat board. Next, wrap an Ace bandage or duct tape around your leg to secure the stabilizer in place.

The next step is to attempt to survive with a broken leg. If you are already in your safe zone, you should have enough supplies to last you through the healing process. If you are in the middle of nowhere, you are going to have to fashion yourself a pair of crutches and attempt to make it to a location where there is food, water, and shelter. Good luck with that!

Broken Ribs

A broken rib hurts like a motherfucker, but unless it's protruding into your lungs, the injury is not life-threatening. To help reduce the pain and aid the healing process, it can be beneficial to brace your chest by heavily taping the rib cage. However, the most important thing you can do is to breathe normally. It might be excruciatingly painful to do so, but constantly taking short, shallow breaths can eventually lead to pneumonia, which will be much more likely to kill you than a broken rib.

Broken Fingers and Toes

Broken fingers and toes are easily treated using the "buddy taping" method. This is where you place the broken finger or toe next to a healthy finger or toe, and tape them together so they are side by side. In case you didn't get this, I am not talking about taping a finger to a toe or vice versa. If your finger is injured, tape it to the finger right next to it. For the best results, do not tape your fingers or toes completely straight. Make sure they have a slight bend.

Major Broken Bones

There are certain bones that will most likely lead to death when broken. For example, pelvic fractures are usually the result of serious trauma, like a high-speed car accident or when you get thrown off a twenty-foot cliff. For these types of injuries, you will want to perform surgery on the back of your head using a bullet. Either that or suffer an agonizing death.

Your Teeth

Your mouth can be a real motherfucker, especially when you fail to clean its contents for six months. That's why I had you include toothpaste in your Go Bag. If you blew through that tube and forgot to pick another one up while pillaging homes, it is only a matter of time until your mouth turns against you. The shitty thing is that your mouth rarely gives you signs to let you know trouble is coming. One evening you go to bed feeling fine, and the next morning you are crying like a baby, unable to chew your eggs. If this happens to you, the first step is to locate the cause of the pain, as it could be the beginning of a cavity, an abscess, or even the dreadful scurvy that plagued British sailors.

Cavities are pretty easy to spot, at least when they have progressed to the point where they are causing you pain. Just grab a mirror and look for the tooth that has started to turn black. Unfortunately, you won't have a dentist around to shoot you full of Novocain and give you a filling, so you will have to cowboy the fuck up and be a man. Yep, I'm talking about yanking that rotten tooth out of your head. Here is how you do it:

STEP 1: Locate the rotten tooth.

STEP 2: Apply some type of pliers around the tooth; a Leatherman tool works great for this.

STEP 3: Depending upon the location of the rotten tooth, you want to pull either straight up or straight down. You may need to employ a slight rocking motion to loosen it.

STEP 4: Once the tooth pulls free, pack the hole with a piece of alcohol-soaked cloth.

STEP 5: Place the tooth on a necklace, and then brag to anyone who will listen about how you yanked that very tooth from your skull. Skip the part where you cried like a big fucking pussy and wet yourself.

If you search all of your teeth and none of them appear to be rotten, you may have a disgusting abscess hiding in your mouth. The warning signs are fever, swollen red tissue, pain when chewing, and a permanent bad taste in your mouth. Abscesses are much like zits in that they are enclosed pockets of pus. However, if you ignore the abscess hoping it will go away like an annoying pimple, it will most likely continue to grow, destroy surrounding tissue, and possibly even kill you. To avoid such an outcome, you must drain the abscess by sterilizing some sort of cutting instrument, either with alcohol or over an open flame, and then lance that bad boy so the pus and blood can drain. Once the opening is empty, pack it with some type of clean material, such as pieces of a boiled sheet. To prevent infection, you want to put fresh material into your mouth every day, as well as rinse the abscess with anything cleansing you may be able to scrounge: hydrogen peroxide, mouthwash, alcohol, urine, or drip some of that boiling water right into the hole.

Scurvy is also relatively easy to spot: look for spots on your skin, spongy gums, and random bleeding. Ignore these warning signs too long, and your teeth will begin falling out like a meth addict's. Luckily, scurvy is not hard to cure. It is caused by a lack of vitamin C in your diet, so all you have to do it is eat more fruits and vegetables such as oranges, lemons, tomatoes, potatoes, and green peppers.

Excuses for Leaving Others Who Are Injured

If you ignored my advice to travel alone, you are going to need to come up with excuses to leave your traveling mates should they get injured. Although this might seem like it would be very easy, it can be difficult to be quick-witted when someone is clinging to your shirt collar and begging you to save their life and not abandon them. To spare you the added brainpower, I have come up with some canned excuses that I will allow you to use.

1. "Shhhhh, buddy. You're all right. You're gonna be just fine. No, I ain't never gonna leave you. I will be right here by your side, guarding your back. However, I am going to go fetch you some water from that creek we saw a few miles back."

2. "Dude, do you have my wallet? . . . I think I dropped my fucking wallet. Hold on, I'm going to look for that shit really quick."

3. "You hear that! . . . Holy shit, we're saved. That is the Red Cross out there. I hear them shouting for survivors. Hold on, buddy, this is your lucky day. I'm going to round them up real quick. I'll be back in a minute with a stretcher."

4. "I've got to go take a shit."

HOW TO SPOON FOR WARMTH

Assuming you don't abandon your injured buddies while you're traveling on the long road to nowhere, spooning is an excellent way to conserve body heat and stay warm. If it is just you and one other person, you will want to rotate every hour so that both of you get a chance to warm your chest and back. If there are more members of your group, you can either spoon in a circle so that everyone is pressed tightly together, or spoon in a straight line, in which case you will want to treat it as a game of musical chairs where the people on the ends rotate into the line every hour. Below I have illustrated the proper way to spoon, as well as the improper way to spoon.

Proper Way to Spoon   Improper Way to Spoon

5

NO, YOU CAN'T INVITE YOUR FRIENDS—THEY WILL TRASH OUR UTOPIA

Congratulations! If you are reading this portion of the book, you made it to your safe zone and spent the last six months chilling out while the world burned around you. You survived when billions of others did not, and you owe your success entirely to me. Please, take a moment to think about this and thank me in your own way. If you can think of nothing original, let me give you some hints on what might be appropriate reciprocation:

1. Build a large Forrest Griffin shrine, but do not decorate it with lame shit like flowers and wreaths and such. If you feel it absolutely must be decorated, use skulls and animal bones and patches of fur.

2. Name one of the wild animals
    you have adopted over the
    past six months after me.
    However, do not name it Griff or
    Griffmeister or the Griffinator.
    You must name him either
    Forrest or Griffin. I will also
    accept Forrest Griffin. However,
    it cannot be one of the animals
    you are currently husbanding.

3. Search me out in the
    postapocalyptic world and
    become a blind follower of my
    cult. I would promise to make
    you my right-hand man, but I
    will most likely already have
    held a six-day gladiatorial event in which the best men in the
    land fought for this honor. However, I can guarantee that I will
    make you a jester or minstrel. At the very least, you can get a job
    as my castle janitor.

4. Sacrifice your life in my honor. This can be done by slitting your
    wrists, beheading yourself with an ax, or simply jumping off a
    cliff or out of a very high tree. However, if you attempt to sacrifice
    your life in my honor and fail, you will have disgraced me. (P.S.
    Please fax or e-mail me a map of your food stash before you take
    the plunge so things don't go to waste . . . I promise I won't make
    a beeline for it once I receive your e-mail, and I further promise
    I won't use a large hunting knife to dispatch you should you
    change your mind about offing yourself in my honor.)

5. Use my name to describe something really cool. For example,
    when telling people about the time you surfed a tsunami or
    battled a supernatural wolf, say, "It was so utterly Forrest." I will
    also accept, "I Griffined the shit out of that wave and wolf."

Up to this point, your primary goal has just been to survive. But you have been there and done that, right? If you're thinking it's time to get to the good stuff, you are absolutely correct. Currently, you are standing at a crossroads and have a very important decision to make. Do you want to live a life of solidarity and continue to eat nuts and berries to survive, or do you want to be a part of something greater?[22] If you decide you want to strike it out alone like Captain Apollo did in the last episode of *Battlestar Galactica* (sorry if I ruined the ending), or just perch on top of a mountain for the rest of your days and reminisce about all you have lost, that is fine by me. You will get bored as shit and most likely get eaten by a bear. But if you feel that it is your destiny, so be it. However, if you want to be a part of something greater, then you must create your own utopia, which will require some work. Again, Uncle Forrest is here to tell you how to get it done.

Things are going to get pretty complicated pretty quickly, especially when you begin adding people to your circle, but it is important to take things in steps, with the first one being finding a place to build your new utopia. Your safe zone might be good for you, but chances are it's not enough to support life on a large scale. If you have trouble envisioning what this new utopia should look like, just picture the Thunderdome. Of course you will want to remove the midget and his pigs, add a whole bunch of hot chicks, some personal servants, and a church whose fellowship worships your awesomeness. You will probably also want to remove Tina Turner from the picture, as she will undoubtedly challenge your power, and seeing what she put up with from Ike, you don't want to be messing with that bitch. In any case, you get the picture.

THAT CASTLE AIN'T GONNA BUILD ITSELF

Once you find the location of your new utopia, the next step is to get yourself a kick-ass castle. You've worked hard all of your life, am I right? You broke your back doing manual labor for years while chasing the American Dream. But after all that anguish and toil, everything got ripped right out from underneath you, putting you back to square one. The good news is

---

[22] Such as being my manservant.

that there is no more American Dream, and you can do things completely different this time. You can start the (insert name of your country here) Dream. You do not have to play by the rules because there are no more rules. The apocalypse came and wiped them all out.

The trick now is to dream big. How big? I'm talking castle big. I'm not talking about going out and building yourself a castle. You worked hard all your life, remember, and that would involve far too much work. But just because you can't build a castle yourself doesn't mean you won't get one. Here is what you do:

STEP 1: Discover a plot of land that will serve as the holy ground of your new utopia. I recommend picking something far away from cities or developed areas in order to limit outside influences. It's best if this plot of land has some type of structure on it. The structure doesn't have to be in good shape—it simply has to be large enough to house several hundred people. Some suggestions would be country schoolhouses, warehouses in the middle of nowhere, some type of missile silo, or even a large network of caves. Whichever location you decide upon, the main thing is that there be running water and a food source nearby. Of course, the food source could always be another group of people.

STEP 2: Rig up a bus into a Vehicle of Death and begin rounding up survivors. By this point, most people will be lonely, scared, and desperate to be a part of some type of society. How you get them to join you is easy: tell them that you have created a safe community where they no longer have to worry about dying on a daily basis. Even if that is not true, people will most likely believe you. Why? Because they want to believe. You will be surprised how many people get on the bus. However, you probably don't want to force-feed them all matching glasses of Kool-Aid when they first get on, as this will probably freak them out.

STEP 3: Begin designing your awesome castle. If you are considering moving into a preexisting castle, you are missing my point entirely. In addition to wanting life to be easy, you also want to be remembered through the ages. Create a legacy. When people visit England and Wales, what do they do? They visit castles and talk about how great the creators of those castles were, even though they did no actual work. Erecting a stone castle is perhaps one of the most difficult things to do. If you can somehow convince hundreds of people to dedicate years of their lives to building you a castle, you will be remembered for thousands of years as being totally awesome. Not wanting to be outdone by guys in medieval times, I would recommend building a castle that resembles Hogwarts. In addition to being massive, that place is also filled with all sorts of magic. How cool would that be?

The one thing to keep in mind is that you do not want your castle to be cooler than my castle. If it is, and you follow my instructions on how to command your followers to build it for you, then I will most likely bring my army over and destroy it. And you will be able to say nothing because I saved your life with the information in this book.

STREP 4: Start a religion that worships you as some type of god. In the next section, I give detailed instructions how to accomplish this.

STEP 5: Order your followers to build you a castle. Not wanting to step out of line with the great leaders of the past, you want to make sure not to overpay your workers. If you are truly a great leader, you will not have to pay them at all. However, you may want to be like the Indians of Central America and feed them coca leaves (or, if you like to stay with the times, cocaine or meth), as it does wonders to boost productivity and morale. You might also want to throw them a goat or pig every now and then to ensure they do not starve. After all, a dead worker is an inefficient worker.

BECOME A DOG (I MEAN GOD. SORRY, MY DYSLEXIA KICKED IN)

Let me begin by saying that starting your very own religion is not an easy thing to do. There are currently only five commonly recognized world religions—Hinduism, Buddhism, Judaism, Christianity, and Islam—and each of them has its roots buried in thousands upon thousands of years of tradition and development. Back in the day, starting these religions wasn't all that difficult because the people of the long-long ago were about as smart

as the clay-and-stone tablets the laws of their religions were etched upon. Spending their waking hours growing food, preparing food, avoiding the plague, and courting farm animals, the majority of people had no time left over for things as ridiculous as arithmetic or that fancy book learnin'. They might have been able to weather some pretty terrible shit, but they had a serious chink in their armor: anything outside of their dimly lit perspective became a giant mystery.

Anyone who had ever learned how to read, count, or wash their genitals had a serious leg up, and the peasants viewed this small number of "learned" people as superior. How did the educated wield their power? Well, they used it to interpret, disseminate, and enforce the confusing traditions of religion. Seriously, these guys had it easy. The most educated dude in the mix probably wasn't half as "Smart as a Fifth" Grader© today, and they were given free rein to write the book on The Truth. And like all people of power should, they used the blind faith of the masses for their own designs. Sure, they used religion as a way to give purpose and meaning to the community, but they also used it to organize and control its members.

Your goal in creating a new religion is to establish that same type of power, but it won't be easy. You could always burn all the books and wait for the next generation of brainless followers, but then you would be old, and what's the point of having power when you are old? You got to take advantage of that shit while you are young enough to enjoy it. The trick will be coming up with a religion that people actually buy. Unfortunately, the mob is a lot more educated than the one that existed in the long-long ago. The amount of knowledge that has been amassed during the past twenty thousand years of human civilization is staggering, and there are currently 750 million people sharing that information on social networks on the Internet. You need to consider that your flock will have some degree of technical familiarity even if there is nothing to be technical about anymore. They will understand the basics of math, science, and reading and writing, which wasn't the case in ancient times. You must keep this in mind when creating your religion, as you will most likely be asked to explain and defend your system of beliefs to those who challenge your authority.

Luckily, in a postapocalyptic world people will be looking for a new set of rules. With the old religions obviously having failed them, they will want a new leader, and that is where you casually step into the picture. As long as you are an alpha-type survivor with the skills and the knowledge to maneuver successfully through the devastation, which will be the case since you are the proud owner of this book, it will be easy to rise to the status of leader. Once there, you should be able to use your charisma to get people to follow any somewhat moderate belief system you dream up. I mean, if Scientology can get half of Hollywood *allegedly* (I had to put that in there because these guys have rocking lawyers) believing their crazy bullshit, you should be just fine.

Before you get all giddy and begin rounding people up, there are a few things to consider. First, are you going to shoot for the stars or be more realistic in your goals? In other words, are you going to start a religion or a cult?

The smart theorize that the difference between the two is how they interact with general society. If your system of beliefs teaches its members how to live in the world, along with other people, regardless of your system's place in society, and it offers them guidelines on how to do so, then you are most likely the proud owner of a religion. If your belief system is intent on separating its members from their social system, and it encourages them to interact only with other members of your system, then you may be the leader of what is commonly referred to as a cult. If you find this confusing, let me simplify. For example, if you take your girlfriend to parties and home for the holidays, and she actually initiates sex with you, then her name is Religion. If your girlfriend lives in the basement, receives sunlight only through specialized tanning bulbs, and a tin bucket in the corner serves as her only toilet, then her name is Cult.

Before you decide which one to start, there is more to factor in to the equation. Another key difference between a religion and a cult is that religions usually require their members to worship a higher power that is above mankind and its limited comprehension. A cult, by definition, will many times ask its members to worship the messenger, as he is seen as either divine or an incarnation of a divine figure. There are of course inherent risks with whichever strategy you decide to pursue. For instance, if you are just the messenger, others will be able to proclaim messages from that source as well, and thus sects or spin-offs can occur and rival yours, even though they use the same basic belief structure that you created. When you leave things up to interpretation, they will eventually get interpreted. Next thing you know, people are attacking your gates and demanding that you release all your serving wenches from captivity—all that hard work straight out the window!

The only real way to establish a belief system where you are free from external risks is to become the sole appointee and sole messenger of The Truth. This automatically points you in the direction of creating a cult, but that's pretty much how almost all "religions" started out anyway. (Don't tell this to the Catholics—they tend to get all bent out of shape over it.)

Whatever route you take, you will most likely want to be at the center of the action. This can be accomplished by setting yourself up as the sole heir to The Truth from the get-go, which is a lot like trying to get kinky with a chick in bed. If you want her to dress up as the University of Georgia bulldog while you go at her woof-woof style, you got to do that shit within the first few months in the relationship, while things are still new and exciting. If you wait until three years in before exposing your fuzzy-fucker fantasies, she will probably freak out. It is the same with your religion. You've got to establish yourself and your intentions from the beginning to give your religion a foundation. That way, if others proclaiming The Truth pop out of the woodwork later on, you have recourse to arguing that your words are the Real Deal.

However, when establishing yourself as the supreme dispenser or speaker of The Truth, you do run into some risks as well. Many of these are what I call Internal Risks. That is, they are derived from inconsistencies in your actions or weaknesses in your resolve. For instance, if you proclaim that homosexuality and premarital sex are wrong, and then go around screwing all of your altar boys, you've just created a contradiction. This is why any religion that preaches abstinence from things such as sex, pursuit of money, desire for material goods, alcohol, and other such "vices" end up having their fair share of hypocrites, which in turn creates dissension and ultimately turns people away from that religion. In the case of a fledgling religion, it is essential for its founder to maintain actions consistent with the beliefs of the system he espouses. Therefore, I suggest that you pick your codes well so you are sure you can stay true to them. In other words, don't be full of shit.

It has been said in business that the three most motivating factors in selling a person on something are sex, greed, and fear. When it comes to religion, I would throw guilt into the mix as well. If your goal is to control the masses, you must control and define each of these aspects of human nature. Of course, you must also deliver to your followers a sense of satisfaction through the realization of purpose. Luckily, this will be quite easy in a postapocalyptic world. With everything they ever knew or loved burned to a crisp, it will be very easy to convince people that they were chosen to live for a greater purpose. It is your job to give them that purpose and to enhance their experience and feeling of value within the new community. For all practical purposes, assume the roll of strip club owner, and view your flock as an abused group of eighteen-year-old girls searching for a daddy. Give them the attention and purpose they are searching for. If you blank out on how to accomplish this, just remember the words "You are the chosen ones" goes a long way with smaller groups of people who have been through a lot of trauma.

The one thing you don't want to do is make your religion easy to follow. You want to ask your people to give up EVERYTHING. If you design your religion like a four-minute abs video and proclaim it is so easy that anyone can follow it, people will be deterred. For some reason, people like to suffer. They are completely content thinking that in the *next* life they will get theirs, which does wonders for allowing you to get yours in the here and now. During the three long months I spent working as a personal trainer, I scientifically proved that the more people pay for something, the more perceived value that something has. That is why we were thinking about charging five hundred dollars for this book. If HarperCollins had gone for it, you would have undoubtedly thought that it contained the formula for shitting golden apples. I thought it was a great idea, but at least we managed to con twenty-five bucks out of you for a book worth no more than a half-used pack of butt napkins.

This is the same thing you want to accomplish with your religion. Don't underestimate the power of fraternities or of military hazing. You must ask people to give up all their possessions. You must ask them to give you all of their food. Even if you can't eat that much food, you can always burn it or piss on it and give it back to the hungries worshipping at your feet . . . Yes, definitely go with the cult option now that I think about it.

Heed my words—do not attempt to create a system that is altruistic, which means it is actually good for the people. There are simply no incentives. If you create a religion totally in your favor, your flock becomes your personal slaves. In addition to doing all the things you hate, such as foraging and farming and going to the bathroom alone, they will bring you free sandwiches and give you regular blow jobs. It is a pretty sweet deal—just take a look back at all the heads of England's various churches in the long-long ago. Those guys were all fat off eating turkey legs and getting blow jobs (I have no proof for this statement, but it seems right). If you invent a religion that attempts to break the class system and get rich people communicating with poor people, the repercussions for being discovered as a fraud will be the same as for any other fraud—they will torture you to death by making you watch *The Hills* on mushrooms. Might as well get something out of the whole deal.

It's also important to know what your people are thinking, not because you care what they think but because it's another way to wield power. This can be achieved by adding confession to the rituals and system of your religion. These sessions should be recorded or transcribed and filed away for future reference. People often hold out in confessions, so it is important that all of the clergy in your new cult are also trained hypnotists. Once you have the members' deepest, darkest secrets, your flock will feel somewhat trapped. They will fear you. It would be like if I told someone about the time I slept with a post-op tranny. I would never tell anyone that. But if I did, you would have something over my head.

If a member of your group gets uppity, you leak the secrets you have on them to the rest of the group. Eventually, it will get out that that dissension leads to horrible punishment. Of course, if exposing their darkest moments is not enough to keep members from getting uppity, there are other ways to deal with their disobedience.

Why does any of this matter? The castle, dummy. Remember the castle. If you don't have a group of blind followers, who in the heck is going to build it for you? I sure as hell ain't.

MIX-AND-MATCH RELIGIONATOR CHART

I'm not gonna lie: starting your own religion is not easy. It takes at least a solid weekend of work with intermittent breaks to fight off the nomadic hordes. If you start to get frustrated and feel like calling it quits, remember that a sage once said, "Don't be a quitter 'till you hit her in the shitter." Your new system doesn't have to be perfect. As a matter of fact, it can be downright insane. Use a mix-and-match Religonator Chart like the one I've laid out below—it really is that simple. The religion you end up with might not exactly fit your needs and desires, but at least you will end up in power and have control.

This chart contains some of the more, how do you say, fantastic beliefs held by a few of the world's religions, as well as a column for what I like to call the "wild card" beliefs. To build you very own religion, circle one belief from each of the major religions, and to add that individual touch, top it off with two beliefs from the wild card column. Once you have made your choices, blend them together and create an almost ridiculous story line and a group of laws. Just go nuts with it and have some fun. Next, write the main story line on a really old scroll, scratch each law onto a stone tablet, and deposit both of these items somewhere in the desert. Just make sure to remember where you put them because later you will need to "find" them in the midst of a vision or dream.

Christian

- Baby born by virgin.
- Leader rises from the dead.
- Walking on water.

Catholic

- Consume the body and blood of your fallen leader on a weekly basis.
- Encourage young boys to hang out with old, asexual men.

Judaism

- The parting of entire seas.

Hinduism

- Good begets good, bad begets bad.
- Cows are sacred.

Scientology

- Aliens provide purity and clarity to humans. (Or some shit like that. Seriously, if they can get away with this kind of shit nowadays, what with modern technology and plenty of other religious options out there, you can get away with just about anything. *Allegedly.*)

Wild card

- Baby born by man virgin.

FORREST FACTOID

Don't be afraid to go crazy with your proclamations about your new faith. After the earthquake that claimed two hundred thousand lives in Haiti, Pat Roberts claimed that the Haitian people brought the death and mayhem upon themselves by worshipping the devil. If you can say something as fucked up as that and still have people follow your advice, you can say pretty much anything.

HOW DAVID KORESH DID IT
(CREATING YOUR GODLIKE PERSONA)

Getting your belief system set up is a good start, but it's not enough on its own. Now that you have a set of "values" in place, you need to make sure you have the presence to match. I know you've never been one to care much about your appearance, especially after the apocalypse (okay, let's be honest: things weren't great for you before the apocalypse either), but you might want to think about trying a few things to appear your holiest at all times.

Wildman Crazy Hair Doesn't Inspire Confidence (i.e., Nick Nolte)

Anytime you introduce a set of beliefs and ask people to follow them, you must become the focal point of excitement for those whom you wish to entice with those beliefs. Essentially, you must become the life of the party. Although I have never seen you personally, I imagine you have let yourself go a little, especially now that the  apocalypse has hit. You have greasy skin, your drawers smell like a battle-field, and you always have goop caked in the corners of your eyes. Clean yourself up! You don't have to look overly proper, but you do have to look presentable.

My suggestion is to start with your hair. If you have hair, part it on the side so that you have that big wave traversing your forehead. A good head of hair works really well for telling your flock that you have what it takes to lead them to the promised land. However, if you are looking a little more like Matt Lindland these days, do not try to hide the fact that you are bald-ing by growing more hair around the sides and back. This is a clear-cut sign of weakness. Instead, shave your head bald. Even if you have a bulbous-shaped head, you will look wise and a trifle spooky. Spooky is good, trust me.

FORTUNE COOKIE WISDOM

If you truly want to be remembered as a legend, you will want to die as a martyr at the apex of your life. It will leave people with an iconic image of you—young, strong, and virile. If you hang around too long, you will undoubtedly be remembered as that fat, bloated, old guy hustling on the Vegas Strip for a couple of dollars so you can pay your child support. With this in mind, I still have to admit that martyrdom just isn't for me. Seventy-two virgins sounds well and good, but I cannot be responsible for teaching that many girls how to get it on. Personally, I need a girl with a little experience. Not a Vegas prostitute, but not an amateur either. Now if they offered an endless supply of coffee . . .

You Need to Sound Smarter

Another thing you can work on is your accent. When you have a foreign accent, it creates an illusion of superiority and knowledge. The goal is to choose an accent that best represents your belief system. If you are trying to create a religious community that has Hindu or Buddhist roots, you may want to speak like a Vedic Indian or wise Asian. If you base your belief system on a military concept, Texan, German, and Russian accents will help create an effect of power and militaristic credibility. The only accents you do not want to use are Canadian, Swedish, and of course French. Choosing one of these accents will get you stoned to death or burned at the cross. If you are not sure what accent to take on, just switch it up every few years like Madonna.

Whatever you do, do not use your regular voice. Employing an accent creates the "faraway effect," which is where people perceive anything remote from their lives to be more valuable than the things that are around them every day. This is the reason why everyone thought Pride was so good, because that organization was far away in Japan. But when those fighters came over here, and some of them didn't do that well, it shattered the illusion.

Another helpful hint is to speak using only cryptic phrases. Let me give you an example:

DISCIPLE: Forrest, I am hungry. Can I have a piece of meat?

FORREST: My son, we can only know these things in the end.

Crazy Eyes (aka Forrest Whittaker)

Another critical characteristic you need to develop are crazy eyes. Every religious or political leader that has attained the loyalty and blind allegiance of a group or a country has had them. Just think about David Koresh. He wore glasses to accentuate his crazy eyes, and people actually burned to death for him.

Practice in the mirror by staring at yourself for a really, really long time. As a matter of fact, stare at yourself until you are no longer comfortable doing so, and then stare some more. Eventually, you will automatically begin to make strange faces and your eyes will begin to take on the necessary look of intense commitment that your beliefs require. Although your crazy eyes will dissuade nonbelievers from getting near you, they will have the opposite effect on those who are searching for spiritual guidance. To them, the crazier your eyes get, the more they will believe that you have "seen the light."

NOTE TO READER: In no way are we condoning the actions of David Koresh, Jim Jones, or those guys who started that Heaven's Gate shit. We are simply pointing out that a couple of the techniques they used worked quite well, actually. We want you to use those techniques for good. That is what I will be doing.

Not Shaving for Five Years Finally Pays Off: Your Facial Hair

Another thing you may want to incorporate into your leadership getup is facial hair. Most wise men of religious or political movements have either had distinct mustaches or beards. If you are like me and cannot grow an adult beard, that is even better. The scruffier your beard or mustache, the more wisdom people will think you possess. The two looks I would  recommend choosing from are the Fu Manchu beard of the Eastern master or the long beard of the mountain philosopher.

Jesus Was a Snazzy Dresser

Your attire will put the finishing touches upon your
new persona, but it is important to make the right
choice. Instead of picking something you look good
in, ask yourself what you are trying to achieve. A long
robe lets your fledgling converts know that you are a
man of deep thought. Clothing yourself in animal
skins lets them know you are a man of nature. Wearing a turban lets them think that you are without
vices, and wearing a militaristic uniform gives off an
aura of invincibility and power. It is totally up to you,
but just make sure whatever dress you chose to adopt is readily available,
as you will most likely want to outfit all members of your group in similar
clothing. This strips away their individuality and creates greater cohesion

in the community. Remember, you want your
group as a whole to have identity, not the individuals in the group. Dressing everyone the
same also makes it easy to identify outsiders
and kill them.

FORTUNE COOKIE WISDOM

It can also be beneficial to worship some type of crazy idol. I was going to suggest a dead dude on a cross, but apparently that has already been used. Just go crazy with it to see how far people will go. Personally, my religion is going to worship wind chimes. The reason for this is obvious—wind chimes are moved by God's life breath. Fortunately, I will be the only one who can hear God's voice when the wind chimes speak. I will interpret what he is saying and then share that knowledge with my people. The downside to this, of course, is that a community filled with seven thousand wind chimes will probably get pretty fucking annoying. Man, I hate the sound of those things. Reminds me of old people, for some reason . . . So, on second thought, my religion will most likely worship trees. They have been around longer than humans, and they don't even bother trying to communicate with us, which means they are super wise. The downside to this is that trees will be sacred, which means everyone will have to live in mud huts or some shit. However, I will be able to live in a giant hollowed-out tree because that is how I divine with the gods. Yeah, that's a lot better than listening to wind chimes all day.

Putting Everything Together

Below are few examples of how you can put everything together.

FORTUNE COOKIE WISDOM

As the head of your new religion, you'll quickly find that there are real benefits to human sacrifice, as it's a great way to get rid of people trying to usurp power. Ancient Mayans routinely practiced human sacrifice to appease their various gods and to commemorate the coronations of their leaders. In one such sacrificial ritual, they would paint a victim blue, cut under their breastbone with a flint knife, reach into the gaping hole they created, and extract the still-beating heart Indiana Jones style. After the event, the victim would be flayed and his skin turned into a cape, which the priest would wear while performing a ritual dance.

MATING POSTAPOCALYPSE

If you are planning to start a new society, there is going to have to be some funny business happening at the back of the cave when the sun goes down.

Today's mating rituals are confusing and involve many factors, most of which I do not understand. Postapocalyptic mating rituals will be much more primal and focus on immediate survival. Personal hygiene will play a much smaller role in mating, which is good news for most of my readers. In addition, bow-staff skills will have a much greater relevance attached to them. But that doesn't mean that all those Napoleon Dynamite losers will be able to get mates all of a sudden. Females will look for a big, strong, tough animal with good genetics that she can control enough to provide her and her young with food and shelter. Women will be attracted to a protector and a provider, plain and simple.

However, there will still be some similarities between pre-apocalyptic and postapocalyptic customs. For example, today women want a man with a nice house, and postapocalypse they will want a man with a nice shelter that doesn't leak and is not too exposed to the wind and temperature changes. Today they want a man with a good job, and postapocalypse they will want a good hunter . . . Wow, now that I think about it, all those socially inept weirdos that never get women because the only women tough enough to stay with them are lesbians will be the most-prized bachelors. (You hear that, Erich? There is a chance for you.)

What will men be looking for postapocalpyse? Well, in my opinion men should be looking for tough, strong women who are clean and healthy enough to avoid sickness and such. Women that have a little fat (ample ass and tits—okay, that sounds a little harsh when I actually see it on paper, but this doesn't make it any less true) so they can survive during childbirth and the lean winter months. After all, when calories become scarce, it will be great to be fat—not to the point where you can't move, but fat in the sense that you can't see your abs. On second thought, men should probably simply look for any woman that doesn't run from them. Oh, and doesn't have a dirty baby maker.

THE ORIGINAL POWER GEL BY ANTHONY

Female patients often ask me if it is safe for them to swallow their husband's ejaculate during oral sex. The answer is YES! In addition to being completely safe and great tasting (not based upon personal experience, but rather on thousands of hours of research conducted with loose women around the world), it is great for your health. Human male ejaculate is only 10 percent sperm. Among other things, it contains vitamin C (which boosts your immune system), calcium (which makes you grow strong bones), protein (helps you build muscles), zinc (helps prevent a number of health problems), and fructose sugar (a nice energy boost to start your day). If you are still skeptical, I understand completely, but at the very least it can serve as an excellent exfoliant. Ancient Egyptian women routinely allowed their men to blow on their face, and they were renowned for having nice skin.

If you shy away from swallowing because you think it tastes icky, just have your man drink pineapple juice and eat fresh fruit a few days prior to your journey south. This won't make his jizz taste like a lollipop, but it should calm your gag reflex. Seriously, swallowing a mouth load of jizz is a very healthy, natural thing to do, and all women should get accustomed to doing it. It really isn't that bad—just ask Bigger John.

BIGGER JOHN GETS A TASTE OF HIS OWN MEDICINE
BY BIGGER JOHN

Back when I was twenty-seven, I was seeing a former dancer from the Athens area, and she was giving me a blowjob in her parent's house. She asked me to give her some kind of signal or sign to let her know when I was about to blow, but there was no way in hell I was going to do that. Well, I guess she felt the tide rising, and just as the volcano blew, she removed her lips from my pole. I of course let out a tremendous sigh of pleasure, and the next thing I know I have a mouthful of my own cum.

Now, the only reason I am telling this story is because I am sure it has happened to many men. And it is kinda manly knowing that I can blow a load that far—there ain't no dribble dick here, son. But despite being impressed with my distance, I was totally grossed out. I ran to the bathroom, threw up several times, and then grabbed a random toothbrush on the counter and brushed my teeth. It was a pretty rough experience. But truth be told, it was the idea of it that grossed me out more than the actual taste.

POCKET PUSSY

Not one for political correctness, I am going to talk about a controversial topic—the pocket pussy. All men have tried to build one at some point in their life, and all men have experienced horrible repercussions due to their botched experiment (some men may have tried to build a pocket anus. I am not judging, but you are extremely homosexual). Men will be a lot more desperate postapocalypse due to the loss of the Internet, and to prevent them from attempting to construct makeshift devices out of old car parts and rusty nails, I have included a proven pocket pussy blueprint below. Trust me when I tell you this contraption was not designed in haste or developed in some pervert's basement. It was masterminded by Alexander the Great himself, and passed down through the ages by the Freemasons. How did I come across this knowledge? . . . *What travels in the moonlight by way of the eastern pass* . . . enough said.

Supplies

- One latex glove.
- Three pieces of string, approximately twelve inches long.
- Lubricant: whatever is available. (Note: motor oil is precious and should not be used on your dick.)
- Towel.
- Water.

STEP 1 (TOWEL AND GLOVE SETUP): Fold your towel in half and then lay it on the ground. Make sure that the height of the towel is not shorter than your johnson. Next, place the glove at one end of the towel with the cuff approximately three to four inches outside of the towel.

   HINT: Before rolling up the towel, you may want to wet it to make it feel more humanlike. Up to you.

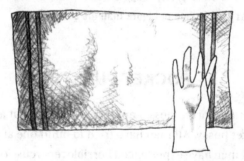

STEP 2 (ROLLING THE TOWEL): Roll up the towel. When done properly, the cuff of the glove should protrude three or four inches from the end.

STEP 3 (FOLDING THE GLOVE): Fold the cuff of
the glove over the towel. This is when the
contraption will begin to resemble a vagina.

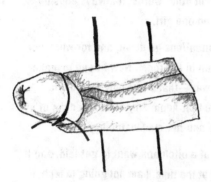

STEP 4 (TYING THE TOWEL): Place three strings approximately two to three
inches apart across the towel. Next, tie the first string to the desired
tightness or looseness.

STEP 5 (ADDING LUBRICANT): Tie the second two strings. Now that your
pocket pussy is complete, add the desired amount of lubricant. Have
fun!

    NOTE: Make sure to remember to change gloves between uses. This
pocket pussy is a onetime deal!

How to Make a Pocket Anus
See instructions above, just add shit.

DICK IN A BOX BY BIGGER JOHN

The sad truth is that when the apocalypse comes, there won't be all that many women left, and so you'll have to get comfortable sharing. Personally, I will not have a problem with this because I am the king of group sex. Unfortunately, it is not "the good kind." In other words, it always ends up being me and two or three other dudes on one girl.

In 2006, I had ten different group sex situations go down, and for whatever reason, each time there was another man in the room. Now I need to make it very clear that I did not set it up this way—that's just how the cookie crumbled. It got so bad there for a while that Adam Singer accused me of not being able to get hard unless there was another man watching.

My whole deal is that I am a horny son of a bitch and want to get laid, and if there happens to be another guy around at the time, I am not going to let him get in the way. Luckily, all these little experiences I've had are going to help me when shit hits the fan. During the apocalypse, every sex situation will most likely be a group situation due the minimal number of women left on the planet, and I will be the first to jump into the mix. If you're nervous about having this type of encounter, I can offer you some advice to make it a little easier.

First off, instead of seeing the other guys in the room as invading your turf, view them as teammates. Anytime you're with a chick, you get nervous about something, such as if you are going to cum too fast or be able to get a stiff enough erection. But when there are other guys present, and you see them as your brothers, your friends, your teammates, they can offer moral support if anything should go wrong. They can provide you with the confidence you need to correct any problem you may be having and get back into the game.

When you acquire this mind-set, you don't see a massive cock as a threat. You simply see it as more cock to get the job done. For example, when playing a game of football, you want the biggest linebackers possible. As long as you have the team mentality, the same thing goes with group sex.

To give you an idea of how a mostly male, group sex situation should transpire, I will share with you one of my funnier gang bang stories. It involved a nurse and my childhood friend Bill. Well, anytime Bill and I tag-teamed a girl, he liked to take the role of director, which was fine by me. So on this particular occasion, we were sitting around the living room, and he says to the nurse, "Why don't you take off John's pants." Sure enough, she takes off my pants. Next he said, "Why don't you start sucking on John's cock." Being the truly wonderful woman she was, she began sucking on my cock. Next thing I hear is, "John, lose the shirt." Without thinking, I removed my shirt. A second later, I realized that he had not been referring to my shirt, but rather the shirt of the nurse. It was pretty damn funny, but what really blew my mind was that the nurse was actually able to laugh with my cock still in her mouth. She could suck a dick and laugh at the same time. What a talented girl.

WHO'S THE BOSS

Once you have effectively set yourself up as the Bringer of the Light and established yourself as the top male of the group, the next step is to create a hierarchy, starting at the bottom floor—your laborers. This job will be filled with the people who have pre-apocalypse skills that are no longer valued postapocalypse. This includes but is not limited to lawyers, writers (yes, Erich will be one of my laborers), bureaucrats, plumbers (buckets will be our new toilets), nuclear engineers, astronauts, pilots, bankers (you will own everything of value), and computer scientists. If you happen to be among this group, sorry, buddy, but you are finally going to have to get your hands dirty. And what the fuck are you doing reading my book—you are smarter than this.

Ironically, the people who had jobs that were considered menial pre-apocalypse will most likely have skills that are extremely valuable postapocalypse. This includes but is not limited to professional fighters, artists (someone has to build your statues and paint your murals—aka, keep record of your greatness), wilderness guides, archers, gunfighters, farmers, and carpenters. You don't necessarily have to put these people in a position of power (you want to control as much of it as you can), but you definitely want to make them feel superior to the laborers. This can be

FORREST FACTOID

I was hanging out with the late Evan Tanner a while back, bitching about how people can be so damn critical. Suddenly Evan gets all quiet, and he says to me, "Jesus of Nazareth walked the earth, did nothing but good, and they crucified him for it." That was some pretty heavy shit right there. Needless to say, I quit my bitching.

accomplished by giving them nicer houses, more food, and perhaps assigning each one their own slave laborer. Could you imagine how good it would make a carpenter feel to have his own rocket scientist as a slave?

Your middle class will be made up of people who have skills that neither gained nor lost value postapocalypse. This group will exist solely of strippers and prostitutes.

Lastly, you want to assemble your group of lieutenants. This is where a lot of leaders go wrong. Instead of picking their most loyal subjects to serve in this role, they pick the most ambitious. Although ambitious people often prove to be excellent advisers and will go to great lengths to corral your people into a tightly knit group, they will almost always attempt to overthrow you when you are at your weakest. And since they have a lot more interaction with the people on a daily basis, they can often raise a fairly decent-size army to help them with their task.

To avoid such an outcome, assign all ambitious people to horrible jobs such as pig farming or butt wiping, and fill your lieutenant positions with the dumbest members of your lot. (In other words, follow the path of George W. Bush, not Julius Caesar.) They might not be great advisers, but do you really need an adviser? Hell no, you don't. You also don't need senators or congressmen or anyone else who tells you what is best for your flock. After all, they are your flock. For all intents and purposes, they are your cattle. Before you found them, they were dirty, scared, and confused. They will of course forget this fact, but whipping them back into shape is easy. All you have to do is stage a famine or crisis or war, or make terrible decisions that lead you to a real famine or crisis or war. Anytime people feel threatened, they tend to come together and place blind faith in their leader. Just look at the faith we placed in George W. Bush after 9/11. Enough said.

THE ETCHING ON THE STONE TABLET

One of the nicest aspects about starting your own religion is that it allows you to create laws almost at will. All you have to do is claim that they are of divine origin or suggest that they must exist in order to remain in Divinity's favor. No matter the absurdity of the law you make, no judge in his right mind will attempt to overrule it or say it is unconstitutional. After all, it would be the same as saying God is unconstitutional, and if you have structured your laws correctly, such a crime is punishable by death.

I know it might seem like a good idea to have an anarchistic society, but it simply won't work. Without laws, society cannot function because there is no order. However, I am not saying that you should go crazy with laws. And you especially don't want to make all the laws in your own favor. You want to create certain laws that help solve issues that commonly arise in the community, such as who is allowed to join your group and who isn't, and how to deal with those who cause harm or bring disorder. But there have got to be some benefits to sitting at the helm of this whole thing, and my suggestion is to get a little creative. I am not saying you should enact a law as self-fulfilling as making all women visit you in your bedchambers the day they turn sixteen (if you are thinking, "Damn, that would be sweet," then yes, you are indeed a pedophile), but you definitely want to pass laws that make your life easier or at least less annoying.

Once you create these laws, no matter how absurd, you must enforce them with an iron fist. Personally, I am not one for hurting others, except perhaps for punching people in the face or trying to break their arms with submission holds . . . oh, and maybe once in a while trying to crack a rib with a solid Thai kick, and then also getting real joy out of delivering a stout punch to the liver so the recipient pisses blood for a week . . . but besides all that, I'm not really a guy who likes to dispatch punishment. However, when creating a society, your new utopia, it is absolutely necessary to create consequences for insubordination. You don't want to get all crazy with things, like burning someone at the stake for not bowing the proper number of times when worshipping your awesomeness. You must be fair when doling out punishments in order to keep order and faith in your system. In other words, the punishment needs to fit the crime.

There is always the good old "eye for an eye" type of justice. If someone steals, they get their hands cut off. If someone lies repeatedly, they get their tongues cut out. If someone screws another man's woman—well, you get the picture.

Many smaller groups simply ostracize their members, exiling them to a life on their own, and in a postapocalyptic world this would undoubtedly be a scary proposition. (Note: Ostracize means to shun or ignore, not make your people dress up and act like ostriches. Just letting you know as these things can sometimes get confusing.)

Below I have included some of the laws that I will enact in my post-apocalyptic community, as well as the punishment people who break those laws will receive.

1. **LAW:** Men can't dye their hair.
   PUNISHMENT: Public stoning. If you are wondering why not death by hanging, beheading, or crucifixion, let me tell you. First off, stoning seems like a pretty terrible way to go, especially if the people can't throw that good and it takes them a while to put you out of your misery. Second, it makes everyone the killer. If you kill someone by beheading, the blame lies solely with you and the executioner. If you get everyone to partake in the festivities, they all have blood on their hands.

2. **LAW:** Women are not allowed to flirt with men they do not plan to have sex with.
   PUNISHMENT: They must become strippers.

3. **LAW:** You must pitch in by your own free will on community projects, such as building schoolhouses, temples to worship me, and of course my castle.
   PUNISHMENT: While everyone else in the community does man's work, you have to serve them lemonade in a pink dress and hold the bucket for them when they need to relieve themselves. Oh, and you must eat your meals out of the same bucket.

4. **LAW:** Don't wear white after Labor Day.
   PUNISHMENT: Uppity bitches will make fun of you.

5. **LAW:** Stupid people must use condoms. And yes, this includes me.
   PUNISHMENT: They have babies they have to take care of.

6. **LAW:** No ostentatious showing of wealth. (I made this law
   because I just learned the word "ostentatious" and had to use it
   in a sentence in order to remember it.)
   PUNISHMENT: Have to extirpate all their wealth (not sure if I used
   "extirpate" correctly).

7. **LAW:** No hurting coffee plants in any way.
   PUNISHMENT: Death on the spot. However, stoning is not allowed
   because it may damage one of the plants.

8. **LAW:** Women are not allowed to use their left foot during the full
   moon. (I would get more into this, but it is very personal.)
   PUNISHMENT: None at all, but I am begging you not to do it. (The
   begging is a part of it all.)

9. **LAW:** Women cannot use words such as "small" or "tiny" or
   "microscopic" or "babylike" when referring to a man's genitalia.
   It hurts a guy's feelings.
   PUNISHMENT: That man is the only lover you may take for five years.

10. **LAW:** All pets must be properly maintained.
    PUNISHMENT: Must spend a week in an animal's cage, getting
    treated as you treat your animal.

11. **LAW:** No driving and texting at the same time.
    PUNISHMENT: Chances are there will be no working cell phones
    or vehicles, but you don't want to mess around with this one
    anyway. Punishable by stoning.

12. **LAW:** No smoking in public places.
    PUNISHMENT: Death by stoning.

If you have trouble coming up with your own laws, the Ten Commandments are a pretty good place to start. Currently, I follow approximately six

and a half of them. In case you have forgotten what they are, let me refresh
your memory:

1. *You shall have no other gods before me.* In the case of the
   apocalypse, that God will be me, Forrest Griffin. (Just kidding,
   real God. Please don't smite me. It was a joke.)

2. *You shall not make yourself a carved image—any likeness of
   anything that is in heaven above, or that is in the earth beneath,
   or that is in the water under the earth.* This is the wild card
   commandment. I'm not quite sure what it means, and I am
   sure others won't either. Basically, I will define it to suit my
   immediate purpose. For example, if I catch someone shitting
   on my lawn, I will shout, "You shall not make yourself a carved
   image."

3. *Remember the Sabbath day.* Although the Sabbath is currently
   every Saturday, I like to sleep in on the weekends. I also feel four
   times a month is a little extreme. As a result, my Sabbath will be
   every other Wednesday.

4. *Do not take the Lord's name in vain.* I'm actually a firm believer
   in this one. Although my last book contained about six thousand
   swearwords, I didn't take the Lord's name in vain once.

5. *Honor your father and mother.* Basically, this means honor your
   father and then, if you have any goodwill left over, throw it to
   your mother. I never understood this—mothers birth you, feed
   you from the teat, raise you, shower you with warmth, and do
   everything in their power to protect you even after you become
   a filthy adult. Seems a little unfair to me. After all, fathers are the
   ones you run and hide from when they get home from work.

6. *You shall not murder.* This is a good one, but I feel it needs a little
   more clarity. In my religion, it will strictly state, *Do not murder
   me, Forrest Griffin.*

7. *You shall not commit adultery.* Everyone should abide by this,
   unless, of course, the chick is super hot and freaky. Just don't get
   caught.

8. *You shall not steal.* Again, this one needs to be defined. You will not steal from me, Forrest Griffin. However, you may steal from others and give to me, especially if the thing you stole was a warm cup of coffee.

9. *You shall not bear false witness against your neighbor.* I am not quite sure what this one means either, but I assume it has something to do with sleeping in your neighbor's bathtub, which is not a good idea.

10. *You shall not covet your neighbor's house; you shall not covet your neighbor's wife, nor his male servant, nor his female servant, nor his ox, nor his donkey, nor anything that is your neighbor's.* Basically, this is most awesome commandment of the lot. It is solely designed to keep the elitists in a position of power. However, it is kind of worded strangely. It seems to get all sexual there with the neighbor's wife part, but in the same sentence they mention male servants, oxen, and donkeys. Most likely, there were some pretty sick fucks back in the day. I mean, who wants to covet a donkey? A deer, on the other hand . . .

YOU GUESSED IT—A SERIOUS SECTION IN A DICK-JOKE BOOK

How did society get to this point? How are all these intelligent people running around, believing in religions that are based on ideas and concepts and beliefs that cannot be proven. I know, I know. You just gotta have faith. I have been hearing that all of my life, but if I have faith that tomorrow morning I will awaken with the athletic endowments of LeBron James, it just ain't going happen.[23] The fact of the matter is that faith cannot make morons into astronauts, so why will it make the concepts of any religion any more true? That's why when I talk at schools I do not tell the kids that they can do anything. Instead, I say, "If you work really, really hard, perhaps you can be the first one in your family to graduate high school. No, you cannot be an astronaut—sorry, that is not really an option for you.

---

[23] I do that every night, and wake up disappointed every morning.

NAKED ETIQUETTE

Around the time I was working on this section of the book, I got a workout in at the Las Vegas Health Club and then hit the showers. About halfway through, the hairy man showering next to me asked some random guy in the locker room if he would be so kind as to soap up his back. I looked over and saw this hairy man hand a complete stranger a little washcloth and then turn around. You could tell the guy who had been asked to perform this service was in complete shock, and not knowing exactly how to behave, he did as he was ordered. He quickly soaped up the guy's back, handed the washcloth back, and then scurried out of the locker room. I had to use all my willpower not to scream at the hairy man next to me, "What the fuck are you doing?" It bothered me to such a degree that I felt it was necessary to include a few Naked Etiquette laws.

Naked Etiquette Law 1: If you are naked in a public place such as a locker room, speaking to other people is strictly forbidden. Do not talk to me, and do not look at me. Keep your mouth shut and your eyes glued to the wall in front of you. However, I will accept talking while in the sauna, even if you are naked. This helps pass the time and has a less "rappish" feeling associated with it.

Naked Etiquette Law 2: This law is very similar to the first law, but I felt I needed to get very specific just so there was no confusion. Even if you are half naked, which tends to occur when you are at a urinal, talking is strictly forbidden.

Naked Etiquette Law 3: Shaking hands in any place where urination or defecation commonly takes place is strictly forbidden . . . Come on, people, get your head in the game.

Let's work on maybe getting a bachelor's degree or maybe a trade you are really good at. Baby steps, kids."

The thing that gets me is that the people who try to spread religion usually aren't the smartest among us. Just look at any late-night evangelist—every single one of these guys would get creamed in a third-grade spelling bee. But with all of that said, I too have recently found religion.

Does that make me a hypocrite? Yes, probably does, but I have certainly been worse things. I believe in God because when I pray to Him, when I say, "Please take away my fear, my anxiety, my pain," it seems to happen. So when I think about it, I guess faith is not really that blind after all. There really does seem to be something there. I mean, if I do something good and selfless, it feels good. When I do bad things, it feels bad. Sure that could be programmed into me by society, but it could also be God, so I'm going with that one. Besides, now that I am going to church, I will get to go to heaven. In your face, old, agnostic ways!

However, I have to admit that being a nonbeliever was a whole lot easier. I used to be a militant agnostic, which is where you think, "I don't know, and neither do you." Agnosticism appealed to me because its whole belief system could be summed up in that one statement. And what comeback did people have? Since they were unable to prove any of their beliefs here on earth, it all came back to faith. What helped sell me on religion is Pascal's Gambit. Now, I have an interesting take on this idea because I learned about it in Sunday school as a kid, and my brain has taken a LOT of abuse since the fifth grade, but I didn't bother to look it up because I like my personal recollection. Pascal's Gambit is basically this: if you follow the basic tenets of any moderate religion, you will have a better life, you will be more adjusted to society, and you'll help move things along for the betterment of all. You will also be happier, and if there is in fact a God and a heaven, you will get to meet Him and go there because you followed the rules.

On the flip side, you have the atheist's gambit. (And just so you know, I am most likely making this all up, even though in my head I honestly feel it is something someone told me at one point at time.) The atheist's gambit states that religion is restrictive and destructive. To prove this point, all you have to do is look at one of the hundreds of wars that have been fought over religion, such as the never-ending battle raging between Pakistan and India (seriously, why can't the Buddhists and Confucianists just get along!). If you abolished all the religions, the majority of wars would simply end. Sure, the leaders could find other methods to rally their people to fight for their selfish causes, but they would never be able to mobilize the same number of them. So the atheist's gambit basically states that without religion, people will stop all the fighting. They would start living for the moment and stop focusing on getting theirs in the next life.

Personally, I find Pascal's Gambit to be more attractive. After all, I am not killing anyone in the name of religion. If you use a little common sense, it should be easy to figure out that killing people in the name of your religion is probably pretty wrong. As a matter of fact, anytime you use religion to justify a bad action, it is wrong. All religions have done it, even the Mormons. Back in the long-long ago, they used to kill other settlers and take their shit, and it was done in the name of religion. I have no intention of killing people and taking their shit, so I think I am pretty much okay. Sure, it is rough to believe in God and heaven when you see millions of people die before they've even had a chance in life, like all the kids who lost their lives in the Southeast Asian tsunami or over in Haiti when they had that massive earthquake. I mean, I would understand if God smote me down tomorrow because I am a dirty fucker, but all those kids . . . How do you explain that? The answer I have come up with is you don't. If you look too deeply into anything, contradictions are going to pop up. It is just a fact of life. You just got to do what feels right, and recently for me, it has been to find faith that there is in fact a higher power . . . anyway, back to the death and mayhem!

A Note from Forrest

I know this whole section is a little heavy for this kind of book, whatever kind of book it is. But I like to rant about God because I am afraid to die. I want to know what is next, and I think that by ranting about religion, I will somehow see The Light. The good news is that I know for a fact that I am going to heaven; you heathens are fucked.

The other reason for all this religious stuff is that I want to get my book sold in Christian bookstores. Ya, probably not gonna happen. Apparently, you can't cuss in Christian books. It's probably in the Bible somewhere that you can't use profanity, but if this were really important to God, he would have made it one of the Ten Commandments. So it probably isn't any more important than "it is God's will that you should be sanctified, that you should avoid sexual immorality" (from the Bible, p. 418). By the way, from that passage I just quoted, do you get that it's wrong to have premarital sex, because I didn't get it no matter how many times sister Mary-Joy explained it to me . . . Look up Thessalonians 4:3.

GIVE THEM THE GAMES!

I like to think that I learned lots of things from the movie *Gladiator*, but honestly, I probably only learned one: win the hearts of your people, and you will win their allegiance. That said, this lesson clearly didn't work out that well for Emperor Joaquin Phoenix, but then again, he did spend most of that movie whining about Russell Crowe, so he wasn't exactly a winner to begin with. Let's just say winning the allegiance of your people is a very important concept to remember when building your new utopia. I know you want to get your castle built as quickly as possible, but it can't be all work and no play for your people. You must keep them entertained. Back in Roman times, they used to accomplish this by hosting massive gladiatorial events where armed combatants fought with each other, condemned criminals, and even the most insane wild animals. While these events did wonders to keep people entertained, they were extremely expensive and did little to help the state acquire more riches.

If you learn anything from my book, I hope it is that it is wise to kill two birds with one stone whenever possible. I know what you are thinking: "How could hosting such barbaric tournaments ever help the state?" In order to answer this question, I must ask one in return. What is the number one burden of every society throughout the history of mankind? If you answered drug addicts or criminals, you are absolutely wrong. The number one burden has and will always be the elderly. Due to my infinite wisdom, I have devised a way to not only entertain the mob, but also solve the problem of what to do with elderly, a problem that will inevitably arise after the apocalypse.

Before you start imagining all sorts of horrible shit about me, let me be very clear. In no way, shape, or form am I suggesting we arm the elderly with swords and shields and let them have at each other. That is a disgusting

FORTUNE COOKIE WISDOM

Oftentimes in life when confronted by two choices, the harder of the two is most likely the right answer . . . Also, he who falls asleep with itchy butt wakes up with stinky finger.

thought, and I look down on you for even entertaining it. What I am suggesting is much more humane: MMA for the elderly. That's right, it came from my mouth first, mixed martial arts for the elderly. Surprised you haven't already seen it on Spike TV or pay-per-view? I am as well. It is absolutely genius. Not only do you provide sports entertainment for all your hard workers, but you also help the elderly to pull their own weight and remain active members of society. Now, before you scoff at this idea, just remember that Randy Couture and Mark Coleman have been proving this to be a viable concept for years now. To turn it into a resounding success, all you will need to do is structure the organization correctly. The first step to doing this is developing training camps.

MMA FOR THE ELDERLY

Back in Roman times, the majority of their gladiators were either criminals or paid volunteers. This is perfect! After the apocalypse comes, Walmarts will no longer exist, which means every elderly person will be out of a job and sign up for The Games on their own accord. Each "student" will receive food and housing, as well as all the training they need to turn them into fine-tuned, partially mobile, semi-asthmatic, fighting machines. The setting will be that of a peaceful retirement community. All you have to do is make a few small adjustments. For example, replace their naps with rigorous sparring sessions, their pinochle tournaments with takedown drills, their hour of *Ricki Lake*[24] with conditioning routines, and their kite-flying lessons with hill sprints. Other than these few small alterations, it will be retirement paradise. No longer will their existence be a burden on the state. They will have purpose! Forget about helping an old person across the street—turning them into an MMA fighter will help them in life.

---

[24] Does anyone actually watch *Ricki Lake* anymore?

Once you have developed half a dozen camps, immediately begin initiating rivalries. For example, steal all the walkers and wheelchairs in Camp A, and then blame it on Camp B. Next, steal all the pudding from Camp B and blame it on Camp A. Pretty soon, they will hate each other and begin shouting at each other from across the street (yes, in my imaginary world these camps are apparently right across the street from each other). In addition to building up the fights, such tactics will also create unity in each camp. However, it is important that you let everyone know right off the bat that sooner or later members from the same camp will have to fight each other, and there can be no excuses like, "We are gin partners, there is no way we can fight each other." If they get uppity about this, just threaten to return things to how they used to be, which is where they got pampered all day by nurses and got to sleep nineteen hours a day. That will get them back into line.

Before you begin hosting events, it is important to alter the rules from what they are today. The first thing that needs to be addressed is the length of the rounds. Currently, MMA fights consist of five-minute rounds, and it will take both contestants in a geriatric MMA fight that long to hobble out to the center of the cage. To resolve this issue, you can either triple the time of each round or start both combatants in the center of the cage. If you want the contests to be entertaining, I strongly suggest the latter.

The second thing that needs to be addressed is the use of weapons. I'm not talking about guns or knives or anything like that, but rather wheelchairs and oxygen tanks. Obviously, some of the warriors are going to need these devices to simply make it to the ring, and you must decide before the action begins if they will be allowed to use them in combat. For example, will it be allowable to run over your opponent's leg with a wheelchair or bludgeon your opponent with an oxygen tank? Personally, I recommend outlawing any such actions, and handling the foul much like groin kicks or eye gouges are handled today. Give the contestant who got run over or bludgeoned five minutes to recover, and then remove one point from the perpetrator should he prove to be a repeat offender.

Another issue to address is the use of eyeglasses or spectacles. Remove these from the contestants, and it would turn the stare-downs into squint-downs. Personally, I recommend allowing the combatants to wear eyeglasses because not only will it allow them to find their target, but it

WAYS TO KNOW IF YOU ARE A FUCKING FIGHTER

1. You might be a fighter if you have an orthopedic surgeon on speed dial.

2. You might be a fighter if you've ever given a stripper ringworm.

3. If you've ever worn Tapout shorts on a first date, you might be a fighter.

4. You may be a fighter if you play more than nine hours of video games a day.

5. If you take your shirt off at the office, you may be a redneck. If you take your shirts and pants off while at the office, you may be a fighter.

6. If you bleed on a daily basis, you may be a fighter . . . If you bleed on a daily basis and have a tendency to lose limbs, you may be a lion tamer.

7. If you feel comfortable using another man's toothbrush, you might be a fighter.

8. If your favorite thing about a one-night stand is getting to use the chick's body wash, you might be a fighter.

9. If you get into a bar fight in a grocery store, you might be a fighter.

10. If you've ever attempted to pay for a Subway sandwich with an autographed picture of yourself, you may be a fighter.

11. If you use more Icy Hot than deodorant, you might be a fighter.

12. If you've ever said, "He didn't hurt me, I just slipped onto his fist," you may be a fighter.

will also dramatically improve the entertainment value of the match. After all, can you think of a more entertaining display of dominance than the classic Smashing of the Glasses? I certainly can't.

Next you must assess protective gear. In order to keep the event from turning barbaric, the wearing of adult diapers must be allowed. Inform the combatants that they can be worn either under their fighting shorts or in lieu of the traditional trunks—much like sumo wrestling diapers have been worn for centuries.

Another essential piece of protective gear is the groin cup. However, when you are talking about pitting the elderly against one another in combat, this poses a unique problem, as their balls are much longer than younger MMA fighters. We all know that the cup size, thankfully, is not based on the size of one's package, but rather on the actual size of the pubic area itself (but always stick with a medium or large, okay?). But when dealing with the elderly, the container of the cup needs to be extra bulbous in order to effectively hold the elongated testicles. To get an idea of how large, place an orange in a stretched-out tube sock and hold it up by the cuff. You will see what you are up against here. Luckily, the manufacturing of mouthpieces will not be necessary for obvious reasons.

Strength is also something you must consider, as old people do not have a lot of it. Although many of them will be vicious in their attempts, most will be lacking the physical strength to cause any type of damage to their opponent. To remedy this situation, it will be necessary to enlist the participation of what I like to call "the Enhancer." The Enhancer will be a neutral person armed with some type of striking object, say a branch or some type of thick stick. If one opponent is obviously trying to throw another, and it is deemed that the attempt is technically sound, but failing due to a lack of strength, then the Enhancer would proceed to knock the other person over with his stick. Another example would be if a fighter delivered a Thai kick that barely produced any force; in this case the Enhancer would of course administer a sound thwack to the spot where the weak kick had landed. Thus, the Enhancer's entire job will be to upgrade the force of the strikes to a realistic, true fight level.

Once all the rules are in place, the next step is to increase the level of the Spectacle itself. This means that you are going to want it all—the grand fighter entrance, the ring girls, the works! First off, you want to make sure that the fighters are pumped up before heading to the ring. This can be accomplished by turning their hearing aids up to the maximum level, and also making sure that the fighter's entrance song properly represents him. May I suggest some produce a good polka by Lawrence Welk? This will get both the fighter and crowd revved up for sure. To ensure that the fighters make it to the cage before the song ends, I suggest having them ride down to the cage on Rascals. If you paint the rascals with flames or shark teeth, this might actually be pretty cool and entertaining as well.

So as you can see, the concept of MMA for the elderly is really quite exciting when put to paper. And just remember, if you can entertain your herd, they will always follow. If the elderly get bored with MMA for the elderly, you can always introduce them to a new assortment of games. One suggestion would be jousting on Easy Glides. Just get creative and go crazy. The world is your oyster! And to answer your question, no, I don't think it was a waste of time for Erich and me to sit around for hours and figure out the best ways for old people to fight each other.

DE-EVOLUTION

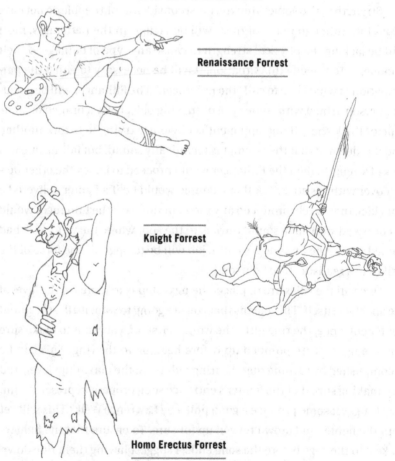

Renaissance Forrest

Knight Forrest

Homo Erectus Forrest

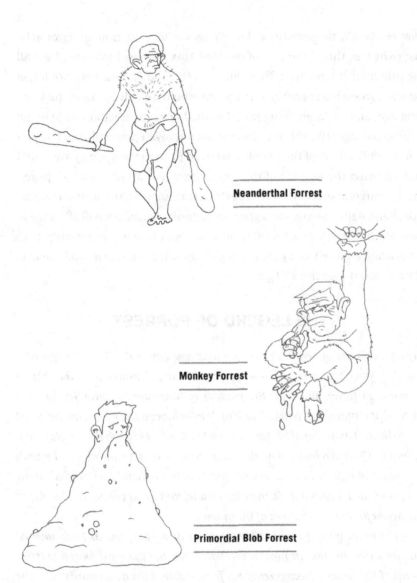

Neanderthal Forrest

Monkey Forrest

Primordial Blob Forrest

There are archaeologists who believe that human civilization has not evolved in a progressive fashion, but rather got knocked back to a Stone Age type of existence numerous times due to apocalyptic events such as the eruption of super-volcanoes and asteroids impacting the surface of the earth. It makes sense if you think about it. If a disaster was severe and it cast the small pockets of human survivors into a desperate struggle for the bare essentials, the majority of knowledge we have accumulated would be lost (why yes, this is the plot of the Mad Max movies. I told you, I got all the info for this book from these films . . . Oh, and *Rambo.* Let's not forget *Rambo*). In such a scenario, our present would quickly become the long-long ago, and children being raised in the barren wasteland would begin writing passages like the one above about our mysterious culture. The personal recollections of the people who lived prior to the apocalypse would end up being the legends of the new culture. For all practical purposes, the apocalyptic survivors would be the future ancients to the next civilization. Personally, I see this as a great opportunity because it will allow me to pass on whatever legacy I want to my descendants. It is my opportunity to immortalize myself as a god, much like Zeus, Jupiter, Osiris, and the like. Here is how my legend will go:

THE LEGEND OF FORREST

My legend is one of death. In the long-long ago, before the Great Hunger and Not Very Much Water, I was a revered general that led the armies of the Empire to many victories. But with the passing of time, the Emperor fell ill, and instead of handing the reins of his kingdom to his evil son Chubaka, he asked me to be the Guardian of his lands upon his death. Through the employment of magic, Chubaka learned of his father's wishes, and he murdered him with his sword of light before his father's final command could be ratified in the People's Court. Chubaka claimed the throne, and I was condemned to die in the arena for the amusement of the masses.

The name given to me in the arena was Bruce Lee, and as I vanquished one foe after the next in mortal combat, I became the most feared warrior in all of the Games. Recognizing my formidable skills as a swordsman, the supreme master, Raden, recruited me to fight in a tournament against supernatural beings that wished ill upon humanity. I fought through a gauntlet of strange fighters with the powers of the Scorpion, the Reptile, and one who could freeze his opponents with a single conjured blast of ice. I called upon the great Force, the fantastical energy that connects all life, and suddenly I was filled with the power of a hundred men. I slew each of the supernatural beings as if they were mere children and the world was, for a time, safe.

I became rich from these conquests, and I enjoyed the spoils of my victories. I continued to spill the blood of many men and dwarves, increasing my hit points daily. But with wealth came great responsibilities. As a member of Wu-Tang Clan, I saw it as my duty to protect the city and its inhabitants from evildoers, and when a crime wave fell upon us, I reacted. Using my vast fortune, I designed never-before-seen weapons, all of which mimicked the vicious fighting nature of the bat. I created a suit that allowed me to glide through the air, a belt equipped with various doodads of destruction, and I traveled from crime scene to crime scene in a black chariot that allowed me to race forward at great speeds across paths of smooth rock.

As my wealth and arrogance grew, I took greater risks. One afternoon I was approached by a stout, shiny-headed man who wished to wager for my beloved "chariot." Thinking that no mortal could defeat me, I agreed to a race. We flew like the wind down a stone path, our machines screaming with power, but alas, the man with the chromelike dome defeated me. Being a man of my honor, I bestowed upon him a pink contract for my beloved chariot, and retreated to the caves of Mordor to grieve. I cast aside all my earthly possessions, all my wealth, even my honor. All I brought with me was a single golden ring, my precious.

When I emerged many years later, it was to a strange and wondrous world. The gears of change had been busy in my absence, and there now existed boxes that could transport images and sounds across great distances. One day the leaders of every country appeared on these boxes, and their message was earnest: beings from another world were descending upon us. They traveled in ships the size of cities, and they had made their intentions clear: the moment they arrived, they would exterminate the entire human race.

I was earth's only hope, but realizing that the Empire had betrayed me by casting me into the arena, they could not ask me to fight for them. Instead, they employed trickery and sent Colonel Sam Trautman, a dear old friend who I had served under in the great war on the planet Avatar. He assured me that I would be under his command, and if I went to battle, I would get what I truly desired, which was for my country to love me as much as I loved it!

Knowing we were outnumbered fifty thousand to one, Trautman and I commandeered an enemy craft, a metallic hawk that flew faster than lightning itself. We took to the sky, but we did not attempt to engage the enemy forces, as we were just one and they were many. Instead, we flew our stolen craft directly into their mother ship, pretending that we were one of their own. It was there that we learned that the bowels of their ships were actually flesh and blood. Instead of driving a stake down into the heart of that ship, which would do little because of its massive size, I released a virus that traveled not just throughout the mother ship, but also throughout all the enemy vessels. In a matter of minutes, I had saved the planet!

But alas, there was not enough time for me to fly my foreign bird away before the enemy ships exploded, so I was forced to travel into a strange device they called the Stargate, and it transported me to a different universe. I was set down on a small desert planet, and the primitive inhabitants mistook me for a god. They showered me with jewels and women, but after many years of basking in these luxuries, I left my tribe of Ewoks and searched the sky far and wide for a passageway back to my homeland. Alas, I found it, another Stargate in all that sky, in all that dark. I gripped destiny's hand, and together we flew through the passageway, and in a matter of moments I once again recognized the stars around me.

But something was amiss. A massive mountain of pure rock was hurtling toward my homeland from the heavens. I knew that if this monolith impacted my world, it would surely destroy it with great floods, earthquakes, volcanic eruptions, and firestorms. The Great Danger lay just below my machine, and so I brought the craft down upon the chaotic surface. A team of my comrades had already arrived on the rock, led by a man named Bruce Willis. They had drilled a deep hole into the core of the object and were preparing to blow it to bits with an explosive device. When the timing device failed to operate, it became clear that one of us had to stay behind and manually detonate the weapon. Someone had to lay down his life for our home world. I told the others to go. Leave me behind and I would carry out this final task. I only asked them to tell my wives that I loved them all.

After my comrades had flown away into the darkness, I pressed the button that would reunite me with my ancestors of yore, including the great warriors Jackie Chan, Chuck Norris, and Dwayne Johnson. The subsequent explosion decimated the rock on which I had chosen to die, but alas, I did not perish. I was hurled into a cloud of rock and debris, and with my godlike strength,

I clung to a small fragment of stone as it spun wildly outward. Once I was clear of the discharge, the ride smoothed and I realized I was heading toward my home planet. I rode that rock down as a returning conqueror, steering it to its destination. I managed to maneuver my horse of stone toward a vast blue ocean, took the deepest breath I've ever taken, and then hit the water. The force of the impact pushed me down hundreds of feet. My world faded to black.

I awoke to find that I had grown webbed feet and gills, and that I was breaking underwater. As my vision cleared, my eyes were met with the strangest sight. A small yellow square sponge and an enormously obese pink starfish were staring at me with wide eyes. Once they realized I was all right, they burst into hysterical laughter and ran away cackling at the top of their lungs.

I had no idea where I was. In fact, it came as quite a surprise when I wandered outside and realized I had been in a dwelling made from a giant, hollowed-out pineapple. At any rate, I seized the opportunity and swam desperately toward the surface hundreds of kilometers above.

I swam for a great many days, and when I finally stood on solid land, my entire country stood before me, and the president himself bestowed upon me the Medal of Valor, our highest honor. I settled in with my wives and my dog, Boba Fett. We've lived in harmony ever since, but I will stand prepared, as I always have, to once again defend my lands, my women, and you, my children of the corn.

EPILOGUE

Most kids don't give death much thought, but around the age of ten or eleven, I became obsessed with it. With a single terrifying dream, I transformed from a happy-go-lucky runt into one terrified son of a bitch. Before you make a judgment call about my manliness, let me give you the details of this nightmare. I was at my biological father's house down by the coast, and somehow I fell off the edge of a pier that stretched out over a sandy beach. Except instead of the pier being seven feet high, it was more than a thousand.

I'd had falling dreams before, and like most people, I would always wake up just prior to impact. Not this time. My body slammed down into the unforgiving surface and I died. I could feel my body broken in fifty places, and assuming that this little accident had really happened, I figured that in a matter of seconds my brain would shut off and my spirit or whatever would head toward a bright light. That's not what happened. I remained utterly lucid. I could feel hundreds of shattered oyster shells digging into my back. I could hear seagulls crying and waves breaking in the distance. I could smell the ocean air. I was just as coherent as I had been before making this great fall, but I was utterly paralyzed. I couldn't move my body, blink, or communicate. For all intents and purposes, I was fucking dead.

I lay there for a great long while, and eventually people came and scooped up my broken body. They carried me away, brought me to a funeral home, and I was placed in a coffin. Next thing I know, I am in the ground, and I could hear dirt being shoveled onto my box, putting me into the ground for all eternity. I tried to scream, "I am still alive!" but no words came out of my mouth. All I could do was lie there and listen to the voices of my family grow more distant.

Despite my being placed underground, there was still light in the coffin. I should have realized that this meant I was dreaming, but I was too terrified by that point. Logic had been shut off and all I had left was my horror. I'm not sure how long I lay there, but pretty quickly there came noises around me. That noise was the maggots burrowing into my rotting flesh, consuming my body. Their numbers grew with each passing minute, and soon I was engulfed, my arms and legs and torso being removed bit by bit.

My life was not the same for a great long while when I awoke from that dream. For a week or more I walked around in a daze, and just when I began to feel that perhaps I could leave it in the past, I had another similar dream. My death was exactly the same—I fell off that skyscraper pier and crashed down into all those oyster shells, but this time, instead of putting me in a coffin and burying me, they loaded me onto the metal shoot of an incinerator. My head had been propped up on something, so I could see down the length of my body. As my feet entered the fire, searing pain shot through me. My entire family stood around me with grim faces, and I tried to scream at them to pull me out of the fire, but just as with the first dream, I couldn't move or make a sound.

When I awoke from that one, I knew there would be no going back to my haphazard, blissful childhood. While other kids thought about the upcoming weekend and all the fun stuff they had planned, I thought about death. No matter where I was or what I was doing, anytime my mind drifted, I would think, "Forrest, you are going to die, and you know exactly what will happen. Nothing. You will be stuck in a body you can't use, and maggots will eat you. You will see and feel every horrible thing to come." I got paranoid about everything, especially getting onto the school bus. I would break out in sweat every time I had to climb those stairs because I was certain that the bus would crash and I would die. At night, instead of passing out the instant I hit the bed like normal, I would just lie there in a twilight sleep, reliving those terrible dreams over and over. And when I did fall asleep, I always woke up scared.

For seven or eight months, I lived in a constant state of fear. In my first book, *Got Fight?*, I told a story about that time in my life. I was in a locker room before basketball practice, and this jock who had made it his life's purpose to fuck with me began making fun of my attire. I guess he thought my shirt was too tight and my shorts too short. He had been on my ass for a while, and realizing that his mother had recently died, I said, "Does it make you feel better, picking on me? Does it take your mind off the fact that the maggots are eating your mother right now?" I'm sure a lot of people thought I was the asshole of the century for saying something like that, but that's where my mind was at this time in my life. I thought about maggots all day and all night, and about the fact that it was only a matter of time until I heard them eating my flesh.

The horror became so unbearable, I went searching for answers. I was in Catholic school at the time, so I talked to the priests. In fact, my desperation had reached such extreme levels, I thought about becoming a priest. I would do anything it took to avoid the terror I had experienced in my nightmares. The priests I tried gave me the heaven run-around as usual, but nothing they said was real or tangible. Those fucking nightmares were more real that heaven, and so I didn't buy into anything they said. I was stuck with my misery.

There was a time there when I thought that ending up in a loony bin might be a very real possibility for me, but then one night while I was rehashing the nightmare over and over, it took a different turn. Just as all the other times, I was lying in a coffin and could hear the maggots eating my body, but strangely the terror had left. Instead of panicking at the thought of my decomposition, I focused on the maggots, and I could feel my energy or life force or whatnot inside of them. I felt my energy burrowing through the ground, and then a bird scooped that energy up. Before long, I could feel myself take the form of a muscle in a bird's wing. I was soaring through the skies, and it felt wonderful. At the same time, I could feel another part of my (I want to say "chi," but that is lame) energy being absorbed into the roots of a tree. In a matter of just a few hours, as I was lying there in bed, the terror left me. Just like in *The Lion King*, I came to terms with the great cycle of life. I didn't see a bunch of dancing and singing wild animals, and Simba never made an appearance, but I was over-fucking-joyed, to say the least.

I don't want to say that I accepted death, because I didn't and still haven't. I realize that one day my life will have run its course and I'll die, and end up as the muscle in a bird's wing. Although I have always liked muscles and want to experience the exhilaration of flight, I want to delay this day as long as possible. Deep down in my heart, I am still that eleven-year-old kid sitting in the darkness of his room, listening to Nine Inch Nails and burning himself with a lighter. I think about death more often than I should, but the results are much more positive than they once were. The idea of death makes me thankful that I am alive right now, allows me to enjoy each day, and makes me realize that I have to do whatever I can to hang on to life.

The downside is that when you focus on trying to stay alive, it causes you to take a much harder look around you and you see the possible dangers. And when I look around me these days, what I see looks bleak. Personally, I see a giant neon sign blaring in the sky, and its message is very simple: people have gone too far. Just like every person's life runs its course, so does every society. When a forest gets old, it develops a massive amount of undergrowth that threatens all the life within it. To keep the forest from withering and dying, Mother Nature sends in our happy friend fire, which wipes out the excess brush and undergrowth, puts nutrients back into the soil, and allows the forest to start the life process over again. But when you stop Mother Nature from doing her job and beat back all the flames, then, when another fire eventually comes, it is catastrophic.

It wipes out not only the underbrush, but also the entire forest, leaving nothing but a charred moonscape.

I don't know how close our society is to having run its course, but to me it looks like there is a lot of fucking underbrush choking the life out of us. Eventually there will be a correction; a massive reset button will be pushed. It's just a matter of time. When you get to the point where there are too many people using too much of our resources, it puts a burden on the earth, and good old Mother Nature is going to implement a correction. We can beat back the flames all we want, but eventually that fire is going to find its way through our meager blockades and cleanse the surface of the earth. With my mind focusing so heavily on death, it makes me think about that fateful day, and I personally want to be one of the ones who survive, which is the reason I wrote this book. I want to feel what it is like to be the muscle in the wing of a bird, but not just yet. I want to be a part of a tree rustling in the wind . . . just not yet.

APPENDIX

Believe it or not, I actually read quite a few books, and one of my favorites is Stephen King's *On Writing*, which teaches you how to write books good . . . or is it write books *well*? In either case, with only two books under my belt, I am not so ostentatious to think that I could teach you how to write a book. I can, however, give you an idea of how to sell a book concept. To illustrate this, I have included the proposal we sent to HarperCollins to get this book picked up. If you're not a quazi-celebrity and your goal is to get a publisher to give you actual money (personally, I requested them to deliver the cash in actual sacks with dollar signs printed on the front of them), I suggest you select your words more carefully, make the proposal make sense, and pretend you actually know something about the subject you are writing on, but hopefully this will give you a good idea of where to start.

P.S. You should watch *Where the Buffalo Roam*—it made me want to be a writer of words.

FORREST GRIFFIN'S SURVIVAL GUIDE TO THE APOCALYPSE

Forrest Griffin and Erich Krauss

Authors of the *New York Times* Bestselling *Got Fight?*
(currently No. 5 on Advice, How-to, and Misc.)

" . . . and that's one of the nights when I learned that if you're going to pay a stripper to punch you in the face, you'd better make sure that she's not wearing any large, gaudy rings."

—FORREST GRIFFIN

"Everyone should carry a gun, especially if you have a small penis like me. The second amendment was not designed to protect yourself. It was written—and I read this in my NRA magazine, so you know it's not biased—to protect us from the Government. They are crazy and oppressive and will one day lead us into the apocalypse."

—FORREST GRIFFIN

Why is Forrest Griffin, the former Light Heavyweight Champion of the Ultimate Fighting Championship (UFC) and *New York Times* bestselling author of *Got Fight? The 50 Zen Principles of Hand-to-Face Combat*, writing a book on how to survive the apocalypse? Seriously, why the hell not? Most children dream about a sparkly world filled with unicorns and stardust where everyone is kind and friendly to each other. Some of those children even grow up to write terrible books about magic and wizards and little boys named Henry (or is it Harry? Fuck, I always forget that shit . . . I know I just jumped from third person to first person, but I figured that you, as an editor, would put two and two together. If you didn't, put down my proposal now and back away from it slowly. You are mentally challenged, and under no condition will you be allowed to publish *my* book.)

Fortunately, Forrest did not fantasize about little boys named Henry. While getting his face rearranged by bullies in school, he dreamed about the near-extinction of mankind and all of the fantastic repercussions that come with it. Think about it: with grooming and personal hygiene no longer a prerequisite to social acceptance, you can let your mutton-chops grow and live out your secret sexually twisted fantasy of becoming Wolverine, which in turn would allow you to dry hump a broad assortment of four-legged creatures with impunity. You could kill squirrels with your bare hands, practice throwing knives all day, and never have to say "excuse me" after farting.

But most important, you could drive down the freeway without worrying that a 125-pound douche bag will somehow grow balls of steel and cut you off. And if one of the four remaining 125-pound douche bags should cut you off, there would be no one stopping you from pulling out one of the six forty-five caliber handguns protruding from your home-made utility belt and dispensing some vigilante justice. Once the douche bag is good and dead, you could strip naked, paint yourself in his blood, and go sprinting down the road singing any one of Madonna's top hits. Most important, you wouldn't be judged or arrested for any of these actions, which is what currently tends to happen. (Note to Editor: My agent said that the intro had to be dramatic, a real ball-grabber. How am I doing?)

Sure, there might be other authors who claim to be able to write a perfect apocalyptic survival guide, but none of them are destined to be a postapocalyptic leader. This is not a joke—it has already been written. When Forrest was fifteen, his mother informed him that while he was in the womb, she had crazy dreams about him walking over a barren wasteland of a thousand corpses, followed by a group of lost souls. She truly believed that this meant he would lead mankind into a new age. Of course, she told him this after the first Terminator movie had come out, which led him to believe that his mother had trouble deciphering between "dreams" and the "movie she had just seen."

He proposed his doubt, but she held fast. (Note to Editor: This actually really pissed me off. I was like, "Mom, why do you have me taking piano lessons then? Why not have me learning something more valuable, like how to be a ninja or a Jedi warrior?" And it wasn't like I was even good at the piano. The first day, my teacher said, "I can't rightly take your money because I know for a fact that you will never play the piano." Maybe my mom kept me going because it was free, I don't know . . . but you could imagine how humiliating this was for the future post-apocalyptic leader.)

Unlike John Connor in the Terminator movies, Forrest did not depend on his mother to teach him how to traverse a soiled planet. To prepare himself physically, he joined the secret society of the Webelos (if you read my last *New York Times* bestseller, then you know I was quickly ejected from this survivalist society for chucking a can of soda pop at my scout master's head, but we will leave this fact out of this book so that the reader thinks I was a super-badass boy scout).

To make himself mentally tough, he purposely got rejected by every hot girl in high school and let everyone, including smaller children, severely pummel his face on a regular basis. To train his skin to handle the darkness of a nuclear winter, he spent all his free time in his bedroom with the lights out, listening to Nine Inch Nails and softly weeping to himself.

When he grew into a man, his mother's words were not forgotten. He became a police officer and learned how to shoot to kill. And to ready himself for the inevitable day when all the ammunition has been exhausted on roaming bands of marauders, he became a professional fighter and learned how to kill with his mitts. (I know what you're thinking—*really, you became a cop and a fighter solely because you wanted to prepare yourself for the apocalypse?* If it's going to help sell this book for half a million bucks, then yes, it's a hundred percent true.)

To complete his training, he teamed up with author Erich Krauss, a survival expert who spent ten years of his life living in the Amazon rainforest and other godforsaken terrain. (Seriously, this guy is fucking crazy. He sleeps in a closet, pisses into an old milk jug, and lulls himself to sleep with visions of the downfall of man. I was kidding about a lot of the other stuff, but I'm being serious about this . . . Krauss is nuts; I was also being serious about the half a million bucks.)

Having spent the last four months riling up each other in the deserts outside of Las Vegas (really, it was more like a couple of hours a week, but who's counting?), they have completed the outline to their manifesto—*Forrest Griffin's Survival Guide to the Apocalypse.* In its pages you will learn to prepare yourself pre-apocalypse, such as constructing your getaway bag, which should include an assortment of weapons to help you get out of the city, as well as an assortment of sexual toys that will help you kill time once you're sitting in the middle of the fucking desert. It will teach you how to handle the various types of apocalypses, including viral, nuclear, economic, and natural disaster. It will inform you on how to do all sorts of really smart survival-type thingies.

And did I mention zombies? Yeah, it will have all sorts of methods for killing zombies with your hands. And for the readers who think the death of 99.9 percent of all people is somehow a bad thing, it will look at the upside of living in a barren wasteland, such as being able to leave your most humiliating stories behind you. Forrest will reveal his most traumatic moments, including the time he had sex with a post op. In case you are not hip with the lingo kids, a post op is a man who has had his junk removed, his Adam's apple shaven down, the whole dealeo. If he didn't believe that the apocalypse was coming and all you fuckers would die, would he admit that? I think not. (Public Service Announcement: Be aware of post ops—some can pass as women for two or three nights of sexual intercourse before you realize something is amiss.)

If you still doubt Forrest's future role as the Messiah of all mankind, he only has two words for you—ketchup packets. Even before he learned of his mother's visions, he had a hoarding mentality and would constantly steal ketchup packets. If you're smart, then you instinctively know that hoarders are survivors. Just look at squirrels—they hoard everything, and they've been around longer than sharks (not sure if that is true—might want to get your fact checker to look that shit up).

For now, all you need to know is that when the world ends, Forrest will be King, so bow down, bitches. Blow off one lesson as stupid or idiotic, and you could end up as a whore to a leather-clad motorcycle gang that travels the desert looking for oil. Seriously, Forrest is going to fill that empty head of yours with some knowledge. And let me tell you, he's got some knowledge to spill. That summer in the Webelos, he didn't spend all his time jacking off. He picked up some *skills*. There is no escaping the coming of the end. When that day arrives, tucking that small pecker of yours between your legs and clicking your heels together won't bring back your loved ones or all your shiny toys. You're in the wasteland, motherfucker, so become a soldier in Forrest's legion and pillage your way into the new age. This is Forrest Griffin's *Survival Guide to the Apocalypse*.

NOTE TO READER

If you are standing in the bookstore, reading the last chapter in an attempt to save a whole bunch of time and some money, please stop reading immediately and go to the checkout line. I say this because I want you to actually buy my book so I get that $38 in royalty money.

PSS. Seriously dude, close the book and go buy it!

PSSS. I'm standing right behind you, and I'm starting to get pretty fucking pissed off. If you read another word without shelling out some cash, I am going to hurt you.

PSSSS. I'm really sorry about getting so harsh before. Totally uncalled for, and I don't blame you if you dislike me now. But I really want you to like me, and I think you buying this book will really help my goal. I am begging you, brother. Please!

PSSSS. I really don't care if you buy this book or not. I hate everyone, my writing sucks, this book sucks, I don't have any friends. I'm going home to sleep for two days.

PSSSSS. I just woke up and I feel much better. Mood swings, you know. Did you buy this book yet?

ABOUT THE AUTHORS

FORREST GRIFFIN is one of the top-ranked light-heavyweight mixed martial artists in the world. He won the first season of *The Ultimate Fighter* in 2005 and has been one of the most beloved UFC fighters ever since. He is the day man, fighter of the night man, and champion of the sun. He is also a master of karate and friendship for everyone. But calm down, ladies, Forrest and his main squeeze, Jaime, live in Las Vegas.

ERICH KRAUSS is a professional Muay Thai fighter and the author of more than twenty-five books, including Anderson Silva's *The Mixed Martial Arts Instruction Manual: Striking*. He has written for the *New York Times*, and is the founder and publisher of Victory Belt Publishing. He lives in Las Vegas.